Hiking Ohio

A Guide to the State's
Greatest Hikes

Second edition

Mary Reed

FALCONGUIDES

GUILFORD, CONNECTICUT
HELENA, MONTANA

AN IMPRINT OF ROWMAN & LITTLEFIELD

To all the Ohio conservationists, past and present,
who have had the foresight to protect our wild places.
Without them this book would not be possible.

FALCONGUIDES®

Copyright © 2003, 2014 by Rowman & Littlefield

FalconGuides is an imprint of Rowman & Littlefield.
Falcon, FalconGuides, and Outfit Your Mind are registered trademarks of Rowman & Littlefield.

Unless otherwise credited, all photos are by the author.
Maps created by Melissa Baker © Rowman & Littlefield.

Library of Congress Cataloging-in-Publication Data
Reed, Mary T., 1968-
  Hiking Ohio : a guide to the state's greatest hikes / Mary Reed. –
Second edition.
      pages cm. – (State hiking guides series)
  Summary: "Many with full-color maps and photos! Each book includes:
Up-to-date trail descriptions with mile-by-mile directional cues
Detailed trail maps and GPS coordinates   Difficulty ratings and
average hiking times   A Trail Finder for best hikes with dogs, with
children, for great views, or for wildlife viewing   Information on fees
and permits, contacts, attractions, restaurants, accommodations, and
canine compatibility   Leave No Trace and wilderness safety tips and
techniques "– Provided by publisher.
  Includes bibliographical references and index.
  ISBN 978-0-7627-8178-2 (pbk.)
  1. Hiking–Ohio–Guidebooks. 2. Trails–Ohio–Guidebooks. 3. Ohio–
Guidebooks. I. Title.
  GV199.42.O3R444 2014
  796.5109771–dc23
                                    2013034601

Printed in the United States of America
Distributed by NATIONAL BOOK NETWORK

Contents

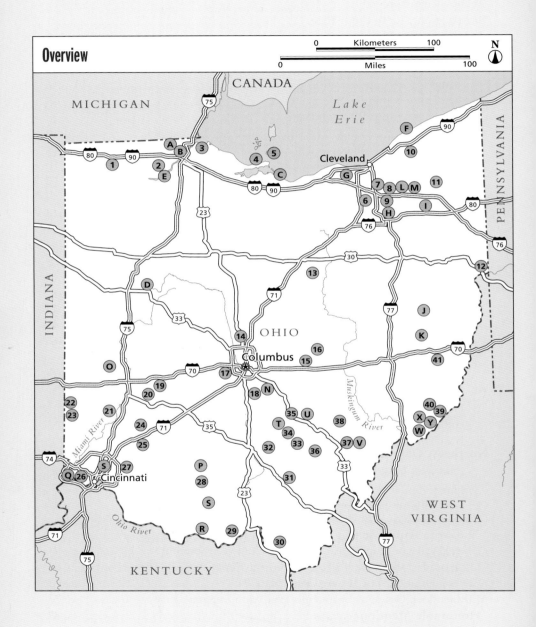

Overview

Central Ohio

Southwest Ohio

Acknowledgments

Thanks to prAna for providing clothing for my "models" to wear in this book. There are too many public and private land managers and naturalists to acknowledge by name. Thanks to you all for giving me information and tips on your area and again for reviewing my finished entries. A thank you also to the many Buckeye Trail Association volunteers who provided help with this manuscript. Thanks to Katie Benoit Cardoso, Imee Curiel, and Ellen Urban at Globe Pequot Press for their work on this project from beginning to end. Thank you to the people who hiked with me, including Chris Swarr, Ron Kittle, Deborah Berlekamp, Sasha White, Erik Dahlstrom, Suzanne Tkach, Alexa Fischer, Ian Fischer, Jim Reid, Mike Watson, and Marcia Goldstein. Special thanks to the trail angels who helped out in a time of need when my car broke down. Those include Sean Patrick Kelly (Bear), Sabrina Gorbett, and Nathan Johnson. Finally, thanks to my partner, Attila Horvath, who served as chauffeur, photography assistant, editor, number-one supporter, and model.

HELP US KEEP THIS GUIDE UP TO DATE

Every effort has been made by the author and editors to make this guide as accurate and useful as possible. However, many things can change after a guide is published—trails are rerouted, regulations change, techniques evolve, facilities come under new management, and so on.

We would appreciate hearing from you concerning your experiences with this guide and how you feel it could be improved and kept up to date. While we may not be able to respond to all comments and suggestions, we'll take them to heart, and we'll also make certain to share them with the author. Please send your comments and suggestions to the following address:

Globe Pequot Press
Reader Response/Editorial Department
P.O. Box 480
Guilford, CT 06437

Or you may e-mail us at: editorial@GlobePequot.com

Thanks for your input, and happy trails!

Introduction: The Buckeye State

Ohio comes from the Iroquoian word meaning "beautiful waters." Indeed, the state is largely defined by water. The Wisconsinan Glacier, which retreated from Ohio 12,000 to 15,000 years ago, gouged out Lake Erie to the north and forced the rivers in the central and southern part of the state to flow south, where they now drain into the Ohio River, the country's ninth longest. Rock deposits and the impressive glacial grooves on Kelleys Island are visible results of the glacier's advance and retreat. Along the former ice sheet's terminal edge, which cuts through the state, now lies one of the most biodiverse areas on the continent, where more than 1,500 plant species grow. In the unglaciated southeastern part of Ohio, forested ridges dominate the landscape.

Evidence of Ohio's human prehistory still exists in the earthworks built by the Adena, Hopewell, and Fort Ancient cultures at the famous Serpent Mound and elsewhere. The state was later home to the Wyandot and Ottawa in the north and the Shawnee, Miami, Mingo, and Delaware in the central and south. The first Europeans were French trappers and British settlers. They all came for the wealth of natural resources in the Ohio territory. The Native American tribes, the French, and the British fought fiercely over Ohio lands at the end of the eighteenth century.

At the time of European settlement, the state was more than 95 percent covered in forests, mostly beech-maple but also oak-hickory and mixed mesophytic forests in the unglaciated southeast portion of the state, with the Ohio buckeye, the state's namesake tree, found throughout. The forests were almost completely felled to fuel iron and charcoal furnaces, access coal seams, and make way for settlement and agriculture. However, a few remnants of virgin forest still remain, and footpaths exist to help you explore them. The largest tracts of second- and third-growth forest are in southeast Ohio, and the state's longest and most secluded trails are here.

Ohio was once home to such animals as the gray wolf, cougar, black bear, wood bison, Carolina parakeet, and passenger pigeon. These species are now either extinct or extirpated (driven out). But if you hike quietly on most Ohio trails today, you're sure to see white-tailed deer, wild turkey, ruffed grouse, beaver, and fox. In the eastern part of the state, the black bear is also making a comeback. There are innumerable bird species, from the ubiquitous state bird, the cardinal, to the less common but growing bald eagle population.

The late nineteenth and twentieth centuries brought a wave of agricultural and urban development to Ohio, seriously diminishing the state's wild areas. To those who haven't taken the time to explore it, Ohio may seem to contain only these urban areas and farmlands. Taking to the trails—whether a short day hike or an extended backpacking trip—is an excellent way to see all the state has to offer. A sampling of hikes presented in these pages will take you along beaches, over boardwalks, through

◀ *Follow the blue blazes on the Buckeye Trail.*

The Ohio buckeye and the yellow buckeye both have compound leaves of five leaflets.

gorges, past waterfalls, into caves, near wildlife, under forest canopies, and through carpets of wildflowers.

Weather and Seasons

Ohio generally offers four-season hiking, especially in recent years with increasingly mild winters and daily winter temperatures that often rise above freezing. The general exception is the snowbelt, east of Cleveland, where cross-country skiing usually replaces hiking in winter. Winter is the time to bundle up and survey the lay of the land. After a winter storm, head to your favorite spot to look at newly formed icicles and a quieting blanket of snow.

Spring is the best time of year in most of Ohio to view wildflowers. Do not be discouraged by the rain! Put on your rain gear and get out in the springtime, because the wildflower show is unparalleled between mid-April and early June. This is also the time when many birds are migrating and nesting. Just be sure to plan ahead and consider what kinds of stream crossings your hike will require, since springtime is also flooding time. Also keep an extra set of dry clothes in the car or back at camp.

Buckeyes

Summer is the best time to tackle the longer hikes and backpacking trips; the days are long and warm. Actually, summer would more accurately be described as incredibly hot and humid, with daytime temperatures often in the sticky 80s and 90s Fahrenheit. And the bugs do swarm, especially mosquitoes! Go to your local outdoors retailer and try out an effective, nontoxic bug repellent. Summer is also the best time to plan hikes that are farther afield, since campgrounds tend to be open seasonally.

Late summer and early fall feature the year's second wildflower season, mostly in open fields. Then the birds begin their southward migration. Fall is a good time to search out hikes with vistas so that you can enjoy the colorful foliage. It's also the driest time of the year, with comfortable temperatures.

Find your favorite spots and visit them in every season to witness the annual cycle of life that continues, whether you are there to witness it or not.

Ohio's Natural Regions

Some 300 to 500 million years ago, Ohio was periodically covered by seas. The sediment that piled up in layers on the sea bottom makes up Ohio's sedimentary bedrock. Three or four ice ages have occurred in Ohio more recently—geologically speaking—over the past two million years. The glaciers that advanced and retreated over the land probably have been the primary force shaping the landscape and its

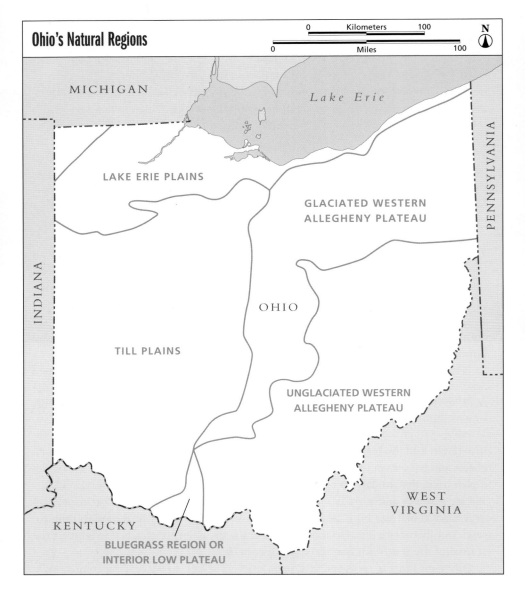

Ohio's Natural Regions

| 0 | Kilometers | 100 |

| 0 | Miles | 100 |

N

MICHIGAN

Lake Erie

LAKE ERIE PLAINS

GLACIATED WESTERN
ALLEGHENY PLATEAU

PENNSYLVANIA

INDIANA

OHIO

TILL PLAINS

UNGLACIATED WESTERN
ALLEGHENY PLATEAU

WEST
VIRGINIA

KENTUCKY

BLUEGRASS REGION OR
INTERIOR LOW PLATEAU

variations. As anyone who observes nature can tell you, it's the "edge" areas—where different conditions (forest, water, fields) or entire ecosystems meet—that harbor the most life. Depending on whom you ask, Ohio has four to six distinctive ecoregions, each with its own distinct geology, climate, and species.

Lake Erie Plains

To the north are the Lake Erie Plains, home to a flat landscape and more than 200 miles of shoreline. Temperatures here are moderated by the lake, and you'll find species that dominate here and not inland. This region was formerly home to the Great Black Swamp, and remnants of the swamp-oak forests hang on in preserves. Look for an abundance of cattails and grasses such as little bluestem, bluejoint, slough grass, and the nonnative, invasive phragmite grass. Showy flowers include wild sunflower, goldenrod, aster, lupine, and wild coreopsis. Ash, walnut, maple, basswood, and sycamore are some common tree species. Shorebirds include an abundance of eagles, terns, gulls, herons, cranes, ducks, and geese.

Western Allegheny / Appalachian Plateau

The Western Allegheny Plateau is Ohio's hill country, located along the east and southeast portions of the state. The glaciated northern Allegheny, or Appalachian, Plateau was covered by the Wisconsinan Glacier. The resulting landscape is characterized by rounded hills, broad valleys, and many wetlands. The unglaciated Western Allegheny Plateau, in southeast Ohio, is home to sharp ridges 300 feet above the valleys. The forests along the Western Allegheny Plateau are often dominated by oak and hickory on the ridges and maple and beech in the lowlands. Many of the east- and north-facing slopes are home to mixed mesophytic forests. Twenty to twenty-five tree species are common, including the aforementioned oak, hickory, beech, and maple, as well as tulip poplar, ash, elm, hemlock, walnut, and locust, but no single species dominates the canopy. More than 1,500 species of flowering plants can be found throughout the region.

The Teays River was the major watershed draining the eastern portion of what's now the United States until the Kansan Glacier (700,000 years ago) dammed the river and reversed drainage patterns. In the unglaciated southeast portion of Ohio, evidence remains in the landscape of the former Teays River valley.

Lexington Plain / Bluegrass

Jutting up from Kentucky into portions of three Ohio counties is the Interior Low Plateau, also known as the Lexington Plain or Bluegrass ecoregion of Ohio. This region shares some features with the Western Allegheny Plateau, since it was also once part of the ancient Teays River watershed and was also unglaciated. The Bluegrass is home not only to sandstone and shale bedrock but also to the more resistant dolomite. The resulting landscape has higher ridges—several hundred feet above the creek valleys—than the rest of southern Ohio. Also characteristic of this ecoregion is the presence of barrens and glades, which are small prairie communities. These were once common but are now rare. Shallow soils support grasses and sedges as well as some oaks and cedars. The Edge of Appalachia preserve, owned by The Nature Conservancy, is an excellent place to explore this ecoregion.

Till Plains

Most of the western half of Ohio is known as the Till Plains, so named for the rich layer of glacial debris, or till, that makes up its fertile soil. The landscape here is flat, and river drainages are shallow. Many of these rivers and creeks have high sustained water flows and support a wide variety of species. Big Darby Creek, west of Columbus, is home to 100 of the 166 fish species found in Ohio. When European settlers arrived, this land was mostly covered in beech-maple forests and dotted with prairie openings. John Deere's invention of the steel plow helped transform this landscape drastically. Today 95 percent of the land in this region is either urbanized or cultivated into large fields of corn and soybeans. A remnant Till Plain forest exists in Hueston Woods, and several city and state parks have worked to restore or maintain remnant prairie lands, which include such species as echinacea (coneflower), prairie dock, and big bluestem grass.

Precautions

Hunting is allowed in most areas covered in this guide. Be sure to contact the land administrators to find out the dates of hunting seasons, specifically firearm seasons. It's probably best simply to avoid areas where hunting is allowed during deer firearm season. However, if you do decide to hike then, be sure to wear hunter-orange clothing.

Poison ivy is everywhere! Wearing long pants is usually enough protection against this irritant. When you finish a hike, wash with cool water and soap and launder your clothing. Your pet can pick up poison ivy oil and pass it on to you, so be sure to wash your dog if it has come into contact with the plant. If you don't already know how to identify poison ivy, it comes in two basic forms: In summer you will see it along edge areas and in full sun as a creeping vine with leaflets of three. The leaves tend to have one noticeable notch, and the stems are reddish; the fall berries are white. The second form of poison ivy grows into huge, hairy vines up the sides of trees. If you are a tree hugger, watch out for the PI!

Land Ownership and Oversight

Wayne National Forest

The Wayne, covering a patchwork of 240,900 acres in southeast Ohio, is a multiple-use area. Environmental groups are battling proposed hydraulic fracturing (fracking) for shale gas, but the USDA Forest Service plans to continue with extraction. Many trails in the Wayne are open to off-road vehicles, horses, and mountain bikes. Hikers are allowed on these multiuse trails, but it's safest and most pleasant to stick to the hiking and backpacking trails. Leashed dogs are permitted, and hunting is allowed.

State Forests

Ohio state forests are largely managed for logging and oil and gas development—with fracking on the horizon—but are also open to recreational opportunities. Most trails, in terms of sheer mileage, are for off-road vehicles and horses, but some parks also have many miles of hiking trails. Some state forest lands are pretty beat up, and some hiking trails skirt clear-cuts. Shawnee State Forest is home not only to some of the largest public-land logging operations but also to Ohio's only wilderness area; a

Dogwoods bloom throughout Ohio in early spring.

backpacking trail allows you to explore it. Leashed dogs are allowed on hiking trails, and hunting is allowed in the forests.

State Parks

Ohio's state parks are managed primarily for recreation, though there are now plans to develop fracking in them. Trails are generally well developed and marked. Most state parks have campgrounds and other resources, such as concessions, beaches, pools, amphitheaters, miniature golf, and so on. Several state parks have lodges. These are good destinations for seeing some of Ohio's scenic treasures without "roughing it." State parks are generally not the best place to find solitude, especially during summer weekends, when campgrounds and trails are usually overrun with people. Naturalist programs are often offered between Memorial Day and Labor Day. Leashed dogs are allowed on state park trails, and hunting is allowed in some parks.

Metroparks

Many Ohio cities have well-developed metroparks. These parks tend to be well managed, with nature centers, naturalist programs, guided hikes, and environmental restoration projects. Most metroparks do not offer camping options. Because of their proximity to large population centers, metroparks often have heavily used trails, but they are generally well maintained in response to this high demand. These are great options for nearby day hikes but not for finding solitude. Leashed dogs are usually permitted in metroparks, but hunting is generally not allowed.

Natural Areas and Preserves

The Ohio Department of Natural Resources maintains a Department of Natural Areas and Preserves (DNAP). These preserves are managed for the land itself, not for you! DNAP preserves exist to protect biologically significant lands. These parcels are generally pretty small but quite beautiful. Camping, pets, and picnicking are not permitted on DNAP lands, but there's an upside to all of this: Trails on state nature preserve lands are among the nicest in the entire state. A number of preserves are accessible by permit only. Contact DNAP for more information (see appendix B). Each preserve is now managed in coordination with a state park, usually the closest park to the preserve.

Private Preserves

A few private preserve hiking trails are covered in this guide. These preserves, although open to the public, may have strict rules to protect the ecological integrity of the land. These, too, are some of the most attractive and biologically significant areas in the state. Dogs are not permitted on some private preserves, and hunting is generally prohibited. Be considerate of preserve rules, and encourage others to do so, too, since these lands are only open to the public at the goodwill of preserve owners. Also consider helping maintain these preserves with a monetary donation.

Difficulty Ratings

Ultimately, you have to know your own strengths and limits when hitting the trail. The following descriptions should serve as guidelines as to what to expect from the ratings used in this book.

- Easy hikes are less than 5 miles in length and are on mostly flat, well-worn trails.
- Moderate hikes can be from 1 to 5 miles in length with steep ascents and descents, or 5 to 10 miles long but generally flat or with moderate ascents.
- Difficult hikes are approaching 10 miles in length or longer and are on hilly terrain.

Contacting Your Representatives

Most of the hikes covered in this book are on publicly owned lands. That public is you and me. Contact your state representative and senator and let them know about your support for public lands. This is especially important now that fracking is competing with recreation for use of these lands. Encourage funding levels that allow these lands to be managed and staffed at full capacity. Also watch closely at how funds are allocated, and follow up on your support for recreational opportunities.

Legislative Public Information Office: (800) 282-0253

State of Ohio home page legislature link: www.legislature.state.oh.us

Volunteering

The most important resource when it comes to Ohio's trails is you. Many of the hikes described in this book were built by volunteers. If you live near a park or preserve, contact the manager and find out if a volunteer trail organization already exists. If it doesn't, start one. Contact the Buckeye Trail Association (740-832-1BTA or www .buckeyetrail.org) for information on trail building.

Getting around Ohio

By Road

They say that there are two seasons in Ohio: winter and road repair. For links to up-to-date information on weather, road conditions, and road closings—or if you have a breakdown or other problem—contact the Ohio State Highway Patrol at (877) 7-PATROL or www.statepatrol.ohio.gov. For more esoteric information on Ohio's transportation system (that is, roads), contact the Ohio Department of Transportation (ODOT) at www.dot.state.oh.us. You can reach the Ohio Turnpike Commission at (440) 234-2081 or www.ohioturnpike.org.

By Air

Ohio is serviced by numerous regional airports. Most flights, however, are concentrated at three major airports: Cleveland, Columbus, and Cincinnati.

- Cleveland Hopkins International Airport, (216) 265-6000, www.clevelandairport .com. The airport is accessible by train from downtown. For more information contact the Greater Cleveland Rapid Transit Authority (RTA) at (216) 566-5100 or www.riderta.com.
- Port Columbus International Airport, (614) 239-4000, www.flycolumbus.com. The airport is accessible by public bus. Contact the Central Ohio Transit Authority, (614) 228-1776, www.cota.com.
- Cincinnati/Northern Kentucky International Airport, (859) 767-3151, www .cvgairport.com. The airport is accessible by public bus. Contact the Transit Authority of Northern Kentucky, (859) 331-8265, www.tankbus.org.
- Akron/Canton Regional Airport, (330) 896-2385, www.akroncantonairport.com.
- Dayton International Airport, (877) FLY-DAY-1, www.flydayton.com.
- Toledo Express Airport, (419) 865-2351, www.toledoexpress.com.
- Youngstown-Warren Regional Airport, (330) 539-4233, www.yngwrnair.com.

The airports also host car rental companies and taxi services to help you get to your ground destination. (Most hikes in Ohio are not accessible by public transportation.) To book your reservations, contact an airline directly by phone or reserve online via the airline's website or a general travel website. Some popular ones are www.travelocity.com, www.expedia.com, www.cheaptickets.com, and www.priceline.com.

AREA CODES

Ohio, a very population-dense state, has ten area codes:

- Toledo/northwest Ohio—419 and 567
- Cleveland—216
- Cleveland east/west suburbs—440
- Akron, Canton, and Youngstown—330 and 234
- Southeast Ohio—740
- Columbus—614
- Cincinnati—513
- Dayton/Springfield and southwest Ohio—937

By Train

Amtrak serves Youngstown, Akron, Alliance, Bryan, Cleveland, Elyria, Sandusky, Fostoria, and Toledo across the northern part of the state. In southern Ohio, Amtrak serves Cincinnati and Hamilton. For information and reservations, log on to www .amtrak.com.

By Bus

Greyhound serves most medium-size and large cities in Ohio. For fare and schedule information, call (800) 231-2222 or log on to www.greyhound.com. All of Ohio's major cities have local bus services.

Visitor Information

For statewide travel and tourism information, call (800) BUCKEYE or visit www .discoverohio.com. Almost every county in Ohio has a local convention and visitors bureau. To find a local bureau, go to the Ohio Association of Convention & Visitors Bureaus at www.oacvb.org.

How to Use This Book

Hiking Ohio is designed to be highly visual and quickly referenced. We've split up Ohio into five regions: Northwest Ohio, Northeast Ohio, Central Ohio, Southwest Ohio, and Southeast Ohio. Each region begins with a section intro, where you're given a sweeping look at the lay of the land. Following each section intro are the hikes within that region.

Each hike within a region begins with a short summary. You'll learn about the trail terrain and what surprises each route has to offer. If your interest is piqued, read on. If not, skip to the next hike.

The hike specifications are fairly self-explanatory. Here you'll find the quick, nitty-gritty details of the hike, including where the trailhead is located, hike distance, approximate hiking time, difficulty, type of trail surface, best hiking season, what other trail users you may encounter, nearest town, any fees and permits required, and other key information. The "Finding the trailhead" section provides dependable directions from a major intersection or a nearby town or city right down to where you'll want to park.

"The Hike" is the meat of the chapter. Detailed and honest, it's the author's carefully researched impression of the trail. While it's impossible to cover everything, you can rest assured that we won't miss what's important. "Miles and Directions" provides mileage cues to identify all turns and trail name changes, as well as points of interest.

At the end of each hike, you'll find sources of additional local information. We'll also tell you where to stay, where—and sometimes what—to eat, and what else to do and see while you're hiking in the area.

"Honorable Mentions" details hikes that didn't make the first line of hikes. In many cases it's not because they aren't great hikes, but rather that they're overcrowded or environmentally sensitive to heavy traffic. Be sure to read through these. A jewel might be lurking among them.

Don't feel restricted to just the routes and trails described here. Show your adventurous spirit and use this guide as a platform to dive into Ohio's backcountry and discover new routes for yourself. (One of the simplest ways to begin this is to hike the trail in reverse. The change in perspective is often fantastic, and the hike should feel quite different. It'll be like getting two distinctly different hikes on each map.)

Slip this guide into your backpack and begin your adventure. Enjoy your time in the outdoors—and remember to pack out what you pack in.

Map Legend

🛡70	Interstate Highway	⊟	Bench
🛡40	US Highway	╳	Bridge
295	State Route	▲	Backcountry Campground
CR 12	Local/County Road	▥	Boardwalk/Steps
====	Unpaved Road	⬗	Boat Launch
====	Gravel Road	■	Building/Point of Interest
⊢—⊢	Railroad	⏶	Campground
— · —	State Boundary	⌒	Cave
·—·—·	Powerline	⏜	Cliff
------	Featured Trail	▭	Lodging
------	Trail	🅿	Parking
——	Paved Trail	╳	Pass
	Body of Water	🛆	Picnic Area
	Marsh	👥	Ranger Station/Park Office
	River/Creek	🚻	Restroom
	Intermittent Stream	📷	Scenic View
	Waterfall	⛷	Ski Area
⟋	Spring	⌶	Tower
	State Forest/State Park	○	Town
	Nature Reserve	20	Trailhead
		?	Visitor/Information Center
		🚰	Water

Northwest Ohio

Northwest Ohio's Great Black Swamp, once more than 100 miles long and 30 miles wide, was one of the last places to be settled east of the Mississippi because of its inhospitable swampy soil, weather, and bug conditions. But settlement did occur, and most of the swamp has since been drained. The soil proved very fertile, and today northwest Ohio largely comprises farmland. Most hikes located here are short, but some of the state's best hiking and bird-watching destinations lie in remnants of the Great Black Swamp. Several Lake Erie islands are nearby, with Kelleys Island providing the most hiking opportunities, as well as views of stunning glacial grooves.

The southern shore of Lake Erie is a bird-watcher's paradise. In springtime, birds migrating to the north must stop before making the long trip over the lake, often taking a day to rest and prepare. Single-day bird counts have numbered in the tens of thousands—for each species! Shorebirds include bald eagles, gulls, terns, herons, swans, egrets, and red-winged blackbirds, just to name a few.

Swamp oak forests stand in small parcels and are home to such animals as fox, muskrat, mink, and weasel. Spring wildflowers are abundant in the wooded portions of this ecoregion; marsh and meadow flowers are most conspicuous in late summer and early fall. Although less than 10 percent of Ohio's original wetlands remain, these lands produce the most diverse wildlife of any habitat in the state. Toledo Metroparks' Oak Openings Preserve, home to sandy soils left behind by glacial lakes, is a great place to see yet more diversity of life in a slightly upland region bordering the Great Black Swamp.

The Ottawa and Wyandot Indians were living in this region when European settlers arrived. In the War of 1812 the American forces under Commodore Oliver Hazard Perry defeated the British in the Battle of Lake Erie. (Perry's Victory and International Peace Memorial stands at Put-in-Bay.) The Erie Canal and later the St. Lawrence Seaway opened the Great Lakes for development, and large cities grew along their shores. Vacation destinations in northwest Ohio are within a half-day's drive of tens of millions of people. Historic, amusement, and nature parks

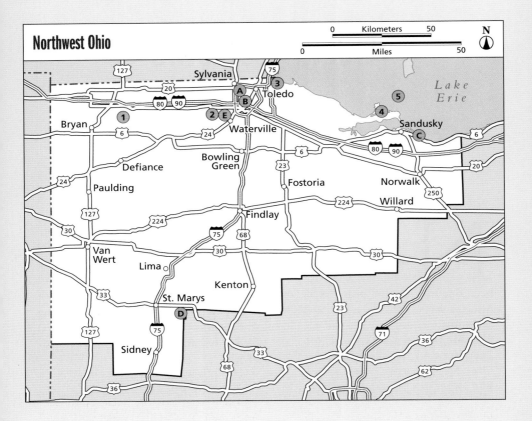

draw tourists, yet seclusion can be found just a few miles into a trail. Look forward to hiking inland among remnant swamp forests, along the sandy shores of Lake Erie, on wetland boardwalks, and among sand dune communities. Most lakeside hikes in northwest Ohio are best tackled in summer. Volatile weather conditions and heavy winds can make cold-weather hiking uncomfortable.

1 Cottonwood to Toadshade Loop

Goll Woods State Nature Preserve

The 170-acre near-virgin forest is a remnant of the Great Black Swamp, characterized by towering trees 200 to 400 years old, with a few specimens as old as 500 years. Hike around the preserve on a 3-mile outer loop; it won't take long to see that you're in a special place. Unusually tall and broad tree specimens include cottonwood, oak, tulip tree, ash, maple, beech, hickory, and linden (basswood). The dark and clear understory is quite swampy in areas and gives you a taste of what the Great Black Swamp was once like, all the way down to the mosquitoes. Take a respite from everyday living to view the process of life, death, and rebirth in a natural ecosystem.

Start: Trailhead next to the parking lot and restrooms
Distance: 3-mile loop
Hiking time: About 1 to 1.5 hours
Difficulty: Easy; flat and clear
Trail surface: Dirt and stone trail
Blaze: None; all junctions are marked.
Best season: Spring and fall, when there's a night frost to keep the mosquitoes down
Other trail users: Hikers only
Canine compatibility: Dogs not permitted

Water: The spigot at the trailhead is dry; bring your own water.
Land status: State nature preserve
Nearest town: Archbold
Fees and permits: None
Schedule: Open daily from dawn to dusk
Maps: Trail maps are usually available at the trailhead kiosk. USGS quad: Archbold
Trail contact: Goll Woods Nature Preserve, Archbold; (419) 445-1775; www.dnr.state.oh.us/location/dnap/goll_woods/tabid/942/Default.aspx

Finding the trailhead: From the junction of SR 2 and SR 66 north of Archbold, continue north on SR 66 for 1 mile to CR F. Turn left (west) and drive 2.8 miles to CR 26. Turn left (south) and drive 0.2 mile to the parking lot on the left. *DeLorme: Ohio Atlas & Gazetteer:* Page 25 D5. GPS: N41 33.29' / W84 21.69'.

The Hike

When the Goll family purchased land for a homestead in northwest Ohio in 1837 (for $1.25 per acre), they probably couldn't have imagined that in less than 150 years their land would be designated a natural treasure—simply because the trees hadn't been cut. In fact, the only reason this small tract of magnificent forest exists is because the Goll family preserved the woods through four generations before selling it to the state in 1966.

The forest at Goll Woods is characterized by towering trees 200 to 400 years old, thick clouds of mosquitoes, and everything in between. This area was the last to be settled east of the Mississippi. It was eventually drained with the help of an extensive ditching project and now is home to almost a million acres of productive farmland. Getting to Goll Woods requires a long drive through what seems to be ceaseless corn-fields, making it hard to imagine the vast expanse of forest that once existed here. Goll Woods was left untouched until World War I, and even then only a few trees were cut. The entire preserve encompasses 321 acres, and the 170 acres of near-virgin timber within the preserve are listed as a National Natural Landmark.

Start the hike just past the trailhead kiosk, which may have self-guided nature trail brochures stocked. Begin by taking a left onto the Cottonwood Trail to make a clockwise loop around the preserve. Unusually tall and broad trees, including the namesake cottonwood as well as oak, tulip tree, ash, maple, beech, hickory, and linden (basswood) tower above, creating a dark and clear understory that's quite swampy in areas. The dark forest and dark swampy bottomlands are what gave the Great Black Swamp its name. This wide variety of evenly distributed tree species is known as a mixed mesophytic forest. Although the land is quite flat, look for very subtle changes in elevation. The wetter soil supports elm and ash, while the drier soil is home to beech and maple. As the swamp was drained over the years, beech and maple trees began to take hold. As the soil continues to become drier, the beech-maple commu-nity will eventually dominate this forest.

Continuing to the Burr Oak Trail, take note of the most impressive big trees, a few of which are estimated to be almost 500 years old. (See the "elder of the woods" at Post 8, which was growing here in the sixteenth century!) Snags stand here and there, providing habitat and food for birds and other animals. Other trees have been blown down during storms and left to rot, helping to create the rich soil that supports this forest. Look and listen for the red-headed woodpecker, common to Goll Woods but not so common elsewhere. In the understory look for the native pawpaw tree and the strong-smelling spicebush, both of which can grow in low light conditions.

The next portion of the route is the Tuliptree Trail, named for the tree that pro-duces yellow-and-orange tulip-like flowers in the spring. Look on the trail for fallen flowers, because you won't be able to see them in the trees themselves—the tall, straight tulip tree prunes itself, and the first branches are 40 to 50 feet above the ground. The tulip tree is one of the oldest tree species on the planet. Fossil records show evidence of tulip trees growing 100 million years ago. Tulips are excellent lum-ber trees, but they were often just burned as settlers cleared the Great Black Swamp.

These remnant tracts of virgin forest are important to scientists and the rest of us because they provide a living record of history, including natural history of fires, droughts, wet years, and so on. These forests also provide a benchmark for what a natural, healthy forest should look like, which is criti-cal when land managers undertake restoration projects. And, of course, these forests are simply remarkable, beautiful places in and of themselves, whether or not we visit them for a respite from everyday life.

▶ **Goll Woods is home to the state champion rock elm tree; that is, the largest of that species in the state.**

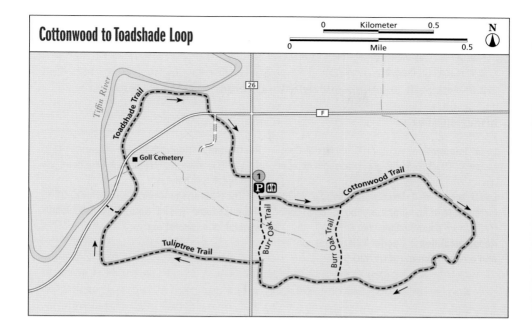

Cottonwood to Toadshade Loop

The final leg of the loop is on the Toadshade Trail, which parallels the Tiffin River for a stretch. Toadshade is a common name for a maroon or green trillium with mottled leaves. Other spring wildflowers found here include bloodroot, columbine, cut-leaf toothwort, phlox, Dutchman's-breeches, wood anemone, miterwort, and the uncommon dwarf ginseng. Later in the year expect to see black-eyed Susan, thistle, jewelweed (spotted touch-me-not), and tick trefoil. As the trail turns away from the river, it enters a pine plantation. This is a fragrant portion of the trail and offers a much-needed respite from the mosquitoes. It's nonnative, however, and will someday be naturally displaced by the native deciduous trees.

Miles and Directions

0.0 Start at the trailhead located beyond the restrooms and the trailhead kiosk. The trail begins at a fork. Take the left fork to begin a clockwise loop around the entire preserve, starting with the Cottonwood Trail.

0.2 Pass a junction with the Burr Oak Trail on the right. Continue straight. **Option:** Take a right to do only the Burr Oak Trail, a 1.5-mile loop.

1.1 At the end of the Cottonwood Trail, come to another fork for the Burr Oak Trail. Take a left.

1.3 Come to another fork. Take a left to begin the Tuliptree Trail. **Option:** Take the right fork to return directly on the Burr Oak Trail for a 2.2-mile loop.

1.4 Cross CR 26 and pick up the trail on the other side, a little bit to the right.

1.9 Arrive at the junction with the Toadshade Trail. Continue straight. (The Tuliptree Trail continues to the right.)

2.0 Pass a junction with an access trail from the left.

2.2 Come to CR F. Turn right and walk about 100 yards along the road and then pick up the marked trailhead on the other side.

2.6 Pass a seasonal river-overlook deck on the left.

2.7 Cross CR F again.

3.0 Arrive at CR 26. Cross the road and return to the parking lot where you began.

Hike Information

Local information: Wauseon Chamber of Commerce, (419) 335-9966, www.wauseonchamber.com

Local events and attractions: Sauder Village historical farm and crafts, Archbold; (800) 590-9755; www.saudervillage.com

Accommodations: Sauder Village has an inn and a campground; (800) 590-9755.

Restaurants: Homestead Ice Cream, (419) 446-2663, www.homesteadicecream.com; try their Black Swamp flavor.

The Barn at Sauder Village, (800) 590-9755

Organizations: Toledo Naturalists Association, www.toledonaturalist.org

2 Oak Openings Hiking Trail

Oak Openings Preserve Metropark

If you're an über-hiker, tackle it in a day, but if you're a mere mortal, take two days to explore this long and winding path. The Oak Openings Hiking Trail is simply one of the best long hikes in the state. It takes you near inland sand dunes, characteristic of the Oak Openings region, home to beaches thousands of years ago when Lake Erie was much higher than it is today and its shores extended this far.

Start: Springbrook Picnic Area
Distance: 15.4-mile loop
Hiking time: About 5 to 8 hours
Difficulty: Difficult due to length
Trail surface: Flat, well-maintained dirt trail that often crosses other trails and roads
Blaze: Yellow
Best season: Apr through Oct
Other trail users: Hikers only except for very short sections that join horse trails
Canine compatibility: Leashed dogs permitted

Water: Available at both the Springbrook and White Oak picnic areas along the trail
Land status: Toledo Metropark
Nearest towns: Whitehouse, Swanton
Fees and permits: None
Schedule: Open daily from 7 a.m. to dark
Maps: Metropark map shows all trails in the park. USGS quads: Swanton, Whitehouse
Trail contact: Oak Openings Preserve Metropark, Swanton; (419) 407-9700; www .metroparkstoledo.com

Finding the trailhead: From I-475 southwest of Toledo, exit on US 24 west (exit 4) and drive 4.4 miles to SR 64 (exit 63) in Waterville. Turn right (north) and drive 8.3 miles to the Springbrook Picnic Area parking on the left (watch for turns on SR 64). The Springbrook sign is parallel to the road, so it's easy to miss. *DeLorme: Ohio Atlas & Gazetteer:* Page 26 D2. GPS: N41 33.39' / W83 52.41'.

The Hike

The Oak Openings Hiking Trail—known to many locals as the Scout Trail, because it has historically been used and maintained by Boy Scouts—is not for the faint of heart, coming in at 15.4 miles in length. Walk near inland sand dunes (a signature characteristic of the Oak Openings), in oak woodlands and pine forests, through canopy openings and prairies, along creek beds, past attractive ponds, and on sandy trails.

Oak Openings refers to the region that reaches from the Maumee River to Detroit, northwest of Toledo. The region extends about 120 miles in length. It's characterized by a ridge of sand that sits atop clay soil. The sand was deposited by a series of glacial lakes and glacier meltwater. Today there are some spots where the inland sand dunes still shift and move and pile as high as 35 feet above the clay subsoil. In

other places the water table rises to just 3 feet below the surface. Native Americans once regularly set fire to the woodlands understory to keep it clear for game hunting. European settlers found that they could drive their Conestoga wagons through the clear understory beneath widely spaced oak trees, thus the name "Oak Openings."

The preserve, at under 4,000 acres, is home to more than 1,000 plant species, a number of which are rare or endangered. These include flowering plants such as Skinner's foxglove and the carnivorous sundew. Rare butterflies found here include the frosted elfin and Persius duskywing. In recent years the federally endangered Karner blue butterfly—no larger than a postage stamp—was reintroduced to the preserve, where it relies on the abundant wild lupine during reproduction. Expect to see some of the park's resident deer, which number in the hundreds. Nesting birds include the state-listed endangered lark sparrow, plus indigo buntings, whip-poor-wills, and bluebirds.

The hike begins and ends at the Springbrook Picnic Area, where the Wabash Cannonball (Rails-to-Trails) Trail bisects the park. Start by walking through the first of many plantations of white, red, and Scotch pines, as well as some spruce and fir stands that were planted by the Metroparks system when it first acquired the land around 1940. Notice how these nonnative species are all in various stages of being replaced with native deciduous forests or open fields. Metroparks is allowing this natural progression to happen and does not intend to plant more evergreens.

The Oak Openings Hiking Trail is thoughtfully designed, rarely joining the bridle trails or following a road. It's mostly flat and on hard-packed dirt. But, as you will see, a main characteristic of the Oak Openings is the sandy soil. It's an interesting experience to walk along the sand in an oak forest. The trail most often winds through native black and white oak with a varying understory. In some places look for a vast, open forest floor covered in cinnamon or bracken fern. In other spots look for the characteristic oak savannas, or oak openings, with widely spaced oak trees and tall-grass prairie species growing underneath, including blazing star, lupine, bird's-foot violet, puccoon, and little bluestem grass. Enter a full-on prairie with no trees and look in spots for yucca, which is well adapted to the sandy soil. The trail passes three attractive bodies of water: Evergreen Lake, Swan Creek, and Springbrook Lake.

You'll have time to reflect on the many who have walked here before you. Archaeologists estimate that humans inhabited the region beginning 12,000 years ago. Recorded history of the Oak Openings begins with European explorers, who used the slightly upland area as part of a transportation route. The region's population was booming around the time the Miami and Erie Canal opened in 1842, but today the main use of the canal towpath is as a right-of-way for hiking trails.

If you're looking for a hike considerably shorter than 15 miles, Oak Openings Preserve Metropark can provide that, too. Most of the preserve's other trails are accessible from the Buehner Center for the Oak Openings. Oak Openings also has an all-purpose trail and a wheelchair-accessible trail. Pick up the park map for more details.

◀ *An oak woodland in Oak Openings Preserve*

Miles and Directions

Note: The trail is long and regularly improved by Boy Scouts. Check with the park for up-to-date trail information. It is very well blazed throughout.

0.0 Start at the Springbrook Picnic Area. Walk to the junction of SR 64 and the Wabash Cannonball bike path. Cross over SR 64 and begin walking east on the paved bike path.

0.1 Leave the paved path by taking a right on the trail into the woods.

0.3 Come to a four-way junction at a fence post. Take a left.

1.1 Go straight at a junction at a fence post. In about 75 feet, take a left. The trail then comes out at the junction of Reed and Manore Roads. Cross the intersection diagonally and pick up the trail on the other side.

2.0 Pass a side trail from the road on the right and continue straight toward mile marker 2. In a few hundred feet, come to a fork. Take the left fork.

2.5 Cross Jeffers Road.

2.9 Cross a footbridge over a tributary to Swan Creek and then cross a horse trail.

3.0 Cross the horse trail again a couple of times.

3.8 Come to a cluster of trail intersections. Continue straight, following the yellow blazes. Cross the horse trail several times.

4.1 Arrive at the Wabash Cannonball Trail Connector and the Lou Campbell Tallgrass Prairie. Take a right and walk on the paved path about 150 feet, then take a left onto the trail that skirts the edge of the prairie. In another 200 feet, the trail turns right, entering the woods.

4.6 Come to a T-intersection and take a left onto a road grade. Pass through a cluster of trail intersections. Watch for the yellow blazes and walk along the edge of Evergreen Lake. **FYI:** This is a good spot for a break, with a picnic shelter and pit toilets. There is no potable water available.

5.2 Come to a T-intersection at the earthen dam. Take a right, cross over the dam, and continue straight. Just before the road, take a left and walk north, paralleling the road.

5.5 The trail hits SR 295. Take a left and parallel the road; do not cross it. Cross over a creek on the road bridge and then reenter the woods on the left.

6.0 Come to a four-way junction. Continue straight. **Note:** The blaze is confusing here. Don't cross the road. Continue straight to mile marker 6.

6.2 The trail comes to Oak Openings Parkway. Take a left and follow the road; do not cross it.

6.4 Cross the park road at a crosswalk, heading north. In about 100 feet, the trail forks. Take the left fork, following the yellow blazes and joining the horse trail.

6.5 At another fork, take the right fork and leave the horse trail.

7.0 Cross Reed Road.

7.7 Come to a junction with the horse trail. Take a right, joining the horse trail.

7.9 Come to the intersection of Wilkins Road and the Wabash Cannonball Trail. Cross diagonally and pick up the trail on the other side, where it joins the horse trail. **FYI:** This is a good spot to set up a car or bike shuttle should you choose to do half the trail at a time. There are a few parking spots here.

8.1 Split off from the horse trail, taking a left.

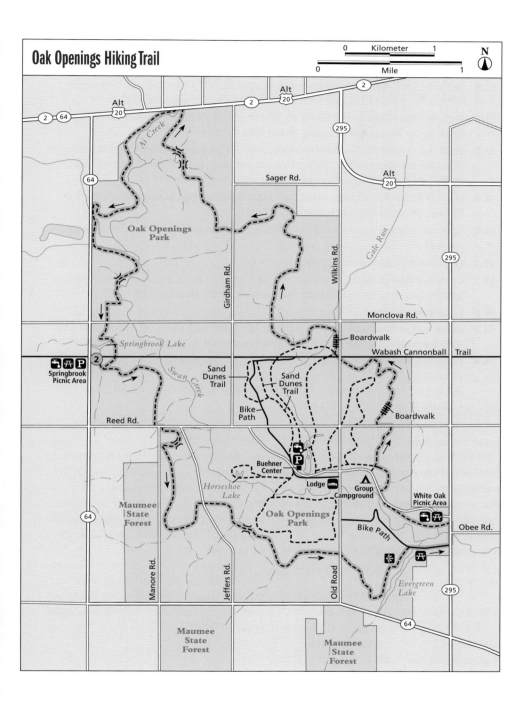

Oak Openings Hiking Trail

Kilometer

Mile

N

Alt 2
Alt 20
2

2 64
Alt 20
2

295

64

Aï Creek

Sager Rd.

Alt 20

Oak Openings
Park

Girdham Rd.

Wilkins Rd.

Gale Run

295

Monclova Rd.

Boardwalk

Springbrook Lake

Wabash Cannonball Trail

2

Swan Creek

Springbrook
Picnic Area

Sand
Dunes
Trail

Sand
Dunes
Trail

Boardwalk

Bike
Path

Reed Rd.

Buehner
Center

Lodge

Group
Campground

White Oak
Picnic Area

Horseshoe
Lake

Maumee
State
Forest

Oak Openings
Park

Bike Path

Obee Rd.

64

Manore Rd.

Jeffers Rd.

Old Road

Evergreen
Lake

295

Maumee
State
Forest

64

Maumee
State
Forest

8.8 Cross Monclova Road.

9.8 After crossing and merging with the horse trail, the Oak Openings Trail leaves the horse trail to the right. This junction is not as well marked as the others.

10.7 Cross Girdham Road.

11.1 At a T-intersection, take a left. In about 200 feet, there is a fork; take the right fork.

11.9 The trail comes out at a decommissioned paved road. Take a right and pass mile marker 12. In a few hundred feet, take a left off of the pavement and onto the trail.

12.0 Come to Airport Highway and take a left. Do not cross the road. After crossing over Swan Creek on the highway bridge, take a left back into the woods.

12.2 Walk behind some homes and take a footbridge over a tributary to Swan Creek. You will then pass an access road on the right (continue straight) and the trail becomes a road grade. Look for the blazes where you leave the road grade to the left.

12.6 The trail becomes a doubletrack dirt road again. Leave the road grade to the left to get on the trail. This junction is not well blazed.

13.0 Pass mile marker 13 and come to a T-intersection. Take a left and join another doubletrack dirt road.

13.1 Leave the road grade and take a left onto the footpath.

13.7 Come to a road grade at a T-intersection. Take a left and cross a footbridge. In a few hundred feet, come to a fork. Take a left and parallel the road. Do not cross it.

15.0 Cross Monclova Road.

15.2 Come to Springbrook Lake at a T-intersection with a dirt road. Take a left and in about 150 feet, take a right off of the road. (There is a connector trail to the group camp on the left.)

15.3 Come to the paved Wabash Cannonball Trail. Take a right and walk back to the trailhead.

15.4 Arrive back at the Springbrook Picnic Area.

Hike Information

Local information: Destination Toledo, (800) 243-4667, www.dotoledo.org

Local events and attractions: The Wabash Cannonball Trail is a 63-mile multiple-use trail from Maumee to Montpelier; wabashcannonballtrail .org. Contact the Northwest Ohio Rails-to-Trails Association, Inc., at (800) 951-4788.

Accommodations: Bluegrass Campground, Swanton; (419) 875-5110; www.bluegrasscamp ground.com

Twin Acres Campground, Whitehouse; (419) 877-2684; www.twinacrescampground.com

The Mill Bed and Breakfast, Grand Rapids; (419) 832-6455; www.themillhouse.com

Restaurants: Loma Linda's, Swanton; (419) 865-5455; www.toledostripletreat.com/loma

Hike tours: Naturalist-led hikes are offered regularly. Call Metroparks of the Toledo Area for up-to-date information at (419) 407-9701 or visit www.metroparkstoledo.com.

Organizations: Maumee Valley Volkssporters walking club; go to www.ava.org/gen3/data/clubevents_results.asp?club=AVA-0532 for a list of events.

Metroparks volunteer program, www.metro parkstoledo.com/metroparks/volunteers

Other resources: The quarterly Metroparks program guide is available at the park or by calling (419) 407-9700.

3 Boardwalk Trail

Maumee Bay State Park

Maumee Bay State Park is home to a 2.4-mile boardwalk that takes you through the heart of a marsh ecosystem. Enjoy this fun little loop that weaves through a swamp forest that gradually gives way to an open marsh. Look for large birds, including white egrets, as well as amphibians and reptiles plus deer. Thick expanses of cattail are dotted with showy swamp rose mallow that provide color in summer and early fall. Take the spur trail to the overlook. It's only about 10 feet high, but that's all you need here. From atop the overlook deck, gaze out over a sea of cattails, with Lake Erie to the north, swamp forests to the south, and development in the distance.

Start: Trautman Nature Center
Distance: 2.4-mile trail system
Hiking time: About 1.5 hours
Difficulty: Easy; short and flat and even wheelchair-accessible
Trail surface: Boardwalk
Blaze: None; junctions are marked.
Best season: Summer
Other trail users: Hikers only
Canine compatibility: Dogs not permitted on the boardwalk trail
Water: Available at the nature center

Land status: State park
Nearest town: Oregon
Fees and permits: None
Schedule: Park open daily until 11 p.m.; boardwalk open dawn to dusk
Maps: Maumee Bay State Park trail map; USGS quad: Reno Beach
Trail contact: Maumee Bay State Park, Oregon; office (419) 836-7758; nature center (419) 836-9117; http://parks.ohiodnr.gov/maumee bay

Finding the trailhead: From SR 2 east of Toledo, turn north onto North Curtice Road and drive 3.1 miles to the nature center entrance on the right. *DeLorme: Ohio Atlas & Gazetteer:* Page 27 C5. GPS: N 41 41.02' / W83 22.04'.

The Hike

If you're a bird-watcher, this is the place for you. The western basin of Lake Erie is situated along both the Mississippi and Atlantic flyways; northward migrating birds gather here in vast numbers in spring. They often stop along the southern shore of the lake to replenish their fat reserves on hatching insects from the marsh before they fly over the lake. The marshes that line Lake Erie are home to about 300 bird species for at least part of the year, and during spring migration tens of thousands of birds gather along the shoreline here. These wetlands teem with animal life among the thick cattail and reed stands. Water levels vary, and trying to walk here can be quite a challenge. The solution: Build a boardwalk.

Swamp rose mallow

Maumee Bay State Park is a special place, in part, because Ohio has lost 90 percent of its wetlands since settlement. Begin the walk from the Trautman Nature Center, which features exhibits on the flora and fauna you will encounter along the board-walk. Interactive exhibits make this a kid-friendly place, and a giant window in the back of the center allows for comfortable bird-watching.

Begin the walk in a swamp forest of swamp white oak, willow, hackberry, and red maple. The ash trees that once lived here are mostly gone due to the emerald ash borer, an insect whose larvae feed on the inner bark of ash trees, killing them. Look for turtles (often seen sunning on a log in the pond nearest the nature center) and amphibians. Soon you will notice the abundant presence of two invasive exotic species, the attractive purple loosestrife and also phragmite grass. The park is spraying herbicides on the phragmite grass in an attempt to eradicate it.

The boardwalk then enters an open marsh. The phragmite grass joins thick expanses of cattail, with showy swamp rose mallow. Take the spur trail to the overlook. It's only about 10 feet high, but that's all you need here. The marsh's largest birds are white egrets and great blue herons, which stand 4 feet tall and have 6-foot wingspans. Other common marsh birds include red-winged blackbirds, kingfishers, green herons, and wood ducks. Look above for bald eagles that nest nearby and sometimes fly overhead. From the overlook, return to the main boardwalk trail and complete a loop back to the nature center.

Maumee Bay has become one of Ohio's most popular state parks, due no doubt to its many amenities: a lodge overlooking the lake, cabins, an eighteen-hole golf course, a campground, and two beaches (one along Lake Erie, the other an inland lake). Nearby natural areas that are more conducive to bird-watching than hiking include Magee Marsh Wildlife Area and Ottawa National Wildlife Refuge.

Miles and Directions

0.0 Start from the side or back door of the nature center and begin walking east on the boardwalk.

0.1 Come to a junction at Post 2. Take a right and walk part of the Short Loop.

0.2 Arrive at a second junction at Post 3. Take another right and walk on the connector section of the boardwalk.

0.3 Hit a T-intersection. Take a right and begin circling the One Mile Loop.

0.6 Pass a side trail on the right that leads to cabins.

0.8 Come to a junction with a side trail to the right to a bird blind. Take the spur to the bird blind, return to this spot, and then continue in a counterclockwise direction.

1.1 Arrive at the junction with the spur trail to the observation tower. Take a right and check out the observation tower.

1.4 Return to the main loop and take a right.

1.9 Finish the One Mile Loop at a junction with the connector trail. Take a right.

2.1 Come to a T-intersection with the Short Loop. Take a right.

2.2 Arrive at a triangular intersection. To the right is the lodge; take a left to return to the nature center.

2.3 Pass the Short Loop trail on the left and continue straight.

2.4 Arrive back at the nature center.

INVASIVE EXOTICS

According to the ODNR Division of Natural Areas and Preserves, about 3,000 species of plants grow in Ohio. Of these, about 75 percent are native to the state. The other 25 percent are exotic plants, meaning that they were introduced from elsewhere, mostly by early European settlers. Some of these exotics are invasive, which means they displace other, native plant species. Among those on DNAP's "hit list" of invasive exotics are Japanese honeysuckle, garlic mustard, multiflora rose (brought here for use as a natural fence—oops!), and, in northern Ohio's wetlands, common reed/phragmite grass and purple loosestrife. You can help avoid further spread of these species by not planting them in your yard and by pulling them out whenever you have the opportunity. Also try to avoid picking up "hitchhikers," carrying seeds from one place to the next.

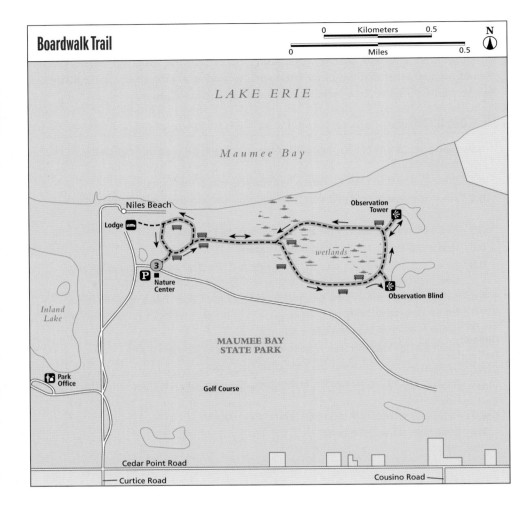

Hike Information

Local information: Toledo Convention and Visitors Bureau, (800) 243-4667, www.dotoledo.org

Local events and attractions: Kite Weekend is the third weekend in July; contact the park for up-to-date information. Magee Marsh Wildlife Area; contact the ODNR Division of Wildlife District 2 offices at (419) 424-5000 or (800) WILDLIFE, or go to www.dnr.state.oh.us/wildlife.

Ottawa National Wildlife Refuge, (419) 898-0014 or www.fws.gov/midwest/ottawa

Accommodations: Maumee Bay Resort/ Quilter Lodge, (419) 836-1466 or (800) 282-7275, www.maumeebaystateparklodge.com

Maumee Bay State Park campground, (419) 836-8828

Restaurants: The lodge's Water's Edge Restaurant, (419) 836-1466

Hike tours: Naturalist-led hikes are offered in season. Contact the nature center for up-to-date information at (419) 836-9117.

Organizations: Black Swamp Bird Observatory, Oak Harbor; (419) 898-4070; www.bsbobird.org

4 South Beach Trail

East Harbor State Park

No matter where you stand in East Harbor State Park, you are no more than 200 yards from the water. East Harbor's 7 miles of trails are mostly located on a peninsula, surrounded by the main body of Lake Erie to the east and natural harbors to the west. Walk along the Wetlands Trail, where boardwalks help when conditions get too muddy. Then hit the South Beach Trail and walk along inland sand dunes under towering cottonwood trees. Watch boats navigating in and out of the channel that links East Harbor and Lake Erie. You have the option to return along the beach. Check out the West Harbor Trail, which narrows to a spit of land less than 20 feet across with West and Middle Harbors on either side.

Start: South Beach parking lot trailhead
Distance: 3-mile loop, with spur loop
Hiking time: About 1 to 1.5 hours
Difficulty: Easy; short and flat
Trail surface: Wide, flat trail on grass, boardwalks, and sand
Blaze: None; junctions are marked.
Best season: Late Apr through late Sept
Other trail users: In winter, trails are open to snowmobiles.
Canine compatibility: Leashed dogs permitted

Water: Available at the North Beach restrooms/concession area
Land status: State park
Nearest town: Lakeside-Marblehead
Fees and permits: None
Schedule: Park open daily until 11 p.m.
Maps: USGS quad: Gypsum
Trail contact: East Harbor State Park, Lakeside-Marblehead; (419) 734-4424; http://parks.ohiodnr.gov/eastharbor

Finding the trailhead: From Sandusky, follow SR 2/SR 269 over Sandusky Bay. When the highways split, take SR 269 north 3.6 miles to the park entrance. Turn right into the park and drive 1.1 miles to the beach area. The road forks here; take a right into the south beach parking lot. *DeLorme: Ohio Atlas & Gazetteer:* Page 28 D3. GPS: N41 33.15' / W82 48.03'.

The Hike

East Harbor State Park is located on the Marblehead Peninsula, which juts more than 5 miles into Lake Erie. This area contains remnants of the Great Black Swamp that once dominated the landscape of northwest Ohio. By the middle of the nineteenth century, timbering and swamp draining had led to the extirpation of such species as ruffed grouse, wild turkey, river otter, bison, wolverine, mountain lion, gray wolf, and even deer. The remaining marshes that surround East Harbor State Park are still home to a relatively high diversity of species, including mammals such as red fox,

woodchuck, and muskrat. A lot of reptiles and amphibians also call this place home, including the green frog, American toad, water snake, fox snake, and painted turtle. The park's main attraction for many hikers, though, is the birding. Look for such species as great blue heron, white egret, mute swan, and black-crowned night heron.

Walk along the Wetlands Trail in, well, a wetland. Growing around you is common reed or phragmite grass, a highly invasive nonnative plant. Some small cedar trees dot the landscape. Walk quietly and bring binoculars in hopes of seeing a lot of bird activity. East Harbor is visible to your right. As you near the end of the peninsula, jump onto the South Beach Trail. This short loop takes you through inland sand dunes beneath towering cottonwood trees. As you circle the edge of the peninsula, you will see boats coming in and out of the narrow harbor channel and trophy homes on the other side of the channel. On your return trip you have the option to walk along the beach.

While you're here, try out the West Harbor Trail. This 1.1-mile out-and-back trip starts along the North Swimming Beach and then curves around to the west, along a spit that's less than 20 feet wide. From this trail West Harbor is to the north and Middle Harbor game sanctuary is to the south.

The entire Marblehead Peninsula is a popular tourist attraction. Several wineries operate in this grape-growing region. From East Harbor State Park, stop at roadside stands or pick-your-own places for fresh fruit. Then make your way to the east end of the peninsula and the famous Marblehead Lighthouse. Johnson's Island, on Sandusky Bay, is the site of a Confederate cemetery. It's a short jaunt to Cedar Point amusement park and a brief ferry ride to Kelleys Island. The Ottawa National Wildlife Refuge is several miles west along the lakeshore.

Miles and Directions

0.0 Start from the trailhead sign near the South Beach parking lot, next to the restrooms. In about 100 feet there's a side trail, which rejoins the main trail a few hundred feet farther on.

0.5 Approach a boardwalk on the left; continue straight.

1.0 Come to a fork at a red post; take a right and walk to a gravel road. Take a right and walk south down the gravel road to the end. **Option:** Continue straight to return directly for a 1.3-mile loop.

1.4 Leave the road and arrive at a fork. Take the South Beach Loop Trail in either direction, and return to this point.

2.7 Return the way you came on the gravel road to the junction on the Wetlands Trail. Take a right and head north.

3.0 Arrive at the terminal trailhead at the parking lot, just south of where you started.

◀ *The beach at East Harbor State Park*
OHIO DEPARTMENT OF NATURAL RESOURCES

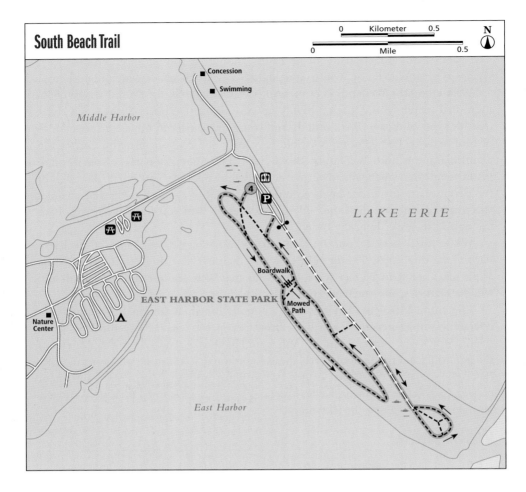

Hike Information

Local information: Marblehead Peninsula Chamber of Commerce, (419) 734-9777, www .marbleheadpeninsula.com

Lake Erie Shores and Islands, (800) 441-1271, www.shoresandislands.com

Local events and attractions: Other activities in the park include camping, swimming, fishing, and boating from a fully equipped marina.

Accommodations: East Harbor State Park campground; call (866) 644-6727 for reservations.

Restaurants: The Crow's Nest restaurant overlooks West Harbor; (419) 734-1742 or http://crowsnestohio.com.

5 North Shore Loop, North Pond, and East Quarry Trails

Kelleys Island State Park and North Pond State Nature Preserve

Explore Kelleys Island by a combination of bicycle and foot to enjoy the unique natural features this charming tourist trap has to offer. Take a ferry to this Lake Erie island and head to the famous Glacial Grooves State Memorial. From there hike on the self-guided North Shore Trail to the water's edge, where you have views of other Lake Erie islands nearby and the horizon beyond. Also check out the North Pond State Nature Preserve on a boardwalk through a wetland. Hit the East Quarry Trail and walk around Horseshoe Lake, which was created when rainwater filled this former limestone quarry. The surroundings are dotted with cedar trees.

To reach Kelleys Island from SR 2/SR 269 west of Sandusky, cross Sandusky Bay to Marblehead Peninsula. When SR 2 and SR 269 split, continue on SR 269 for 2.2 miles to a T-intersection with SR 163. Turn right (east) and drive 5.4 miles to the Kelleys Island Ferry Boat Line parking on the left. Take the ferry to the island. *DeLorme: Ohio Atlas & Gazetteer:* Page 28 D4.
Best season: Memorial Day through Labor Day
Nearest town: Kelleys Island

Fees and permits: There is a fee to take the ferry to Kelleys Island; rates vary depending on whether it's just a person or an additional bicycle or car; (419) 798-9763 or www.kelleys islandferry.com. No fees or permits are required for hiking.
Schedule: Open daily from dawn to dusk. Check seasonal ferry service hours.
Maps: USGS quad: Kelleys Island
Trail contact: Kelleys Island State Park, Kelleys Island; (419) 746-2546 or (419) 734-4424; http://parks.ohiodnr.gov/kelleysisland

The Hikes

Kelleys Island is a bona fide tourist trap, but it has managed to retain its charm and has set aside several natural areas for exploration. The only public transportation to the Lake Erie islands is ferryboat, so just getting to Kelleys Island is fun. Begin with a twenty-minute ferry ride to Kelleys and then explore the 2-by-3-mile island by a combination of bicycle and foot.

From the ferry dock, stop by Inscription Rock, a large limestone boulder where Native Americans carved now-faint pictographs 300 to 500 years ago. Then head north out of downtown on Division Street to Glacial Grooves State Memorial. This excavated spot is known as the world's largest and clearest example of striations caused by glaciers scouring out bedrock. Glaciers produced Lake Erie and the islands in this area.

Glacial grooves at Kelleys Island State Park OHIO DEPARTMENT OF NATURAL RESOURCES

From the glacial grooves to the trailhead for the North Shore Loop Trail, pass an old limestone quarry. The history of Kelleys Island is tied to its natural resource base. Quarrying was once a dominant industry here, and the old quarries remain, some now filled with water. Eastern red cedar trees grow out of this calcium-rich rock and dot the landscape. The land is also suitable for fruit orchards and vineyards, and several wineries exist on Kelleys and other Lake Erie islands. Many people have also made their living fishing the abundant waters of Lake Erie, dominated by walleye, perch, bass, and catfish.

The North Shore Loop is a self-guided nature trail (ask for a map and guide at the campground). Begin by walking alongside the North Quarry, opened in 1830 and operated for more than seventy years. The trail winds by an old loader, used to load crushed limestone onto railcars, and then past an old spoil bank composed of by-products from the limestone crushing process. Walk through second- and third-growth deciduous forests of water-loving cottonwood, ash, and hackberry, identified by its "treads" of corky bark. The evergreens are red cedar. Underfoot, watch out for

▶ Campsites 85, 87, 89, 91, 92, 93, 95, 97, 101, 103, and 104 at Kelleys Island State Park are situated along the water.

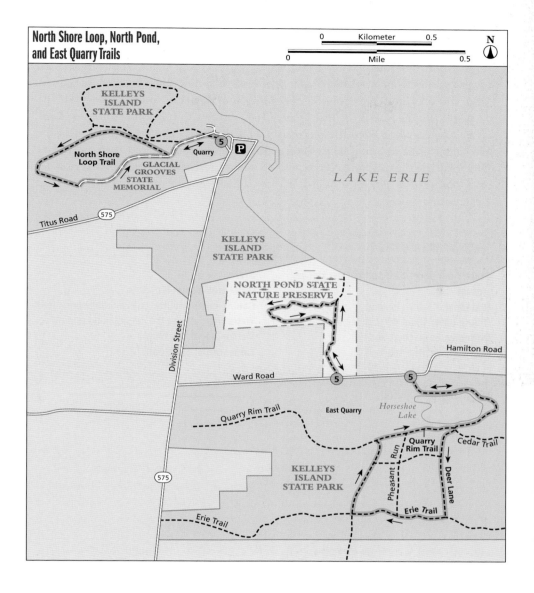

North Shore Loop, North Pond, and East Quarry Trails

poison ivy and Virginia creeper. The trail loops around but has plenty of access trails to the north shore of Kelleys Island.

From the north shore, watch waves crash up against the rocks. If you look closely, you'll see where glacial grooves are evident here as well. To the west you can identify Put-in-Bay by the tall monolith that marks Perry's Victory and International Peace Memorial. Oliver Hazard Perry led US troops in Lake Erie to a victory over the British in the War of 1812, helping turn the tide to an American victory. Return on the loop trail to where you started along Division Street.

Round out a day of hiking by heading down to Ward Road and two more worth-while hikes. The North Pond State Nature Preserve features a 1-mile boardwalk through a lovely forest and wetland. Birding is excellent here; a bird observation tower overlooks the wetland. A spur trail leads to a rare barrier-beach ecosystem. Since this is a nature preserve, you can't bring your dog along on this one.

Just down the road is the East Quarry Trail, which winds around Horseshoe Lake, created when water filled the old quarry. This is an excellent trail for views of the lake and a wetland. You'll be walking mostly on limestone, dotted with red cedars. Due to all the rock and the evergreens, the trail is more reminiscent of western states than Ohio. This is also a self-guided nature trail, so request a map from the state park campground office.

North Shore Loop Trail

Start: Boat parking lot north of the glacial grooves
Distance: 1.7-mile lollipop
Hiking time: About 45 minutes to 1 hour
Difficulty: Easy; short and flat
Trail surface: Dirt trail

Blaze: None
Other trail users: Bicyclists
Canine compatibility: Leashed dogs permitted
Water: Available at the campground and at Memorial Park downtown
Land status: State park

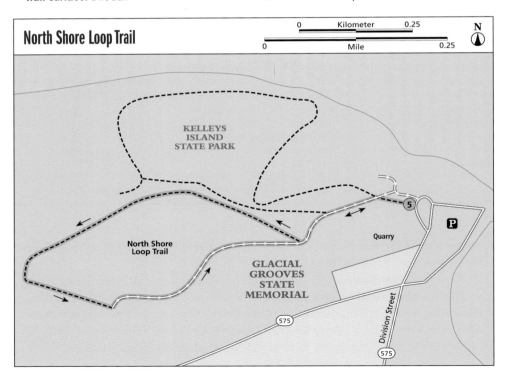

Finding the trailhead: From the ferry dock—by foot, car, golf cart, or bicycle—turn left and continue to the stop sign. Go straight and travel westward on East Lakeshore Drive 0.5 mile to downtown. Turn right (north) onto Division Street and travel 1.7 miles to its end, where there is a parking lot. The trailhead is on the west side of the parking area. GPS: N41 37.06' / W82 42.34'.

Miles and Directions

0.0 Start at the trailhead sign off the parking lot return road. Walk straight past the trailhead sign and in about 25 feet pass a side trail on the left.

0.1 The trail joins a doubletrack road and then forks. Take a right to begin the loop.

0.2 A side trail leads to an old quarry spoil bank (Post 3). Continue straight.

0.6 The trail forks. Take the left fork to continue on the trail, but first take the right spur to the lakeshore. **FYI:** Several spur trails off of the main trail lead to the lake and good lunch spots.

1.1 After passing a half-dozen side trails to the right, the trail curves sharply left (south) and arrives at a T-intersection. Take a left (east).

1.3 Post 9 describes old foundations and quarry roads. Side trails explore these features. Continue straight.

1.5 The trail rejoins the doubletrack road and continues straight.

1.7 Arrive back at the trailhead.

North Pond State Nature Preserve Trail

Start: Trailhead kiosk off of Ward Road
Distance: 1.1-mile lollipop
Hiking time: About 30 to 45 minutes
Difficulty: Easy; short and flat
Trail surface: Recycled plastic boardwalk
Blaze: None

Other trail users: Hikers only
Canine compatibility: Dogs not permitted
Water: Available at the campground and at Memorial Park downtown
Land status: State nature preserve

Finding the trailhead: From the junction of East Lakeshore and Division, travel north 0.9 mile to Ward Road. Take a right and go 0.4 mile to North Pond State Nature Preserve on the left. GPS: N41 36.42' / W82 42.03'.

Miles and Directions

0.0 Start at the trailhead kiosk off Ward Road.

0.2 Come to a fork. Take the right fork and begin a counterclockwise loop.

0.3 Come to a junction with the spur trail to the beach on the right. Continue straight.

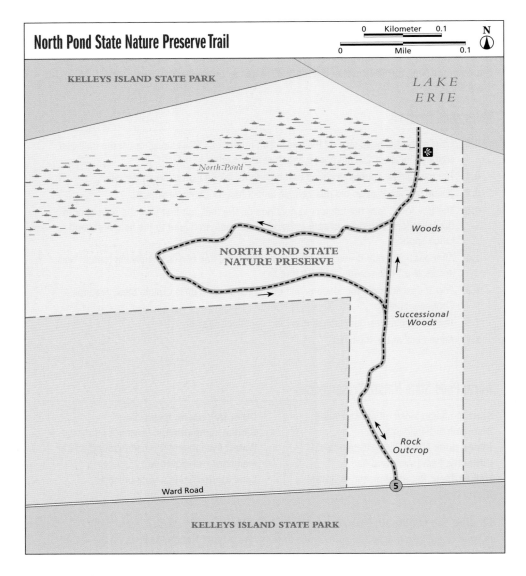

North Pond State Nature Preserve Trail

KELLEYS ISLAND STATE PARK

LAKE ERIE

North Pond

NORTH POND STATE
NATURE PRESERVE

Woods

Successional
Woods

Rock
Outcrop

Ward Road

KELLEYS ISLAND STATE PARK

0.4 Arrive at the wetland overlook deck. Return from the deck and continue in a counterclockwise direction.

0.9 Return to the first junction. Take a right.

1.1 Arrive back at the trailhead.

East Quarry Trail

Start: Trailhead off of Ward Road, marked with a map and a Swimming/Diving Prohibited sign
Distance: 2.5-mile lollipop
Hiking time: About 1 hour
Difficulty: Easy; short and flat
Trail surface: Broad, rock and dirt trail

Blaze: None
Other trail users: Bicyclists
Canine compatibility: Leashed dogs permitted
Water: Available at the campground and at Memorial Park downtown
Land status: State park

Finding the trailhead: From the junction of East Lakeshore and Division, travel north 0.9 mile to Ward Road. Take a right and go 0.8 mile to the trailhead on the right. (If you reach a sharp left in the road, you've gone too far.) GPS: N41 36.43' / W82 41.75'.

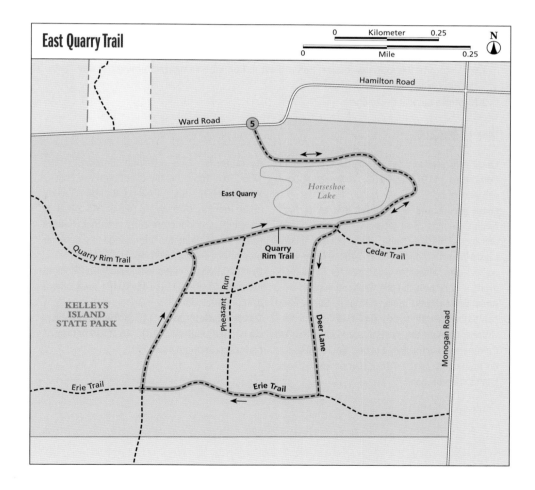

East Quarry Trail

Miles and Directions

0.0 Start at the trailhead, located on the south side of Ward Road. Walk past the sign.

0.1 Come to a four-way intersection just before the quarry. Take a left and begin walking around the quarry.

0.6 Reach another four-way intersection. Take a left, turning away from the quarry. In about 20 feet, reach a fork (Post 4). Take the right fork.

0.7 Pass Post 6 on the left and come to a four-way intersection. Continue straight.

1.0 Pass Post 7 on the right and come to a T-intersection. Take a right.

1.2 Pass Post 9 and come to a junction. Continue straight.

1.3 Come to a four-way intersection. Take a right.

1.4 Pass a side trail on the left.

1.5 Now on a dirt road, pass another side trail on the right.

1.6 Arrive at a T-intersection, now back at the quarry. Take a right. **FYI:** Check out the wetland and views of the lake from here.

1.9 Return to the four-way intersection at Post 4. Continue straight, returning the way you came.

2.5 Arrive back at the trailhead.

Hike Information

Local information: Kelleys Island Chamber of Commerce, (419) 746-2360, www.kelleysisland chamber.com

Local events and attractions: Birding, cycling, fishing, boating, and jet-skiing are all popular activities at Kelleys Island. Check out the Kelleys Island Wine Company; (419) 746-2678 or www .kelleysislandwine.com. Islandfest is an annual event, usually held the last weekend in July.

Accommodations: Kelleys Island State Park campground; call (866) 644-6727 for reservations. Contact the Kelleys Island Chamber of Commerce for a full listing of bed-and-breakfasts on the island; (419) 746-2360 or www.kelleys islandchamber.com.

Restaurants: Kelleys Island Brewery, (419) 746-2314, http://kelleysislandbrewpub.com

Hike tours: The Kelleys Island Audubon Society offers monthly bird walks; (419) 746-2258 or www.kelleysislandnature.com. Contact Kelleys Island State Park for information on summer programs; (419) 746-2546.

Organizations: Kelleys Island Audubon Society, Kelleys Island; (419) 746-2546; www.kelleys islandnature.com

Transportation: Caddy Shack Rentals for bicycle and cart rentals; (419) 746-2664 or http:// caddyshacksquare.com

Honorable Mentions

Northwest Ohio

A Upland Woods Trail, Wildwood Preserve Metropark

Toledo's Wildwood Preserve Metropark could be named Wildly Popular Metropark, and its popularity is consistent with the spirit of its origins. In 1973 a developer's plans were thwarted by the Citizens' Campaign to Save the Stranahan Estate. Two years later the former estate of Champion Spark Plug Company cofounder Robert A. Stranahan became Wildwood Preserve Metropark. Try the 2.3-mile Upland Woods Trail and hike in a forest of maple, oak, sassafras, and witch hazel. Enjoy outstanding wildflower displays from spring through fall as well as wildlife and a floodplain eco-system. Don't be afraid to take the narrower, less-traveled side trails and explore the many verdant streambeds that drain into the Ottawa River.

Trail contact: Metroparks of the Toledo Area, (419) 407-9700, www.metroparks toledo.com

Finding the trailhead: From I-475 northwest of Toledo, exit east on US 20 (exit 13) and drive 1.6 miles to the park entrance on the left. Follow signs to the Metz Visitors Center, where all trails originate. *DeLorme: Ohio Atlas & Gazetteer:* Page 26 C3. GPS: N41 40.85' / W83 40.09'.

B Miami and Erie Canal Towpath Trail: Farnsworth Metropark to Providence Metropark

Nature and history meet along an 8-mile ramble on the Miami and Erie Canal tow-path, which parallels the Maumee River near Toledo. Begin walking upstream from the popular Farnsworth Metropark. Just a couple of miles in, arrive at Bend View Metropark, where you can enjoy views of the towering cottonwoods, sycamores, and maples. Keep an eye out for ospreys and bald eagles. Continue all the way to Provi-dence Metropark for the "canal experience," complete with a mule-drawn canal boat replica, a restored lock and mill, and interpretive guides dressed in period clothing. Shuttle or return the way you came for a 16-mile out-and-back hike.

Trail contacts: Metroparks of the Toledo Area, (419) 407-9700; Farnsworth/ Bend View Metroparks, (419) 878-7641; www.metroparkstoledo.com

Finding the trailhead: From I-475 southwest of Toledo, exit west on SR 24 (exit 4) and drive 5.5 miles to the Roche de Bout Shelterhouse parking on the left. GPS: N41 29.23 / W83 44.11. To shuttle, continue west 8 miles to the entrance to Providence Metropark, also on the left. *DeLorme: Ohio Atlas & Gazetteer:* Page 36 A2. GPS: 41 25.06' / W83 52.12'.

◯ Sheldon Marsh State Nature Preserve Trails

The 2-mile out-and-back trail at Sheldon Marsh is mostly along an asphalt path that was once part of the original automobile road to Cedar Point amusement park. This short jaunt allows you to explore a swamp forest, a cattail marsh, and a barrier beach—a remnant of this once-common ecosystem in the Sandusky Bay region. Springtime brings such showy wildflowers as Dutchman's-breeches, trout lilies, and trilliums, as well as migrating birds, including colorful warblers. Throughout the year this small preserve sees as many as 300 bird species. Look for large, conspicuous birds such as great blue herons and bald eagles. From May 1 to September 30, the beach is off-limits to hiking in order to protect the nesting grounds of the federally endangered piping plover and the state-endangered common tern. The beach provides ideal nesting habitat for these two birds. Across the water Cedar Point's roller coasters rise from the horizon.

Trail contact: Sheldon Marsh State Nature Preserve, Huron; (440) 839-1561; http://ohiodnr.com/location/sheldon/tabid/910/Default.aspx

Finding the trailhead: From SR 2 in Huron, exit north onto SR 6 (Rye Beach Road). At the stoplight, take a left (west); drive 0.6 mile to the preserve entrance on the right. *DeLorme: Ohio Atlas & Gazetteer:* Page 39 A5. GPS: N41 24.53' / W82 36.17'.

◯ Buckeye Trail: Minster to 40 Acre Lake

This is not a wilderness trail; rather it's a 13-mile slice of rural and small-town America. Start just north of the town of Minster and walk through farmland, New Bremen, more farmland, and then through the attractive little burg of St. Marys. Continue to a finish at 40 Acre Lake. This portion of the Buckeye Trail follows the Miami and Erie Canal Towpath Trail; amenities (water, food, restrooms) are available along the way. Be sure to check out the Bicycle Museum in Bremen. Avoid this hike during full summer sun, since it's quite exposed. The St. Marys section of the Buckeye Trail map has detailed directions.

Trail contact: Buckeye Trail Association, Worthington; (740) 832-1BTA; www.buckeyetrail.org

Finding the trailhead (north trailhead): From I-75 near Wapakoneta, drive west 10.5 miles on US 33 to SR 66. Turn north onto SR 66 and drive 2.1 miles to Glynwood Road (Township Road 160). Turn left (west) and drive 1.6 miles to a pullout near the bridge that crosses over the north end of 40 Acre Lake. *DeLorme: Ohio Atlas & Gazetteer:* Page 45 D4. GPS: N40 34.99 / W 84 23.38.

Finding the trailhead (south trailhead): From I-75 between Wapakoneta and Sidney, turn west onto SR 119 and drive 12.5 miles through Minster (watch for the turns—if you hit the railroad tracks, you've just passed the trailhead). Pull off onto the right side of the road and hop on the towpath. *DeLorme: Ohio Atlas & Gazetteer:* Page 55 A5. GPS: N40 24.45' / W84 22.99'.

E Sand Dunes Trail, Oak Openings Preserve Metropark

The 2-mile Sand Dunes Trail in this Toledo Metropark provides a truly unique Ohio hiking experience. In addition to the rare experience of walking in woodland sand dunes up to 35 feet high, you'll find yourself in a park with the state's highest concentration of endangered, rare, and at-risk plant and animal species. Rare species include the Karner blue butterfly. Not rare but still unusual for Ohio are lupine and prickly pear cactus. Begin the hike among oak trees and a relatively open forest floor. After hitting the junction where the trail splits to do a loop, you will come upon the open sand dune area, which is really a sight to behold. The trail begins and ends at Mallard Lake, where there is a nature center and other trailheads.

Trail contact: Oak Openings Preserve Metropark, Swanton; (419) 407-9700

Finding the trailhead: From I-475 exit 4, take US 24 west 4.4 miles to SR 64. Go north on SR 64 for 4.1 miles to SR 295. Take a right and go 0.8 mile to Oak Openings Parkway and take a left. Go 1.2 miles to the Mallard Lake parking area on the right. *DeLorme: Ohio Atlas & Gazetteer:* Page 26 D2. GPS: N41 32.70' / W83 50.74'.

Northeast Ohio

When the Connecticut Western Reserve was admitted into the US Confederation in 1786, this land was already known as "Ohio," a word borrowed from the Iroquois language meaning "beautiful waters." In northeast Ohio today, little more than names are left to remind us of who inhabited or frequented these lands before Europeans: Erie, Wyandot/Huron, Delaware, Ottawa. When US forces and Native American nations signed the Treaty of Greenville in 1795, much of Ohio was opened for settlement. The following year, surveyor Moses Cleaveland landed on the shores of Lake Erie (and, as the joke goes, said "We'll just stay until the weather clears").

The completion of the Erie Canal in 1825, connecting the Atlantic Ocean with the Great Lakes, and then the Ohio and Erie Canal in 1832, connecting Lake Erie with the Ohio River, fueled the population growth of northeast Ohio. The steel industry employed a large segment of the workforce, and by the beginning of the twentieth century, Cleveland (the name was shortened to fit a newspaper headline) was the nation's sixth-largest city. The Cleveland Metroparks system was established in 1917, and today it provides an "emerald necklace" of greenspace around the sprawling metropolitan area. Excellent multiuse and hiking trails ring the city in this well-run park system.

Yet another strip of greenspace connects Cleveland and Akron, surrounding the Cuyahoga River and the old Ohio and Erie Canal. Cuyahoga Valley National Recreation Area was established in 1970, and it was upgraded in 2000 to become Ohio's only national park. Cuyahoga Valley National Park is home to more than 125 miles of trails, including the 20-mile Ohio and Erie Canal Towpath Trail. Northeast Ohioans love their trails, and several hiking organizations get together to hike and help with trail maintenance around Cuyahoga Valley National Park and several cities' metroparks.

The statewide Buckeye Trail begins its route from the north at Headlands Dunes State Nature Preserve and Headlands Beach State Park. A spur from here leads to a 1,400-mile loop around the entire state. A number of other state parks and preserves are concentrated in the Western Allegheny or Appalachian Plateau, which extends

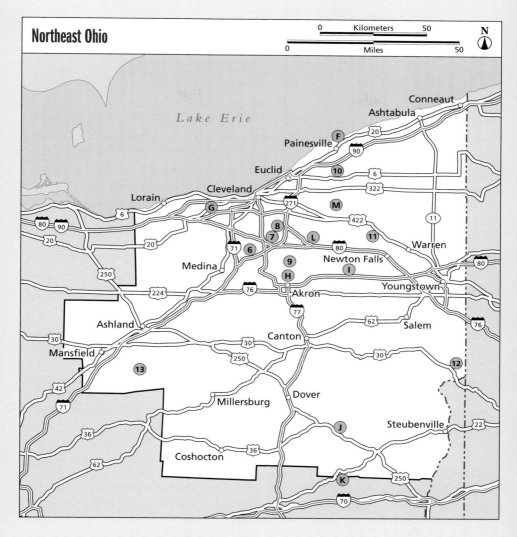

from Pennsylvania into Ohio. Because the last glacier advanced this far, the hills are more rounded here than in the southeastern portion of the state. Natural ponds, bogs, and wetlands are more prevalent, especially closer to the shore of Lake Erie. Wildlife species that once struggled in Ohio are coming back nicely, such as beaver, white-tailed deer, bald eagle, and now black bear.

In far northern Ohio, rivers flow north into Lake Erie; rivers in the rest of the state flow south to the Ohio River. The Muskingum River watershed, south of the state's watershed divide, encompasses much of the landmass in northeast Ohio. The Muskingum Watershed Conservancy District manages 54,000 acres of land in the watershed for flood control, conservation, and recreation. A number of reservoirs, including Tappan and Piedmont Lakes, are home to plenty of lakeside hiking opportunities.

6 Hinckley Lake to Whipps Ledges Trail Loop

Hinckley Reservation

Hinckley Reservation is one of the best known in the Cleveland Metroparks system. The reservation gets its fifteen minutes of fame every year with the return of the buzzards. For locals, its 25 miles of trails are just as popular. Try a 6.7-mile loop around Hinckley Lake (a reservoir created by damming the East Branch Rocky River) and continue on the Buckeye Trail to Whipps Ledges, an area of 40-foot-high Sharon conglomerate rock ledges. In the meantime, enjoy views of the lake, lakeside birds, wildflowers, and forest.

Start: Spillway Pool Picnic Area
Distance: 6.7-mile loop with spur loop
Hiking time: About 2.5 to 3.5 hours
Difficulty: Moderate due to length
Trail surface: Crushed gravel and dirt trail
Blaze: Hinckley Lake Trail, blue heron silhouette; Buckeye Trail, blue paint; Whipps Ledges Trail, oak leaf silhouette
Best season: Mid-Apr through mid-Oct and after a winter snowfall
Other trail users: Hikers only
Canine compatibility: Leashed dogs permitted

Water: Available at the restrooms/changing rooms
Land status: Cleveland Metropark
Nearest town: Brunswick
Fees and permits: None
Schedule: Open daily from 6 a.m. to 11 p.m.
Maps: Buckeye Trail Section Map: Medina; USGS quad: West Richfield
Trail contacts: Hinckley Reservation, Cleveland Metroparks, Hinckley; (216) 635-3200; www.clemetparks.com. Hinckley Boathouse, Hinckley; (330) 278-2160

Finding the trailhead: From SR 303 east of Brunswick, turn south on SR 606 and drive 0.8 mile to Bellus Road. Turn left (east) and drive 0.2 mile to the parking lot on the left, next to the ranger station. *DeLorme: Ohio Atlas & Gazetteer:* Page 41 C5. GPS: N41 13.71' / W81 43.23'.

The Hike

Bird-watchers and other curious folks gather every March to celebrate the harbinger-of-spring return of the buzzards, large bald-headed scavengers, also known as turkey vultures. The Annual Return of the Buzzards is a park event every March 15, when the buzzards supposedly return like clockwork. The celebration motto is "No one spots a buzzard until the Official Buzzard Spotter spots one first!"

The central feature of Hinckley Reservation is Hinckley Lake, a dammed reservoir on the East Branch Rocky River. This body of water provides good birding year-round, where great blue herons, kingfishers, ducks, and Canada geese are as common as the buzzards. The Hinckley Lake Loop Trail encircles the entire reservoir, providing

Great blue herons frequent Hinckley Lake. ATTILA HORVATH

good views of the lake, its human and avian visitors, deciduous and evergreen forests, and plentiful wildflowers. This well-used lake and its surrounding trails are enjoyed by hikers, joggers, cyclists, anglers, canoeists, and kayakers (you can rent canoes and kayaks from the boathouse).

The trail begins near the swimming area below the dam spillway and generally hugs the lakeside all the way to the river. You will pass wetlands, home to more birds as well as willows, cattails, and grasses. As you hike, disregard the various side access trails to the main (crushed gravel) trail and to fishing spots. Look for water lily in the lake and forget-me-not, St. John's wort, and Canada lily along the trail.

At the source of the lake, cross the road and jump on the Buckeye Trail (BT), which serves as a connector path to the Whipps Ledges Trail. This short section of the statewide BT is an attractive narrow footpath that parallels the edge of the East Fork Rocky River for a stretch. In this sunny, wet area look for horsetail (scouring rush), wild rose, and willow.

The trail then joins Whipps Ledges, another highlight of Hinckley Reservation. The trail starts at the bottom of these 40-foot Sharon conglomerate outcroppings, which are made up of rounded quartz pebbles cemented into sedimentary sandstone. The quartz pebbles come from ancient streams that rounded their shape and deposited them in layers. Beech and maple trees grow up between the many rock ledges and passageways, where you can expect to see rock climbers on nice days. The trail continues up a stone stairway to the top of the ledges. Oaks and hickories grow up here, and you can peer down to where you climbed from.

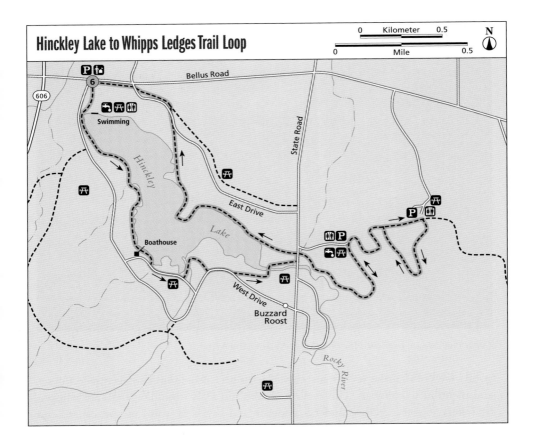

The last leg of the trail rejoins Hinckley Lake's east side, where stands of spruce join the deciduous forest. Walk along the asphalt all-purpose trail to finish the loop. Hinckley Reservation is home to more than 25 miles of hiking, bridle, and all-purpose trails to explore on another day.

Miles and Directions

0.0   Start on the asphalt all-purpose trail where it begins along Bellus Road. Walk south, toward the spillway.

0.1   From the bottom of the spillway, take the stairs to the top and reach a four-way intersection. You'll see the first blue heron blaze ahead. Walk straight through the intersection and begin paralleling the lakeshore. Stay on the broad crushed-gravel path and walk past numerous side access and fishing trails.

0.4   The trail forks. Take the left fork, staying near the lake.

1.2   Pass a junction on the left and continue straight toward the boathouse. Walk straight along the asphalt access road, past the boathouse, and to the all-purpose trail. At the all-purpose trail, take a left and pick up the crushed-gravel path again. Pass the restrooms.

1.3 As you walk into the picnic area, look for a junction to the right. Take this unmarked trail to the right through a small wetland. Walk straight to the all-purpose trail again. At the all-purpose trail, take a left and parallel the trail to the end of the reservoir.

1.5 Pass a picnic area on the left and cross over a footbridge on the all-purpose trail. Just past the footbridge, reach a junction. Take a left and pick up the crushed-gravel path, blazed now with both the heron and the blue Buckeye Trail (BT) blaze.

2.3 Come to a T-intersection with the all-purpose trail. Take a left and follow the all-purpose trail over the bridge.

2.5 At a four-way intersection, take a right and cross State Road at the Whipps Ledges picnic area sign. Walk past the sign to a split-rail fence. At the fence, pick up the BT to the right, marked with a blue blaze.

2.8 At the river's edge, reach a fork. Take the left fork and ascend the slope.

3.1 Come out at a picnic area, behind the restrooms. Turn right; in about 50 feet the trail forks. There are no visible blazes here; take the right fork, where the trail is more level.

3.3 The trail approaches the ledges. Take a left here and walk along the bottom of the rocks.

3.4 Between two rock faces, follow stone steps to the top of the rocks. At the top of the steps, take a right, turning away from the blue blaze. In about 50 feet, come to a post with blazes for both the BT and Whipps Ledges. Disregard the arrows on the post and continue straight ahead.

3.5 The trail forks. Stay right and continue to the picnic area. (**FYI:** Water is available here.) Come to a T-intersection with a dirt path and a post. Take a right and follow the trail into the woods.

3.8 The trail forks. Either fork descends to the top of the ledges. At the top of the ledges, turn right and return to the intersection for the BT and Whipps Ledges. Take a left and return to the top of the stairs. Return the way you came to reach State Road.

4.9 Cross State Road and pick up the crushed-gravel path again, marked with the blue heron blaze.

5.9 Pass a side trail on the right and continue straight into a patch of spruce trees.

6.0 Cross East Drive and join the all-purpose trail. Follow it to the end of the road.

6.5 Come to a T-intersection with Bellus Road. Turn left and cross East Drive, staying on the all-purpose trail, paralleling Bellus Road.

6.7 Arrive back at the trailhead.

Hike Information

Local information: Medina County Convention and Visitors Bureau, (800) 860-2943, www.visit medinacounty.com

Local events and attractions: The annual Return of the Buzzards is celebrated every March 15 and again the following Sunday (unless, of course, the 15th is a Sunday). Cuyahoga Valley National Park is less than 10 miles east of Hinckley Reservation; (330) 657-2752 or www .nps.gov/cuva.

Hike tours: Naturalist-led walks are available; contact the park for up-to-date information.

Organizations: Buckeye Trail Association, Worthington; (740) 832-1BTA; www.buckeye trail.org

Other resources: Cleveland Metroparks produces a newsletter, *Emerald Necklace*, available online, at nature and visitor centers, and by subscription; (216) 635-3200.

Buckeye Trail: Red Lock to Blue Hen Falls to Boston Store

Cuyahoga Valley National Park

Upgraded from national recreation area to national park in 2000, Cuyahoga Valley National Park straddles a 22-mile north–south section of the Cuyahoga River between Cleveland and Akron. Tracing a line right down the center of it all is a section of the statewide Buckeye Trail (BT). For a relatively long and secluded hike in this popular park, tackle the BT from Red Lock and hike to the historic town of Boston, then return on the canal towpath. Stop at the popular Blue Hen and Buttermilk Falls along the way.

Start: Red Lock parking area
Distance: 8.7-mile loop
Hiking time: About 3 to 5 hours
Difficulty: Difficult due to length and one steep ascent and descent
Trail surface: Dirt trail and crushed-gravel canal towpath
Blaze: Blue
Best season: Mid-Apr through mid-Oct
Other trail users: Hikers only
Canine compatibility: Leashed dogs permitted
Water: Don't rely on seasonal hours of operation at Jaite park headquarters or Boston Store; bring your own.

Land status: National park
Nearest town: Peninsula
Fees and permits: None
Schedule: Open daily from dawn to dusk; visitor centers closed Thanksgiving, Christmas, and New Year's Day
Maps: Cuyahoga Valley National Park map; Buckeye Trail Section Map: Bedford; USGS quad: Northfield
Trail contact: Cuyahoga Valley National Park, Peninsula; (330) 657-2752, (800) 257-9477; www.nps.gov/cuva, www.dayinthevalley.com

Finding the trailhead: From I-77 in Brecksville, exit east on SR 82 (Chippewa Road). Pass SR 21 and drive 0.2 mile to Chippewa Creek Drive. Turn right (south) and drive 1.8 miles to Riverview Road. Turn right (south) onto Riverview and drive 2.4 miles to Vaughn Road. Turn left (east) and drive 0.5 mile, crossing the railroad tracks and the river. Just past the river and on the left is the parking lot for Red Lock. *DeLorme: Ohio Atlas & Gazetteer:* Page 41 B6. GPS: N41 17.35' / W81 33.88'.

The Hike

With more than 125 miles of trails, Cuyahoga Valley National Park is one of Ohio's premier hiking areas. Add a well-developed outdoor adventure infrastructure, and you can easily spend several days or longer discovering all the nooks and crannies of this lush greenway. The two best ways to do this are by cycling the Ohio and Erie Canal Towpath and by hiking some (or all) of the park's footpaths.

Blue Hen Falls

Starting from Red Lock, cross the Cuyahoga River. The beauty of this winding river does not belie the struggles it still has with pollution. (Park literature euphemistically says that water quality "varies.") In late summer you'll be walking in sun-loving grasses and wildflowers such as wingstem, bottlebrush, bergamot, goldenrod, and ironwood. Soon you will walk past the former mill-company town known as Jaite. Today this collection of buildings serves as park headquarters. The trail then crosses the road and steeply ascends to the top of the ridge. Power line rights-of-way provide occasional views of the river valley below.

Atop the ridge, hike in a nicely maturing mixed mesophytic hardwood forest. Occasionally you'll cross cool ravines that are lined by hemlock and musclewood. Spring greens and wildflowers include coltsfoot, jack-in-the-pulpit, mayapple, and ramps (wild leeks). Toward the end of this stretch along the ridgetop, arrive at Blue Hen Falls, pouring into a shale creek bed. Take the spur trail that passes Blue Hen Falls and continue to Buttermilk Falls, a beautiful cascade that's worth the short trip. Return to the BT and cross the road again, then descend steeply back down to the river across from Brandywine Ski Resort.

As you cross the bridge back over the Cuyahoga, look to the north side. You may see the wooden remains of a former dam that long ago impounded water for a mill. Take a break and stop at the restored Boston Store, which is now a canal and canal boat museum. Across from the old Boston Store, pick up an ice-cream cone at Trail Mix general store.

Return to Red Lock by walking north on the crushed-gravel canal towpath. Completed in 1827, the Ohio and Erie Canal linked Cleveland and Lake Erie with Portsmouth and the Ohio River. Towns boomed along the canal, including Cleveland and Akron but also Peninsula and Boston. Look across the river for railroad tracks. Railroads displaced canal transport by the end of the nineteenth century, and now the automobile has rendered this railway a sentimental scenic byway. As you walk north, pass Stanford House (see Hike 8) on the right.

Miles and Directions

0.0 Start at the Red Lock trailhead, off Vaughn/Highland Road. Take the spur to the towpath. At the towpath turn left (south) and cross Highland Road. Turn right and cross the river on the road.

0.1 Just past the Entering Cuyahoga County road sign, take a left and pick up the trail, blazed with a signpost that might be obscured.

0.6 Walk under power lines and cross the railroad tracks. Another trailhead comes in from the right here.

0.7 Come to a junction with Riverview and Snowville Roads. Cross Riverview Road and walk along the edge of Snowville Road. In a few hundred feet, a blue-blazed post points you across the road to the left and into the woods. Ascend to the top of the ridge.

3.1 Cross Columbia Road.

4.9 Come to a junction with the spur trail to Blue Hen and Buttermilk Falls. Take a left onto the spur trail; Blue Hen Falls is almost immediately on the right. Continue downstream.

5.4 Approach an old cement foundation. Walk around to the far side of the foundation, and then cross the stream again. Follow the sound to the top of Buttermilk Falls.

5.9 Return the way you came to the BT, and take a left.

6.0 Walk through a parking area and come to Boston Mills Road. Cross the road and walk along a doubletrack road for about 40 feet. Take a left into the young woods. A large silver maple is blazed blue.

6.2 Come out of the woods and see a building ahead. Walk along the road, but don't cross it. Instead, pick up the gravel road.

6.3 Take a right off the gravel road at a trailhead sign, next to two abandoned buildings.

6.7 Come out at Boston Mills Road and take a right. Cross Riverview Road, and then cross the bridge over the Cuyahoga.

6.9 Walking on the sidewalk now, pass the Boston Store on the right and reach the canal towpath trail. Take a left and walk north.

7.1 Pass a spur trail on the right that leads to Stanford House.

8.7 Arrive back at the Red Lock trailhead.

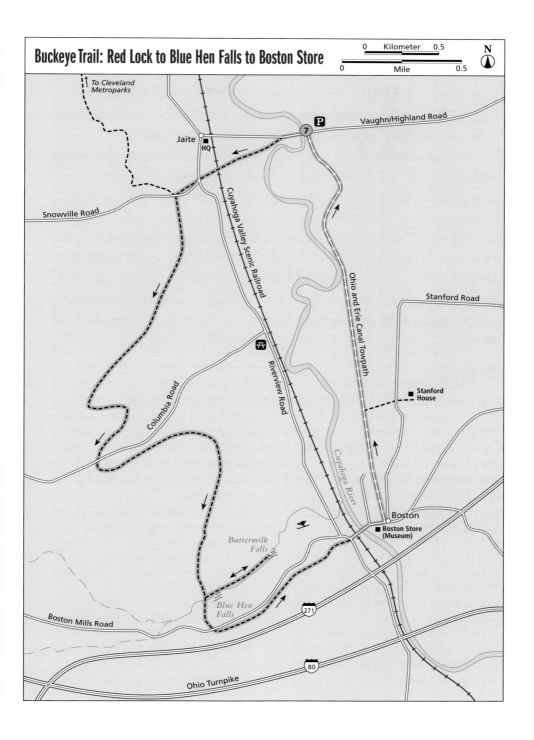

Buckeye Trail: Red Lock to Blue Hen Falls to Boston Store

0   Kilometer   0.5

0   Mile   0.5

N

To Cleveland Metroparks

Vaughn/Highland Road

P

7

Jaite

HQ

Snowville Road

Cuyahoga Valley Scenic Railroad

Ohio and Erie Canal Towpath

Stanford Road

Columbia Road

Riverview Road

Stanford House

Cuyahoga River

Boston

Boston Store (Museum)

Buttermilk Falls

Blue Hen Falls

271

Boston Mills Road

80

Ohio Turnpike

THE CUYAHOGA RIVER

The Cuyahoga River was formed with the retreat of the last ice age glaciers about 12,000 years ago. The resulting changes in landscape rerouted the drainage of this river from a south-flowing body of water to its current U-shape. The 100-mile Cuyahoga begins flowing south but abruptly turns north where it drains into Lake Erie at Cleveland, just 30 miles west of its mouth. The shape lends to the name Cuyahoga, which means "crooked river."

By the mid-nineteenth century, pollution pressures on the Cuyahoga included raw sewage and industrial waste, including oil. The first fire on the Cuyahoga actually occurred in 1936, but the huge blaze in 1969 catapulted Cleveland to national attention as the "mistake on the lake." Even today, the Great Lakes Brewing Company features the Burning River Pale Ale.

With the 1972 Clean Water Act and ensuing EPA guidelines on pollution emissions, the Cuyahoga is no longer a "dead" river. Its headwaters are protected by natural bogs, fens, and other wetlands. It even supports a warm-water fishery. But the navigable portion of the Cuyahoga near its mouth, still lined with industry, continues to suffer serious water-quality problems. Cuyahoga Valley National Park is upstream from this section. Still—don't drink the water.

Hike Information

Local information: Positively Cleveland, (800) 321-1001, www.positivelycleveland.com

Akron/Summit Convention and Visitors Bureau, (330) 374-7560 or (800) 245-4254, www.visitakron-summit.org

Local events and attractions: The Cuyahoga Valley Scenic Railroad has a Bike/Hike Aboard! program where hikers can walk between stations along the 20-mile Ohio and Erie Canal Towpath and return by train for a small fee; (800) 468-4070 or www.cvsr.com.

There is a slew of park-sponsored events throughout the year, though most services are cut back during winter months; http://dayinthe valley.com.

Countryside Conservancy partners with Cuyahoga Valley National Park to sponsor a weekly farmers' market; (330) 657-2542 or www.cvcountryside.org.

Boston Mills/Brandywine Ski Resort; (800) U-SKI-241 or www.bmbw.com

Accommodations: Stanford Backcountry Campsites are 5 primitive campsites in the park open from approximately Memorial Day weekend through Oct, reservable in advance or at the Stanford House office; (330) 657-2909, ext. 119 or www.conservancyforcunp.org/space-rental/lodging/camp-sites.

The Inn at Brandywine Falls; (330) 467-1812 or www.innatbrandywinefalls.com

Restaurants: Fisher's Cafe & Pub, Peninsula; (330) 657-2651; www.fisherscafe.com

Winking Lizard, Peninsula; (216) 831-0022; www.winkinglizard.com

Organizations: Conservancy for Cuyahoga Valley National Park, (330) 657-2909, www.conservancyforcvnp.org

Cuyahoga Valley Trails Council, www.cvtrailscouncil.org

Cleveland Hiking Club, www.clevelandhikingclub.org

8 Stanford House to Brandywine Falls

Cuyahoga Valley National Park

Approaching Brandywine Falls from Stanford House on foot is one of the nicest experiences you can have in the Cuyahoga Valley. Take this 3.6-mile lollipop to the 67-foot cascade, a signature attraction of this national park. Return by paralleling a beautiful valley cut by Brandywine Creek. Stanford House makes a good base for exploring the park's 125 miles of trails, including the 20-mile Ohio and Erie Canal Towpath.

Start: Stanford House
Distance: 3.6-mile lollipop, including observation deck spur
Hiking time: About 2 hours
Difficulty: Moderate due to some hilly sections and stairs
Trail Surface: Dirt and boardwalk
Blaze: Junctions are marked with signs.
Best season: Apr through Oct and after a snowfall in winter
Other trail users: Hikers only
Canine compatibility: Leashed dogs permitted; owners are expected to clean up after their pets.

Water: A tank with potable water is near the trailhead, behind the barn.
Land status: National park
Nearest town: Peninsula
Fees and permits: None
Schedule: Open daily from dawn to dusk except for campers; visitor centers closed Thanksgiving, Christmas, and New Year's Day
Maps: USGS quad: Northfield
Trail contact: Cuyahoga Valley National Park, Peninsula; (330) 657-2752, (800) 257-9477; www.nps.gov/cuva, www.dayinthevalley.com

Finding the trailhead: From I-271 exit 12, take SR 303 east 3.7 miles to Riverview Road. Turn left (north) and drive 1.5 miles to Boston Mills Road. Turn right (east) and cross the Cuyahoga River. Take the second left onto Stanford Road. Stanford House is 0.5 mile on the right. Pull into the driveway and park behind the barn. There is a trailhead kiosk.

From I-80 in Boston Heights, exit south onto SR 8. In 0.25 mile turn right (west) onto Boston Mills Road. Travel 4 miles to Stanford Road and turn right (north). Stanford House is 0.5 mile on the right. Pull into the driveway and park behind the barn. There is a trailhead kiosk.

DeLorme: Ohio Atlas & Gazetteer: Page 41 B6. GPS: N41 16.26' / W81 33.36'.

The Hike

Brandywine Falls is one of the most scenic spots in Cuyahoga Valley National Park. The trail begins and ends at Stanford House, an 1843 Greek Revival farmhouse, which is listed on the National Register of Historic Places. This is a great home base for exploring the entire park, especially due to its proximity to the 20-mile multiple-use Ohio and Erie Canal Towpath. Parking, information, camping, and a picnic area are all available here.

Brandywine Falls

Begin the Stanford Trail by walking through an open field and then into an oak-hickory forest. Expect to see a variety of birds, wildflowers, and perhaps a large herd of white-tailed deer. The trail can be muddy in wet weather, but its overall quality is quite good, thanks to local hiking groups who donate their time to trail maintenance. Walk across boardwalks and down wooden steps into a nice valley. Look here for such wildflowers as coltsfoot, trillium, bloodroot, mayapple, corn salad, angelica, and bluet.

Ascend out of the valley to Stanford Road, where you will hear Brandywine Falls before they come into view. A wooden boardwalk and observation deck take you close to the 67-foot cascade, a signature attraction of the Cuyahoga Valley. You may even encounter a wedding party here on summer weekends. The trail then takes you to the lip of the falls, where you can peer closely at the water tumbling over a relatively hard layer of Berea sandstone. The softer layers below, worn over millions of years, are composed of Bedford and Cleveland shales.

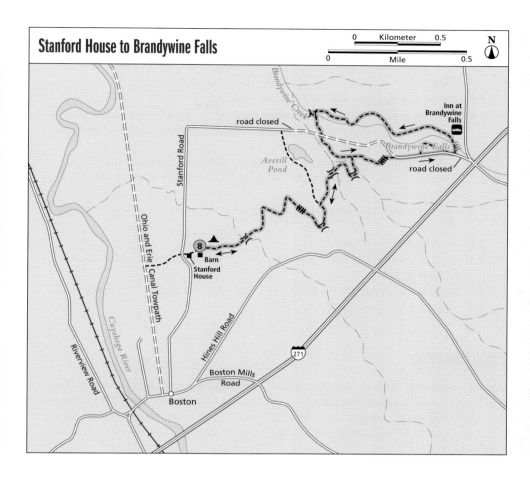

Stanford House to Brandywine Falls

This spot is also the former site of a sawmill, built by George Wallace in 1814. For decades the town of Brandywine thrived. Now little evidence of the mill or the town remains. The Inn at Brandywine Falls is the restored James Wallace House, another option for accommodations.

As you cross the top of the falls, you will walk toward the inn. Here you will pick up the Brandywine Gorge Trail. The path descends into a fairly narrow gorge, cut by Brandywine Creek. Enjoy the shimmering water, hemlocks, rocks, and forests in this very attractive valley. Cross the stream on a footbridge. The trail soon connects with the Stanford Trail, where you will return the way you came.

Miles and Directions

0.0 Start at the trailhead kiosk behind the barn at Stanford House.

0.2 Cross a footbridge over the creek and enter the woods.

0.7 Arrive at the halfway point to Brandywine Falls, marked with a wooden sign.

0.8 Come to a junction with a spur trail to Averill Pond. Turn right to continue toward Brandywine Falls.

1.1 Come to the junction for the Brandywine Gorge Loop. Turn right and ascend the stairs out of the valley.

1.3 The trail dead-ends into Stanford Road. Take a right.

1.4 Take a left at the boardwalk. Follow the boardwalk and then the steps down to the lower observation deck overlooking Brandywine Falls. Return to the main boardwalk. Take a left and walk past the lip of the falls.

1.7 Come to the paved bike and hike trail near the top of the falls. Take a left and cross over Brandywine Creek. Continue along the bike and hike trail as it curves and parallels the creek downstream.

1.8 Leave the paved path and take a left onto a gravel path, marked with a Brandywine Gorge trail marker.

2.3 Cross the creek on a footbridge.

2.4 Come to Stanford Road again. Cross the road to the left of the gate, and pick up the trail on the other side.

2.5 Return to the junction with the Stanford Trail. Take a right and return the way you came.

3.6 Arrive back at Stanford House.

Hike Information

Local information: Positively Cleveland, (800) 321-1001, www.positivelycleveland.com

Akron/Summit Convention and Visitors Bureau, (330) 374-7560 or (800) 245-4254, www.visitakron-summit.org

Local events and attractions: The Cuyahoga Valley Scenic Railroad has a Bike/Hike Aboard! program where hikers can walk between stations along the 20-mile Ohio and Erie Canal Towpath and return by train for a small fee; (800) 468-4070 or www.cvsr.com.

There is a slew of park-sponsored events throughout the year, though most services are cut back during winter months; http://dayinthe valley.com.

Countryside Conservancy partners with Cuyahoga Valley National Park to sponsor a weekly farmers' market; (330) 657-2542 or www.cvcountryside.org.

Boston Mills/Brandywine Ski Resort; (800) U-SKI-241 or www.bmbw.com

Accommodations: Stanford Backcountry Campsites are 5 primitive campsites in the park open from approximately Memorial Day weekend through Oct, reservable in advance or at the Stanford House office; (330) 657-2909, ext. 119, or www.conservancyforcvnp.org/space-rental/lodging/camp-sites.

The Inn at Brandywine Falls; (330) 467-1812 or www.innatbrandywinefalls.com

Restaurants: Fisher's Cafe & Pub, Peninsula; (330) 657-2651; www.fisherscafe.com

Winking Lizard, Peninsula; (216) 831-0022; www.winkinglizard.com

Organizations: Conservancy for Cuyahoga Valley National Park, (330) 657-2909, www.conservancyforcvnp.org

Cuyahoga Valley Trails Council, www.cvtrails council.org

Cleveland Hiking Club, www.clevelandhiking club.org

9 Ledges Trail

Cuyahoga Valley National Park

This easy 2.3-mile loop is a fun trail that takes you along the base of striking Sharon conglomerate rock ledges and then out to an overlook that provides an expansive view of the Cuyahoga Valley. The vista is especially nice in the fall, but the trail is good year-round, with spring wildflowers, cool hemlock coves in summer, and attractive ice formations in the winter.

Start: Happy Days Lodge
Distance: 2.3-mile double loop
Hiking time: About 1 hour
Difficulty: Easy; short, and mostly flat
Trail surface: Dirt and stone
Blaze: Junctions are marked with signs.
Best season: Apr through Oct; attractive but icy after a winter storm
Other trail users: Cross-country skiers (in season)
Canine compatibility: Leashed dogs permitted; owners are expected to clean up after their pets.

Water: Available year-round in the restrooms at the Ledges Shelter
Land status: National park
Nearest town: Hudson
Fees and permits: None
Schedule: Open daily from dawn to dusk; visitor centers closed Thanksgiving, Christmas, and New Year's Day
Maps: USGS quad: Northfield
Trail contact: Cuyahoga Valley National Park, Peninsula; (330) 657-2752, (800) 257-9477; www.nps.gov/cuva, www.dayinthevalley.com

Finding the trailhead: From I-77 in Richfield, turn east onto I-271. Travel 6.2 miles to SR 303 and turn right (east); drive 4 miles to the Happy Days Lodge. Take a left into the parking lot, then follow a pedestrian underpass to the visitor center. From the visitor center, walk to the south side of the parking lot to the trailhead kiosk. *DeLorme: Ohio Atlas & Gazetteer:* Page 41 C6. GPS: N41 13.80' / W81 30.52'.

The Hike

If you've never hiked the Ledges Trail in Cuyahoga Valley National Park, you're in for a treat. Just a few miles south of downtown Cleveland, you can hop on this short trail and walk along the base of tall Sharon conglomerate ledges before climbing to the top for a sweeping vista of the Cuyahoga River Valley. Begin and end at one of the several excellent visitor centers located in Ohio's only national park.

Beginning with Yellowstone National Park in 1872 and continuing for the next century, the National Park Service concentrated its lands in beautiful but remote settings, often inaccessible to the vast majority of the nation's population. But the 1970s saw a trend toward establishing parks close to urban areas. In 1970 Cuyahoga Valley National Recreation Area was established, and in 2000 the Cuyahoga Valley was upgraded to a national park. Around 1978 Cuyahoga Valley National Park took over administration of what had long been known as Virginia Kendall Park, named after the mother of Haywood Kendall, a wealthy Clevelander who owned the property in the early 1900s.

Begin and end the popular Ledges hike at the Happy Days Lodge, built by the Civilian Conservation Corps in the late 1930s as a day camp for area children. Today Happy Days is only open for special events like concerts and lectures.

The Haskell Run Trail begins by descending into a creek valley. In the spring look for skunk cabbage, sometimes poking through a late snow. Soon you will begin the Ledges Trail. For the most part, this trail skirts the bottom edge of tall Sharon conglomerate ledges. Sharon conglomerate is made up of sedimentary sandstone with small quartz pebbles embedded throughout. These white, round pebbles were shaped by moving water during the Pennsylvanian period 320 million years ago. Sediment slowly piled up in seas that once covered Ohio. The quartz pebbles tumbled down the rivers and into the sea and were embedded in the sediment. In time (a lot of time), the sediment formed into Sharon conglomerate sandstone. You will want to include time in your hiking schedule to explore the many nooks and crannies of these geological attractions, including Icebox Cave, named for its cool temperatures. Bring a flashlight if you want to explore the 50-foot-deep cavern.

At about the halfway point, the trail ascends gradually to the top of the rock outcropping to the Ledges Overlook. This is an excellent lunch spot, where you can sit on a broad rock outcropping and take in an expansive view of the Cuyahoga Valley. (Keep a close eye on children and pets here.) The valley is forested, with maple and beech mostly in the low-lying areas. These species give way to mostly oak and hickory on the ridgetops. The cool temperatures around the ledges also support hemlock trees. This spot is especially nice during fall, when leaves are changing color. The trail descends again to the bottom of the ledges, which you follow on the other side to return to Haskell Run and Happy Days Lodge.

Miles and Directions

0.0 Start the Haskell Run Trail at the trailhead kiosk behind the Happy Days Lodge. Follow the gravel path.

0.1 Come to a T-intersection. Follow the sign to the right and walk along the wide, hard-packed trail down into the valley.

0.3 Reach a junction fork with the connector trail. Take a left here to head toward the Ledges Trail. Ascend the stairs.

0.4 Come to the junction with the Ledges Trail. You can walk this loop in either direction; taking a left, walk toward the Ledges Shelter. In a few hundred feet, approach steps to the right

Ledges Overlook ▶

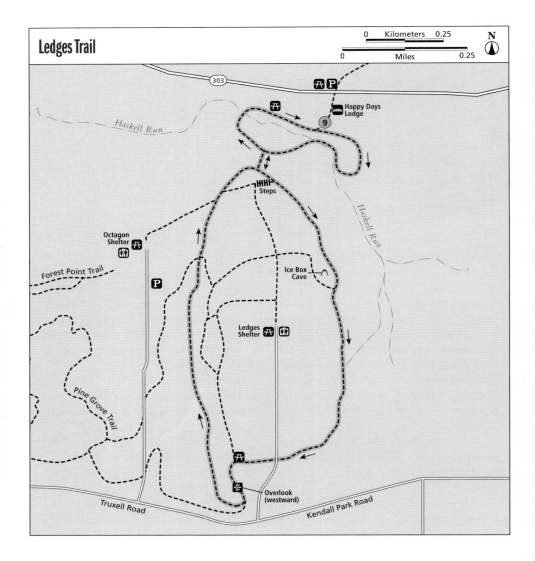

Ledges Trail

0   Kilometers   0.25

0   Miles   0.25

N

303

Haskell Run

Happy Days Lodge

9

Steps

Octagon Shelter

Haskell Run

Forest Point Trail

Ice Box Cave

P

Ledges Shelter

Pine Grove Trail

Overlook (westward)

Truxell Road

Kendall Park Road

that take you to the Ledges picnic shelter. Take a few minutes to explore the rock outcroppings here. Then continue straight, toward Ice Box Cave.

0.6 Come to Ice Box Cave on the right. Then pass another junction for the Ledges picnic shelter on the right; continue straight.

1.0 Cross a paved access road to the shelter. Stay on the gravel path, passing an open field on the right.

1.1 Come to a T-intersection and follow the signs to the left for the Ledges Overlook. Continue in the same direction past the overlook.

1.2 Reach another T-intersection. Take a right and continue your descent to the junction with the Pine Grove Trail connector. Come to a fork and stay to the right, following signs for the Octagon Shelter.

1.7 Pass a spur trail on the left for the Octagon Shelter. Walk upslope a little to join the rocks again, and continue in the same direction (north).

1.8 Another spur from the Ledges Shelter comes in from the right. Continue straight about 100 feet to steps taking you down and a little to the left, passing another spur trail on the left.

1.9 Take some steps down to a footbridge and approach a signpost leading you straight. **FYI:** Informal trails to the right explore the ledges some more.

2.0 Come to a fork and take a left, following the signs for Happy Days Lodge and the Ledges Trail. When you reach the Haskell Run Trail, take two lefts to complete the loop.

2.2 The trail emerges from the woods. From here walk across the grassy field back to the lodge.

2.3 Arrive back at the Happy Days Lodge.

Hike Information

Local information: Positively Cleveland, (800) 321-1001, www.positivelycleveland.com

Akron/Summit Convention and Visitors Bureau, (330) 374-7560 or (800) 245-4254, www.visitakron-summit.org

Local events and attractions: The Cuyahoga Valley Scenic Railroad has a Bike/Hike Aboard! program where hikers can walk between stations along the 20-mile Ohio and Erie Canal Towpath and return by train for a small fee; (800) 468-4070 or www.cvsr.com.

There is a slew of park-sponsored events throughout the year, though most services are cut back during winter months; http://dayinthe valley.com.

Countryside Conservancy partners with Cuyahoga Valley National Park to sponsor a weekly farmers' market; (330) 657-2542 or www.cvcountryside.org.

Boston Mills/Brandywine Ski Resort; (800) U-SKI-241 or www.bmbw.com

Accommodations: Stanford Backcountry Campsites are 5 primitive campsites in the park open from approximately Memorial Day weekend through Oct, reservable in advance or at the Stanford House office; (330) 657-2909, ext. 119, or www.conservancyforcvnp.org/space-rental/lodging/camp-sites.

The Inn at Brandywine Falls; (330) 467-1812 or www.innatbrandywinefalls.com

Restaurants: Fisher's Cafe & Pub, Peninsula; (330) 657-2651; www.fisherscafe.com

Winking Lizard, Peninsula; (216) 831-0022; www.winkinglizard.com

Organizations: Conservancy for Cuyahoga Valley National Park, (330) 657-2909, www .conservancyforcvnp.org

Cuyahoga Valley Trails Council, www.cvtrails council.org

Cleveland Hiking Club, www.clevelandhiking club.org

10 Old Valley to Highlights Trail Loop

Holden Arboretum

Put on your botanist hat at Holden Arboretum, where you can walk around manicured gardens of trees, shrubs, and flowers. A member of the American Association of Museums, it truly is a museum of plants, with more than 120,000 species documented. Add to the 600 cultivated acres another 3,000 acres of natural areas, and there's plenty of space to stretch your legs on 20 miles of trails. Be sure to include trails in the arboretum area on your hike, where you will find flowering plants throughout the growing season.

Start: Corning Visitor Center
Distance: 3.4-mile loop
Hiking time: About 1.5 to 2 hours
Difficulty: Moderate due to length, steep sections, and creek crossings
Trail surface: Gravel, dirt, and boardwalk
Blaze: Old Valley Trail, cedar waxwing bird; Highlights Trail, none (junctions are marked)
Best season: Apr through Oct
Other trail users: Hikers only
Canine compatibility: Leashed dogs permitted
Water: Available at Corning Visitor Center

Land status: Private arboretum
Nearest towns: Kirtland, Mentor
Fees and permits: There is a daily admission fee except for arboretum members.
Schedule: Open daily from 9 a.m. to 5 p.m. except Thanksgiving, Christmas Eve, Christmas, New Year's Eve, and New Year's Day
Maps: Holden Arboretum map; USGS quads: Chesterland, Mentor
Trail contact: Holden Arboretum, Kirtland; (440) 946-4400; www.holdenarb.org

Finding the trailhead: From I-90 exit 193 east of Cleveland, take US 306 south 0.9 mile and take a left onto Chillicothe Road. Go 0.1 mile to Kirtland Chardon Road and take a right. Go 3.5 miles to Sperry Road and take a left to enter the arboretum. Go 1.3 miles to the visitor center entrance on the left. Drive to the guard shack and pay the entrance fee, and then park. From the parking lot, walk to the visitor center. *DeLorme: Ohio Atlas & Gazetteer:* Page 32 D1. GPS: N41 36.68' / W81 18.10'.

The Hike

Start your visit to Holden Arboretum at the Warren H. Corning Visitor Center, home to the museum store, nature exhibits, a library, and an information desk staffed with knowledgeable people. Pick up a visitor guide and trail map, which includes a chart of peak viewing seasons for different trails and garden collections. Right behind the visitor center, check out the Arlene and Arthur S. Holden Jr. Butterfly Garden.

When you hit the trails, the "collected" part of the arboretum—the cultivated gardens with native and imported specimens—is a great first stop. You'll see native northeast Ohio forest trees (maples, beeches, oaks) as well as specimens from as far

Asters in bloom along the Highlands Trail

away as China and Russia (paperback maple, Siberian crabapple). Each collected plant is tagged with its scientific name. Expect to see wildflowers from wild geranium and jack-in-the-pulpit in the spring to goldenrod and aster in the fall. The collections include gardens dedicated to one taxonomic group of plant. For example, you can walk through the rhododendron, arborvitae, viburnum, conifer, and lilac collections. You can also draw inspiration for your home garden: Holden researchers help breed woody landscaping stock for regional conditions.

The many plant species at Holden offer food and habitat for animals as well. In addition to the butterfly garden, the property is a stop along Ohio's Lake Erie Birding Trail and is home to a successful bluebird conservation program. On the garden and woodland trails, expect to see not only birds but amphibians and mammals, including white-tailed deer.

The Old Valley Trail takes you through a portion of the 3,000-acre "natural areas" at Holden—that is, minimally managed mixed hardwood forest that is left in a natural state. Enjoy some solitude on miles of trail through hardwoods and hemlocks near Pierson Creek. Some of the most interesting hiking at Holden is accessible only on guided tours. Check out the arboretum's schedule to find when you can join a tour of Stebbins Gulch, a National Natural Landmark that is home to five different and visible geologic rock units—that is, units of rock with distinctly different origins or age—and several forest zones.

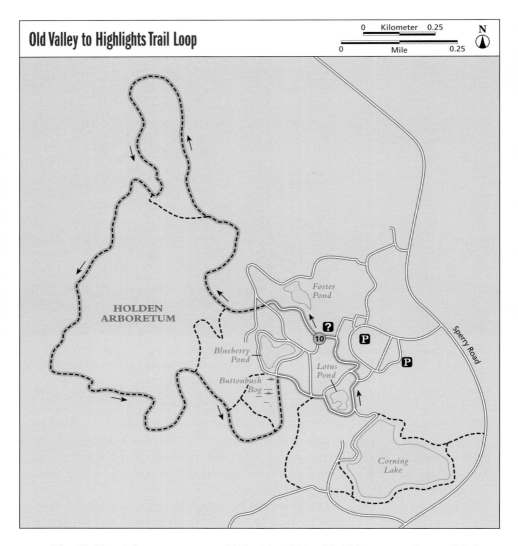

Old Valley to Highlights Trail Loop

0   Kilometer   0.25

0   Mile   0.25

N

Foster Pond

HOLDEN ARBORETUM

❓

🔟

P

P

Blueberry Pond

Lotus Pond

Buttonbush Bog

Corning Lake

Sperry Road

The Holden Arboretum was established in 1931 with 100 acres, made possible by a bequest from the late Albert Fairchild Holden. He wanted to honor his daughter, Elizabeth Davis Holden, who died in childhood from scarlet fever. Since then, members of the Holden family as well as other dedicated individuals helped to grow the arboretum's endowment and acreage, which now stands at 3,600 acres.

Miles and Directions

0.0   Start at the Corning Visitor Center. Head west and south along a paved path, passing the Thayer Center, until you arrive at a junction for multiple trailheads. Take a right here and walk along the gravel path to another junction. Follow the trail straight ahead that is marked for the Woodland, Boardwalk, Pierson Creek, and Old Valley Trails.

0.1 Walk down wooden steps to a T-intersection. Take a left and walk to another T-intersection. This time, take a right. Follow the posts blazed with a cedar waxwing (bird). Walk by Foster Pond on the right. Stay on the main trail, avoiding side paths to the pond.

0.2 Cross two gravel roads in quick succession. Continue straight.

0.3 Come to a T-intersection. Take a right, following the Pierson Creek and Old Valley Trails.

0.5 Come to a junction and take a left. Pass Royal Fern Bog on the right.

0.6 At a three-way junction, go right and begin the Pierson Creek Loop.

1.4 Finish the Pierson Trail Loop at a junction with the Old Valley Trail. Take a right.

1.9 Come to a junction with the Strong Acres loop. Take a left, following a sign for the Old Valley Trail.

2.1 Pass an unmarked side trail on the right. Continue straight.

2.5 Cross a creek and then arrive at a boardwalk loop. You can go either way; the loop connects again straight ahead. The boardwalk then comes to a four-way intersection. Take a right, walking up the wooden stairs. At the top of the stairs, continue straight while trending right. Follow signs for the Old Valley Trail and the visitor center.

2.6 At a junction, take a right to stay on the Old Valley Trail.

2.75 Pass a junction for the Daus Memorial Overlook on the right. Continue straight.

2.8 Come to a fork. Take the left fork to continue on the Old Valley Trail and then come to a four-way junction. Go straight, following signs for the visitor center. **FYI:** In May, take the trail to the right to the blooming rhododendron garden.

3.0 Come to a T-intersection. Take a right and hop on the Highlights Trail, which is a gravel road. Walk to a three-way intersection and continue straight. Stay on the main road. **FYI:** There are paths off of the gravel road that lead to various gardens.

3.1 The road comes to a T-intersection. Take a right, following a sign for the Highlights Trail, and walk around Lotus Pond in a counterclockwise direction. Cross a footbridge and stay left, by the lake.

3.3 Come to a side road on the left. Take this left, following signs for the Highlights Trail. Walk to the smaller Lily Pond and take a right.

3.4 Arrive back at the paved path where you began.

Hike Information

Local information: Lake County Visitors Bureau, (440) 975-1234 or (800) 368-LAKE (5253), www.lakevisit.com

Local events and attractions: Holden Arboretum hosts hike tours, lectures, classes, and events throughout the year; contact the arboretum for details.

Restaurants: Willoughby Brewing Company, Willoughby; (440) 975-0202; www.willoughby brewing.com

Accommodations: Geauga Park District's Big Creek Park in Chardon has tent camping and lean-to

sites; call (440) 286-9516 for reservations; www .geaugaparkdistrict.org/parks/bigcreek.shtml.

Hike tours: Holden Arboretum offers naturalist-led hikes, including to areas such as Stebbins Gulch that are only accessible on guided tours. Contact the arboretum for more info.

Other resources: Holden is home to the Warren H. Corning Library. You may use materials in the library; members may check out materials like field guides.

11 Cascade Falls to Devil's Icebox

Nelson-Kennedy Ledges State Park

Once you've dropped down to your ideal weight from your summer hiking regimen, head over to Nelson–Kennedy Ledges State Park and hike through trail sections with such names as Fat Man's Peril, The Squeeze, and The Narrows. These ledges and mini canyons are not for the claustrophobic or acrophobic, but they are ideal for a day of summer fun. Explore the Sharon conglomerate outcroppings and slump blocks in a beech–maple–hemlock forest. Walk by waterfalls and through caves; climb to the top of the rocks and then back down. All told, you can cover 3 miles' worth of trails, but the scenery is so good, you should plan extra time for exploring.

Start: Northern trailhead, across from the picnic area
Distance: 1.8-mile trail system
Hiking time: About 1 hour
Difficulty: Moderate due to some steep or slick terrain and tight squeezes
Trail surface: Dirt and rock
Blaze: White, red, yellow, and blue
Best season: This is a nice summer hike when the trails are dry yet cool.
Other trail users: Hikers only
Canine compatibility: Leashed dogs permitted

Water: Available in the picnic area
Land status: State park
Nearest towns: Garrettsville, Parkman
Fees and permits: None
Schedule: Open daily from dawn to dusk
Maps: USGS quad: Garrettsville
Trail contact: Nelson-Kennedy Ledges State Park, c/o Punderson State Park, Newbury; (440) 564-2279; http://parks.ohiodnr.gov/nelsonkennedyledges

Finding the trailhead: From I-271 in North Randall, turn east on US 422 and drive 26 miles to SR 282. Turn right (south) and drive 1.7 miles to the Nelson-Kennedy Ledges parking lot on the left. *DeLorme: Ohio Atlas & Gazetteer:* Page 42 B3. GPS: N41 19.43' / W81 02.21'.

The Hike

The formation of Nelson–Kennedy Ledges began when ancient streams smoothed and tumbled quartzite pebbles downstream, then deposited them into a sea that once covered most of what is now Ohio. These pebbles became embedded in sediment, and today's resulting rock is Sharon conglomerate sandstone. When the Wisconsinan Glacier retreated from Ohio some 12,000 years ago, it left a thick layer of debris that covered most rock outcrops. The outcrops at Nelson-Kennedy Ledges, however, remained exposed. The process of weathering through freeze and thaw cycles has created slump blocks, where parts of the cliff have slumped off and are now lying on the ground nearby.

The hike begins immediately among the slump blocks and ledges. Walk through a forest of hemlock, beech, and maple while winding around the many rock faces. Make your way to Cascade Falls, which tumble 35 feet down the rock face. Under Cascade Falls is Gold Hunter's Cave, which got its name during a gold rush of sorts around 1870. But as it turns out, the gold diggers who came here found only fool's gold.

Reverse direction and walk through a dark cave named Old Maid's Kitchen. Work your way out of the cave, then shortly down the trail do a limbo move to walk under the aptly named Dwarf's Pass. In springtime these cool recesses are home to abundant wildflowers, including red trillium, spring beauty, Solomon's seal, and hepatica. A multitude of ferns grow out of the rocky soil and directly out of the rocks themselves. Look for the common wood, Christmas, and maidenhair fern, as well as the less common polypody, grape, and marginal shield fern.

The trail soon reaches the top of the ledges and continues through a mature maple-beech forest. From this vantage you can look down on the two-part Minnehaha Falls and into the slot canyon the falls create. The upper falls are 20 feet high; the lower falls are 35 feet high. Cliffs are as high as 60 feet, so exercise caution, especially if you're hiking with children. This portion of the trail loops back and returns to the bottom of the ledges, where the passageways narrow considerably. The next part of the path has a couple of very small squeezes that aren't even big enough for both you and your day pack. After wiggling through these tight spots, enjoy the cool damp and the acoustics of Devil's Icebox. From here return farther downslope into a cool-weather-loving forest that includes hemlock, Canada yew, and yellow birch. End the hike at the southern trailhead next to the parking lot.

Miles and Directions

0.0 Start from the northern trailhead, across the road from the picnic area. Facing the trailhead signs, take off to the right and follow the yellow-blazed trail around the ledges to Cascade Falls.

0.1 A boardwalk leads to Cascade Falls. After viewing the falls, retrace your steps for about 100 feet to a fork. Take a right, staying near the rocks and ascending slightly. Then walk into the Old Maid's Kitchen cave.

0.2 Exit the cave to the left, just past the boardwalk. Outside the cave, take a right. At the end of the rock face to your right, turn right again into the rocks and then follow another boardwalk through Dwarf's Pass. After crossing a second boardwalk, continue straight and ascend out of the cool rock shelters.

0.4 Walk atop the rocks to a four-way intersection, marked with white blazes. Take a right.

0.7 Before reaching the chain-link fence, the trail curves to the left, overlooking some nice views from the top of the rocks, including Minnehaha Falls.

0.8 A wooden footbridge to the right allows you to peer into the mini-slot canyons below. Walk to the footbridge then turn back, looking for the white blazes.

1.0 Return to the four-way intersection. Take a right and walk about 100 feet. To the left is a metal yellow hiker blaze. Across from this blaze, look for a narrow squeeze between two rocks, marked with a faint red blaze. Walk through this opening.

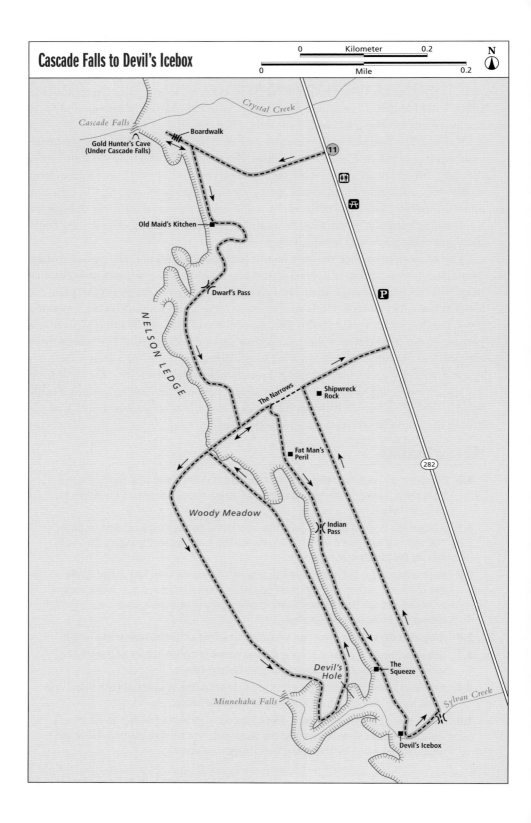

Cascade Falls to Devil's Icebox

Kilometer
0   0.2

Mile
0   0.2

N

Crystal Creek

Cascade Falls

Boardwalk

Gold Hunter's Cave
(Under Cascade Falls)

11

Old Maid's Kitchen

Dwarf's Pass

NELSON LEDGE

The Narrows

Shipwreck
Rock

Fat Man's
Peril

Woody Meadow

Indian
Pass

282

Devil's
Hole

The
Squeeze

Minnehaha Falls

Sylvan Creek

Devil's Icebox

P

1.2 About 50 feet past another narrow squeeze, come to a fork. Turn right and head upward. At the top of the rocks, there's a red-blazed beech tree. Just past the beech tree, descend into the gorge again. **Note:** Be careful here; it's a slick spot.

1.3 Come out of the last squeeze and look left for a blaze. Beyond that, a double blaze indicates a turn to the right.

1.4 Arrive at Devil's Icebox. After exploring, walk downstream toward a footbridge. Instead of crossing the footbridge, turn left and walk north for the return trip, following the blue blazes.

1.8 Come to a T-intersection. Take a right and walk toward the road to arrive at the southern trailhead, across from the parking lot. Follow the road north to the northern trailhead.

Hike Information

Local information: Streetsboro Visitors & Convention Bureau, (330) 422-1770 or (888) 558-5580, www.streetsborovcb.com

Local events and attractions: Eagle Creek State Nature Preserve, Garrettsville; (330) 527-5118; http://ohiodnr.com/location/dnap/eagle_creek/tabid/888/Default.aspx

Tinkers Creek State Nature Preserve, Aurora; http://ohiodnr.com/location/dnap/tinkers/tabid/912/Default.aspx

Accommodations: Punderson State Park in Newbury has a lodge and campground; (440) 564-2279; http://parks.ohiodnr.gov/punderson.

West Branch State Park campground, Ravenna; (330) 296-3239 or (800) 644-6727 for reservations; http://parks.ohiodnr.gov/west branch

Restaurants: Main Street Grille and Brewing Company, Garrettsville; (330) 527-3663; www.msg-brew.com

12 Vondergreen Trail

Beaver Creek State Park

Little Beaver Creek was the first designated Wild and Scenic River in Ohio. It's also a national scenic river, and it does not disappoint. The 10-mile out-and-back Vondergreen Trail follows the edge of Little Beaver Creek, providing views of whitewater, steep forested slopes, and plentiful wildlife. The hike begins and ends near Gaston's Mill and Pioneer Village. It also follows the route of the former Sandy and Beaver Canal, so you will walk by old canal locks as well. The park is excellent for wildlife viewing; if you're quiet and lucky, you might see a bald eagle or a black bear.

Start: Steel bridge near the pioneer village
Distance: 10-mile out-and-back or 5-mile point-to-point shuttle
Hiking time: About 3.5 to 5 hours
Difficulty: Moderate to difficult due to length and some poor trail conditions
Trail surface: Mostly flat creek-side trail of dirt, rocks, and mud, with a couple difficult to navigate portions
Blaze: White
Best season: Mid-Apr through mid-Oct
Other trail users: Mountain bikers; horses on some sections

Canine compatibility: Leashed dogs permitted
Water: Available at the parking lot
Land status: State park
Nearest towns: Calcutta, Rogers
Fees and permits: None
Schedule: Trails open daily from dawn to dusk.
Maps: USGS quad: East Liverpool North
Trail contact: Beaver Creek State Park, East Liverpool; (330) 385-3091; http://parks.ohio dnr.gov/beavercreek

Finding the trailhead: From East Liverpool, travel on SR 7 north and US 30 west until they split. Turn north onto SR 7 and drive 2.3 miles to Bell School Road, marked with a brown state park sign. Turn right (east) and drive 1.2 miles to Echo Dell Road, also marked with brown state park signs. Turn left (north) and drive 1.5 miles. Pass the park office and the pioneer village on the left. Turn right into the parking lot. *DeLorme: Ohio Atlas & Gazetteer:* Page 53 C7. GPS: N40 43.67 / W80 36.67.

Option: To set up a shuttle, travel east on Bell School Road 2.8 miles to Cannon's Mill Road, marked only with a brown group camping area sign. Take a left and drive 2.1 miles to the group camp parking lot on the left. *DeLorme: Ohio Atlas & Gazetteer:* Page 53 C7. GPS: N40 42.30' / W80 35.13'.

The Hike

Begin the hike with a visit to Gaston's Mill and Pioneer Village, located near the trailhead. Built in 1830, Gaston's Mill was one of six mills constructed along this stretch of Little Beaver Creek (and one of eighty in Columbiana County). During its heyday, the mill ground almost 200 barrels of flour daily. The mill operates today for visitors.

Lusk Lock, aka Simon Girty's Lock ATTILA HORVATH

Around the mill, visit the log cabin, chapel, one-room schoolhouse, blacksmith shop, trading post, and covered bridge.

From the pioneer village, walk by a restored lock on your way to the trailhead. This is the first of several locks and dams you will see along the hike, since the path also follows the route of the former Sandy and Beaver Canal. Following the construction of the Ohio and Erie Canal in 1825, a number of "feeder" canals were built to access this successful transportation route. The Sandy and Beaver, one of these feeder canals, enjoyed less success. Privately funded and not completed until 1848, the Sandy and Beaver had to compete with rail transport from the start. The canal operated for only four years, until a reservoir dam broke upstream and the ensuing floodwaters ruined a large portion of the canal. The Vondergreen Trail is named after one of the canal's lock keepers.

Walk past the lock and then cross over the red steel bridge. Pick up the trailhead on the other side and begin walking downstream. As you hike, look for the different types of sedimentary rocks present here, predominantly sandstone, shale, and limestone. The area has abundant clay, which made it the ceramics capital of the country from the mid-1800s through the 1930s. This creek valley is unique in that it's the only one in the United States where geologists have found evidence of all four major glaciations that have occurred in North America over the past two million years. This evidence is the distinctively different rock and mineral deposits left by the retreating glaciers.

From the vantage point of this rocky trail, it's hard to imagine that white-tailed deer and beaver were extirpated (driven out) from Ohio. Both species flourish here today, and black bears are being sighted more and more often. Also look for red foxes, raccoons, and skunks. Overhead, keep an eye out for another comeback species, the bald eagle, which has been found within the park. Great blue herons, kingfishers, and ducks also make the creek their home. In the evening listen for screech, barred, and great horned owls. Walk quietly and you're likely to see and hear wildlife, especially around the edges of the day.

▶ Extirpated species are those that are driven out of a certain place (such as the Ohio Valley) but still survive elsewhere. Once-extirpated species that have returned to Ohio include beaver, black bear, river otter, wild turkey, trumpeter swan, and osprey. Some of these came back on their own; others were reintroduced.

Toward the center of the trail, where there is a large bend in the creek, conditions get cozy. Understory plants tickle you as you walk by. Smell the spicebush when you disturb it, but also keep an eye out underfoot for poison ivy. In fact, it's best to wear long pants along this trail. Touch-me-not (jewelweed), a poison ivy antidote, also grows thick here. Other common flowering plants include purple-flowering raspberry, cow parsnip, Canada violet, phlox, and daisy fleabane. Growing along the banks are water-loving sycamore and silver maple trees.

Some of the old dams and locks are becoming overgrown, but it's still clear what kind of craft and engineering it took to build the canal. Gretchen's Lock is identified with a sign along the trail. Take a short side trip to visit it and reflect on Gretchen's story: Gretchen Gill came from Europe with her mother (who died on the voyage) and her father, E. H. Gill, who was the Sandy and Beaver Canal engineer. Gretchen caught malaria and died during construction of the canal, and her father entombed her casket in the lock. When Gill decided to return to Europe, he excavated the casket to rebury it at home. On the return trip, the ship sank. Gretchen's ghost is one of several said to still haunt the old canal.

"BURN IT WHERE YOU BUY IT."

You've probably seen this sign or its relative, "Don't move firewood—it bugs me." These public education efforts are a response to the invasion of the emerald ash borer, an insect that has had a devastating effect on ash trees in at least fifteen states and two provinces, killing millions of trees. When you move firewood from one place to another (say, one county to another), you take the risk of helping spread this pest if you pick up one as a "hitchhiker." Not moving firewood is a good practice in general, as other pests could very well become problems in the future.

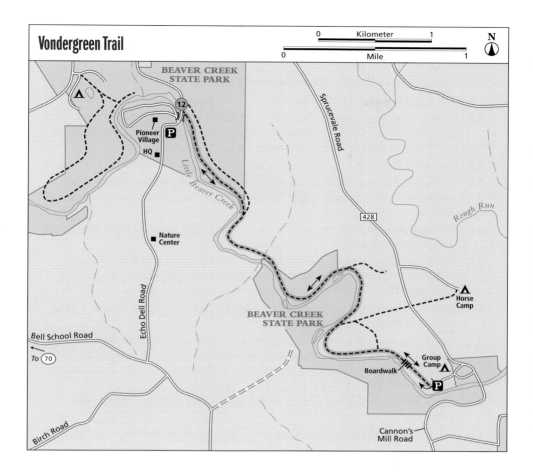

Vondergreen Trail

BEAVER CREEK
STATE PARK

Pioneer Village

HQ

Nature Center

Echo Dell Road

Little Beaver Creek

Sprucevale Road

428

Rough Run

Bell School Road

To 70

BEAVER CREEK
STATE PARK

Horse Camp

Boardwalk

Group Camp

Birch Road

Cannon's Mill Road

Other famous and infamous characters seemed to have chosen this beautiful place to meet their demise. During the Civil War, Confederate General John Hunt Morgan and his Morgan's Raiders beat a swath almost completely across Ohio from west to east before being captured near the present-day park. In 1934, shortly after being named "Public Enemy Number One," gangster Pretty Boy Floyd was killed here by East Liverpool police and federal agents. There's a sign marking the spot, just upstream from Hambleton's Mill, located near the east trailhead of the hike. Today's visitors, in contrast, enjoy a safe and peaceful place to hike, fish, and canoe.

Miles and Directions

0.0 Start on the east side of the steel bridge spanning Little Beaver Creek. The trailhead is marked with signs for the Upper and Lower Vondergreen Trails. Take a right and descend to the creek to begin the Lower Vondergreen Trail. **Option:** For some diversity, turn left and walk up the road a couple hundred feet to the Upper Vondergreen trailhead. Both trails meet up in about a mile.

0.6 Cross a horse trail. Continue straight.

1.1 Arrive at the junction with the Upper Vondergreen Trail. Continue straight.

1.4 Pass Grey's Lock on the right.

1.8 Cross straight over another horse trail and then a footbridge.

2.2 Walk past Vondergreen's Lock on the right.

2.3 Come to a five-way intersection. Take the first left, following the sign to check out Gretchen's Lock, then return to this spot. Continue downstream, on the trail blazed orange (horse trail). Pass an access trail to the creek on the right.

2.6 Pass a dam on the left.

2.7 The horse trail veers off to the right, down to the creek. Continue straight, picking up the white blazes again, then pass another lock and hit a fork. Take the right fork, continuing downstream.

2.9 Walk past another lock. The trail narrows but is still fairly easy to follow. Look to the left for some towering rock walls.

3.4 The trail climbs a slope and reaches a shale outcropping. Do not walk down the shale talus slope to the creek. Rather, scramble up the steep, crumbling shale to firm ground again. **Note:** This is a difficult and somewhat dangerous spot; use caution.

3.6 Come to an intersection with the bridle trail. Cross the bridle trail and continue on a faint, unmarked path that still parallels the creek.

4.1 Pass another lock and reach a T-intersection. Turn left and approach a fork almost immediately. Take the right fork, picking up the white blazes again as well as blazes for the North Country Scenic Trail. Pass a sign on the left for the Vondergreen Trail (which, technically, you haven't been on for the past half mile).

4.4 Cross another bridle trail and continue straight along a wide path next to this straight stretch of creek.

5.0 Come to the end of the line at the group campground parking lot. Turn around and return to the trailhead the way you came. **Option:** Set up a shuttle and end the hike here.

10.0 Arrive back at the trailhead.

Hike Information

Local information: East Liverpool Tourism Bureau, (234) 517-7052, www.visitelo.com

Local events and attractions: Gaston's Mill and Pioneer Village, in the park

Little Beaver Creek Greenway Trail, www.bicycletrail.com/Greenway.htm

Accommodations: Beaver Creek State Park campground; call (866) 644-6727 for reservations.

Lock 30 Woodlands RV Resort Campground; (877) 856-2530 or www.ohiorvcamp.com

Organizations: Little Beaver Creek Land Foundation, (330) 420-9507, www.littlebeavercreek.com

Sandy and Beaver Canal Association, http://sandybeaverassoc.org

North Country Trail Association, (866) 445-3628, http://northcountrytrail.org

13 Hemlock Gorge to Lyons Falls Trail

Mohican State Park

Make a 9.3-mile lollipop to explore many of the main attractions at Mohican State Park. Begin by walking the Hemlock Gorge Trail along the Clear Fork of the Mohican River, which runs through a glacial meltwater gorge that's 300 feet deep. Its natural features include sandstone outcroppings, hemlocks, sycamores, oaks, and rare virgin white pine stands. Continue on the Lyons Falls Trail and walk into a recess cave under Big Lyons Falls and then to the top of Little Lyons Falls, which pour into a box canyon. Return on this loop to the covered bridge, where you'll again meet the Hemlock Gorge Trail.

Start: Main campground trailhead for Hemlock Gorge Trail

Distance: 9.3-mile lollipop; optional 3.3-mile hike with shuttle or 6-mile lollipop with shuttle

Hiking time: About 3.5 to 5 hours

Difficulty: Moderate to difficult due to length and a couple of steep sections

Trail surface: Dirt path; some spots often muddy

Blaze: White

Best season: Early May through late Oct

Other trail users: Hikers only

Canine compatibility: Leashed dogs permitted

Water: Available seasonally at campgrounds

Land status: State park and state forest

Nearest town: Loudonville

Fees and permits: None

Schedule: Open daily from dawn to 11 p.m.

Maps: USGS quad: Jelloway

Trail contacts: Mohican State Park, Loudonville; (419) 994-5125; http://parks.ohiodnr .gov/mohican. Mohican Memorial State Forest, Perrysville; (419) 938-6222; http://ohiodnr .com/forests/mohican/tabid/5160/Default .aspx.

Finding the trailhead: From I-71 exit 165, south of Mansfield, take SR 97 east about 20 miles to its dead end into SR 3 (watch for turns on SR 97). Take a left (north) onto SR 3 and then in 0.2 mile take a left into the campground. Go 0.7 mile to the showerhouse on the right; the trailhead is behind the showerhouse. *DeLorme: Ohio Atlas & Gazetteer:* Page 49 D7. GPS: N40 36.81 / W82 18.95.

Option: You may want to set up a shuttle between the campground and the covered bridge. Travel 15.7 miles on SR 97. Just past the Mohican Memorial on the right, take a left turn onto FR 58 and travel 1.5 miles, following the signs for the covered bridge. GPS: N40 36.79' / W82 19.01'.

The Hike

The centerpiece of Mohican State Park is the Clear Fork of the Mohican River, which runs through a gorge more than 300 feet deep. The meltwaters from the edge of the last glacier helped to carve out this gorge. Its natural features include sandstone

Covered bridge over Black Fork of the Mohican River

outcroppings, hemlocks, sycamores, oaks, and rare virgin white pine stands that have earned the area National Natural Landmark status.

Too many hikers bypass the Hemlock Gorge Trail and thereby miss some of the park's most rare and interesting offerings. Begin on this trail, noticing the thick layer of moss growing on the north side of the trees, especially the sycamores. Look upslope for the old-growth white pines. Within a mile the gorge broadens to a fairly wide flood-plain, and then the river and slope come together, pinching the trail in between. Watch for spots where the trail washes out here. Trout and bass fishing are popular in the Clear Fork; you are sure to see fishers in the river as you hike. As you finish the trail, you will come upon an idyllic scene of anglers with an old covered bridge as a backdrop. Look for great blue herons and kingfishers, both of which frequent the gorge.

Cross the covered bridge and begin the Lyons Falls Trail. You will walk by water-falls that were once frequented by John Chapman, aka Johnny Appleseed. He carved his name and the date on the sandstone walls of Lyons Falls, but his carvings are no longer visible. Some portions of this heavily used trail are considerably washed out. Other spots can be slick or may skirt the edge of drop-offs. Be careful if walking with children or in wet conditions. Take care to avoid further environmental damage by staying on designated trails.

Begin the trail by walking along the river in a forest dominated by hemlocks, with red oak and beech as well. Soon you will walk upslope and to Big Lyons Falls. The trail takes you into a shallow recess cave, behind a trickling waterfall. You will then approach the top of Little Lyons Falls. These falls drop into a beautiful box canyon. The trail returns to the Clear Fork Gorge, this time atop the rock outcroppings.

Continue by skirting the earthen dam that creates Pleasant Hill Lake—home to eagles and ospreys—and then return to the covered bridge on the other side of the river by way of the Pleasant Hill Trail. From the bridge, return the way you came on the Hemlock Gorge Trail.

Miles and Directions

0.0 Start the Hemlock Gorge Trail from the main campground; find the spur trailhead behind the showerhouse. Walk past the BICYCLES PROHIBITED sign and take a footpath to the wooden trailhead sign. Parallel the river.

2.5 Cross a footbridge and walk into Campground B. Walk along the campground road to the covered bridge.

3.3 Cross the covered bridge and take an immediate right (west) to the Lyons Falls Trail. **Option:** If you set up a car shuttle, you can finish your hike here.

3.8 Come to a junction. Take a left to go to Big Lyons Falls. Walk up the slope, paralleling the tributary.

4.2 Approach Big Lyons Falls, pouring over a shallow recess cave. The trail takes you behind the falls and out of the gorge on the other side on a wooden stairway. Soon you will begin to see blue blazes.

4.5 Arrive at the top of Little Lyons Falls, which pour into a slot-like canyon. The path crosses the waterfall and parallels its drainage.

4.8 Come to a T-intersection. Take a left and descend gradually.

5.0 Come to the end of the trail at the dam. Cross the grass below the dam and pick up the Pleasant Hill Trail. You can see the trailhead sign from the dam.

6.0 The Pleasant Hill Trail ends at the covered bridge. (**Option:** If you set up a shuttle, end the trail here.) Walk along the road again that serves Campground B. Return to the trailhead on the Hemlock Gorge Trail.

9.3 Arrive back at the campground trailhead.

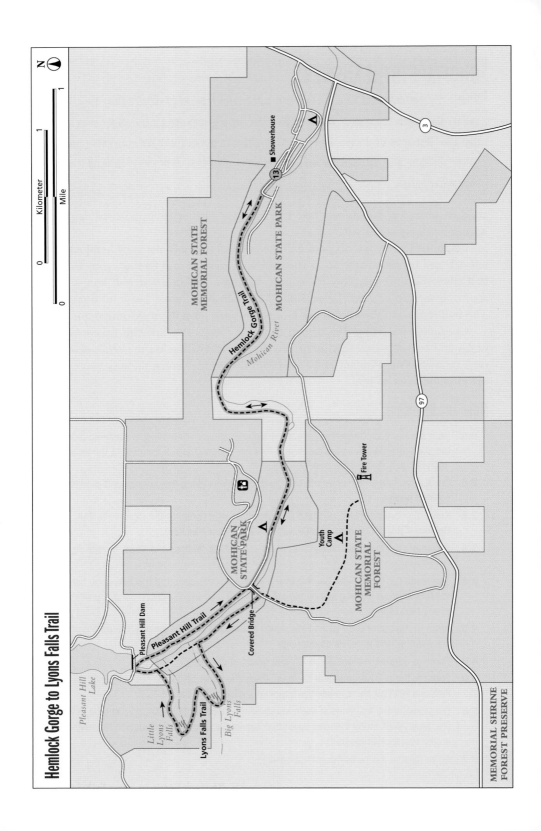

Hemlock Gorge to Lyons Falls Trail

MOHICAN STATE
MEMORIAL FOREST

Hemlock Gorge Trail

Mohican River

MOHICAN STATE PARK

Showerhouse

3

13

MOHICAN
STATE PARK

Fire Tower

Youth
Camp

MOHICAN STATE MEMORIAL FOREST

97

Pleasant Hill Dam

Pleasant Hill Trail

Covered Bridge

Pleasant Hill Lake

Little Lyons Falls

Big Lyons Falls

Lyons Falls Trail

MEMORIAL SHRINE
FOREST PRESERVE

N

Kilometer
0   1
Mile
0   1

Hike Information

Local information: Loudonville-Mohican Convention and Visitors Bureau, Loudonville; (877) 2-MOHICAN; www.loudonville-mohican.com

Local events and attractions: Tree Farm Canopy Tours zipline, (740) 599-2662, www.treefrogcanopytours.com

Malabar Farm State Park, (419) 892-2784, http://parks.ohiodnr.gov/malabarfarm

Accommodations: The trailhead leaves from the developed campground, and a primitive campground is near the covered bridge; call (419) 994-4290 for information or (866) 644-6727 for reservations.

Mohican State Park cottages; call (866) 644-6727 for reservations.

Mohican Lodge and Conference Center; call (800) 282-7275 for reservations.

Restaurants: Bromfield's Dining Room in Mohican Lodge, (800) 282-7275, www.mohicanstateparklodge.com

Organizations: Mohican Trails Club, http://groups.yahoo.com/group/mohican_trails

Honorable Mentions

Northeast Ohio

F Headlands Dunes State Nature Preserve

Mark Twain said, "Buy land, they're not making it anymore." Not true at Headlands Dunes State Nature Preserve. Since ODNR purchased 16 acres in 1976, the nearly 4,000-foot-long Fairport Harbor West Breakwater has impounded so much sand that the preserve has grown to 24 acres. There are no official hiking trails, but walk along the many sandy paths along the shore of Lake Erie. Enjoy views of shifting sand dunes, unusual grasses and flowers, a scenic lighthouse, and the lake itself. This preserve isn't just picturesque, it's also ecologically important. Headlands Dunes is one of the last sand dune plant communities along a river bay in the Great Lakes and is home to unusual grasses, including the state-endangered Great Lakes little bluestem. This is also your chance to begin hiking from the northern terminus of the statewide Buckeye Trail. You can walk from here through Headlands Beach State Park (which is mostly a parking lot with a beach) to Mentor Marsh State Nature Preserve and keep going for about as long as you care to.

Trail contact: Headlands Dunes State Nature Preserve, Painesville; (216) 881-8141; http://ohiodnr.com/location/dnap/headlands/tabid/892/Default.aspx

Finding the trailhead: From SR 2 in Painesville, turn north onto SR 44 and drive 2.6 miles until it ends at the Headlands Beach State Park entrance. Drive straight into the park and take the first right. Travel to the easternmost row in parking lot #1. Walk to the northeast corner of the parking lot to the trailhead sign. *DeLorme: Ohio Atlas & Gazetteer:* Page 32 B1. GPS: N41 45.58' / W81 17.10'.

G Rocky River Reservation

Rocky River Reservation is part of the Cleveland Metroparks "emerald necklace" of greenspace surrounding the city. This long, narrow park is a buffer around the Rocky River as it flows north into Lake Erie. Starting from the nature center, hike south along the river, with views of its shale banks, and then up the steep wooden stairs to a good overlook of the valley below. Heading either north or south, walk the trail pinched between the river on one side and the bike path and road on the other. Like so many other Ohio hikes, this is nice year-round, but especially during spring wildflower and fall foliage seasons or after a winter snowfall. Park naturalists offer guided hikes year-round; contact the nature center for up-to-date information.

Trail contact: Rocky River Nature Center, North Olmsted; (440) 734-6660; www.clemetparks.com

Finding the trailhead: From I-480 in North Olmsted, exit onto SR 252 South. Travel 0.5 mile to Butternut Ridge Road and take a left (east). Drive 0.1 mile to Columbia Road and turn left (north). Drive 0.3 mile to Cedar Point Road and turn right. Descend to Valley Parkway in 0.6 mile and turn left (north). Drive 0.3 mile to the nature center parking lot on the left. *DeLorme: Ohio Atlas & Gazetteer:* Page 40 A4. GPS: N41 26.94' / W81 50.30'.

⊢ Glens Trail, Gorge Metro Park

Straddling the cities of Akron and Cuyahoga Falls, Gorge Metro Park is a long, narrow strip of greenspace that overlooks the Cuyahoga River. Head out on the 3.6-mile out-and-back Glens Trail and find yourself pinched between Sharon conglomerate sandstone outcroppings on one side and the dammed-up river on the other. Enjoy abundant spring wildflowers, and look for white-tailed deer. If you'd like, continue on the Gorge Trail to Mary Campbell Cave, named after a young white girl who lived as a child with her Delaware Indian captors. You can even hop on the Highbridge Trail and walk to Cascade Valley Metropark.

Trail contact: Metro Parks, Serving Summit County, Akron; (330) 867-5511; www.summitmetroparks.org

Finding the trailhead: From SR 8 in Cuyahoga Falls, turn west onto Broad Boulevard and take an immediate left (south) onto Front Street. Drive 1.1 miles to the Metro Park entrance and parking lot on the right. Pick up the Gorge Trail at the trailhead sign next to boulders at the southwest end of the parking lot. Walk across Front Street and pick up the trail again on the other side. *DeLorme: Ohio Atlas & Gazetteer:* Page 41 D6. GPS: N41 07.11' / W81 29.36'.

∣ Buckeye Trail, West Branch State Park

At West Branch State Park, a portion of the statewide Buckeye Trail makes a 9-mile loop around the western third of Michael J. Kirwan Lake (reservoir). Hike the entire loop with two sections on the road, or make it a 7.5-mile horseshoe with a shuttle. Beginning at the junction of SR 14 and West Cable Line Road, follow the blue blazes as you make your way around the south side of the lake in a mostly young forest with beaver ponds along the runs that drain into the lake. The area is also home to glacial kettle lakes. Look for water-loving cattail, buttonbush, and swamp white oak, as well as the usual array of spring wildflowers. Cross the lake by walking along the Rock Spring Road bridge. From here you'll get views of the anglers and boaters who throng to this park, named for the West Branch of the Mahoning River. On the north side of the lake is a picnic area that's perfect for a halfway-point lunch stop. Continue walking counterclockwise on the north side of the lake, where the forest floor is covered in ramps (wild leeks) in the springtime and several fern species year-round. Finish the trail at Knapp Road, where you can pick up your bike or car shuttle or continue walking back to SR 14.

Trail contact: West Branch State Park, Ravenna; (330) 296-3239; http://parks
.ohiodnr.gov/westbranch

Finding the trailhead: From the junction of SR 59 and SR 14 in Ravenna,
turn south onto SR 14 and drive 2.3 miles to West Cable Line Road on the left
and a pullout on the right (west) side of SR 14. Park at the pullout and pick up the
trail across the road. It enters the woods about 150 feet south of West Cable Line. To
shuttle, turn back 0.25 mile on SR 14 to Knapp Road and take a right (east; there
is a gravel parking lot here, and this may be a preferred starting point). Travel 1 mile
on Knapp Road to a pullout and the trail on the right, marked with a blue blaze.
DeLorme: Ohio Atlas & Gazetteer: Page 42 C2. GPS: N41 07.92' / W81 11.24'.

J Deer to Red Fox Trail Loop, Tappan Lake Park

If you look at a map of Ohio, take note of the many sizable permanent reservoirs
located in the Muskingum River Watershed, the result of fourteen flood-control
dams built by the US Army Corps of Engi-
neers between 1933 and 1938. The Muskingum Watershed Conservancy District,
a unique political entity, has a mission to
oversee flood control, conservation, and recreation on the lakes and the entire 54,000
acres of land and water space it manages for
public use. Tappan Lake in Harrison County
is one of the more popular recreation areas
in the district, for hikers as well as other users
like boaters, anglers, and hunters. Beginning
at the campground amphitheater, combine
the Deer, Pine Tree, and Red Fox Trails for a 5.8-mile loop hike that takes you by the
lakeshore and into deciduous and pine forests. Look for old fencerows along the trail,
which are now made up of stately old oak trees. Wildlife and wildflowers are plentiful. Nearby, the Buckeye and North Country Trails make their way through the park.
Camping and cabins are available. There is a day-use fee to enter the park Memorial
Day through Labor Day.

▶ A watershed is an area of land
that drains into the same body of
water, often a river. For example, the
Muskingum River Watershed contains
the Muskingum River as well as the
tributaries that flow into it and the
surrounding land. The Ohio River
Watershed includes the Muskingum,
its tributary.

Trail contact: Tappan Lake, c/o Muskingum Watershed Conservancy District,
New Philadelphia; (330) 343-6647 or (877) 363-8500; park and campground (740)
922-3649; www.mwcd.org

Finding the trailhead: From I-77 in New Philadelphia, take US 250 east 24.4
miles to near the end of Tappan Lake. Turn right (south) onto CR 55 (Tappan-
Moravian Trail—it joins CR 2) and drive 3.7 miles to the park entrance on the right.
Turn into the park and drive 0.7 mile, just past the guard shack, and take a left at the
sign that reads CAMP AREA/BOAT LAUNCHING RAMP/AMPHITHEATER/HIKING TRAILS.
Drive about 150 feet to a stop sign and take a right into Campground 1. Drive on

the campground road 0.2 mile to a stop sign, on the left side of the launch ramp as you face it. Park at the boat launch parking lot and look for the amphitheater sign. That's the trailhead. *DeLorme: Ohio Atlas & Gazetteer:* Page 62 B2. GPS: N40 11.31' / W81 13.72'.

K Buckeye Trail: US 22 to Piedmont Marina Campground, Piedmont Lake Park

The little-used section of the Buckeye Trail that skirts the northwest edge of Piedmont Lake offers some of the best views in the region. You'll likely find solitude along this 8-mile out-and-back segment that skirts the water's edge. Expect to see and hear your watercraft neighbors, though. Try a late-afternoon hike to catch the good light casting its glow on the far side of the lake and the rolling hills off into the distance as you walk through a young deciduous forest and a few pine plantations. Stop at the campground and marina for a halfway-point water or lunch stop. If you're spending some time on the water, too, make your way to the rock that juts out of the lake near Indian Run, where you can see a fossilized snake. Piedmont Lake is one of ten permanent flood-control/recreation reservoirs in the Muskingum Watershed Conservancy District.

Trail contact: Piedmont Lake, c/o Muskingum Watershed Conservancy District, New Philadelphia; (330) 343-6647 or (877) 363-8500; www.mwcd.org

Finding the trailhead: From the junction of I-70 and I-77 near Cambridge, travel north on I-77 for 3.3 miles to US 22. Turn east and drive 22 miles to the trailhead on the right. Just after US 22 and SR 800 split, continue down a hill with guardrails on both sides of the road. The trail starts at a break in the guardrail on the right side of the road. Just after that is a pullout. If you hit the rest area, you've gone too far. Look for the blue blazes. *DeLorme: Ohio Atlas & Gazetteer:* Page 62 C2. GPS: N40 11.36' / W81 13.64'.

L Ledges Trail, Liberty Park, Summit County Parks

This newly developed section of park includes a 1.1-mile trail that takes you through an open field and into the woods with, as the name suggests, 30-foot-high conglomerate ledges trailside. The highlight of the loop is Glacier Cave, which isn't exactly a cave—you can walk into a cool, dark hallway of rock—but provides cool respite on a hot summer's day and interesting views any time of year. The forest is full of maple trees and pawpaw and spicebush in the understory. The rocks are often covered in ferns and mosses. Listen for songbirds and even the squeaking of bats. There is no water available, so bring your own.

Trail contact: Metro Parks, Serving Summit County, Akron; (330) 867-5511; www.summitmetroparks.org

Finding the trailhead: From the junction of US 422 and SR 91 in Solon, turn south on SR 91 and go 3.7 miles to Glenwood Drive. Turn left (east) and go 1.1 miles to the traffic circle. Take the first exit from the traffic circle onto Liberty Road. Go 0.5 mile to the park entrance on the left. Enter the park and drive 0.3 mile to the parking lot and trailhead, marked with a large sign. *DeLorme: Ohio Atlas & Gazetteer:* Page 41 B7. GPS: N41 19.95' / W81 24.70'.

M Ansel's Cave Trail, The West Woods

Seven miles of trails traverse the 900-acre West Woods in Geauga County. Reforested farm fields and wetlands provide habitat for a diversity of plant and animal species as well as a variety of scenery for hikers. Try the 1.5-mile Ansel's Cave Trail, which starts from the nature center and takes you to the namesake Ansel's Cave, a rocky outcrop that purportedly provided shelter to people escaping slavery along the Underground Railroad, returning Civil War soldiers, bootleggers, and a local woodsman named Ansel Savage. After returning to the nature center, tack on the Trout Lily Trail (0.2-mile round-trip) to Sunset Overlook—which, as the name suggests, is quite nice for viewing the sunset over a beaver-dammed wetland.

Glacier Cave, along the Ledges Trail

Trail contact: Geauga Park District, Chardon; (440) 286-9516; www .geaugaparkdistrict.org

Finding the trailhead: From SR 306 and SR 87 in Russell, go east on SR 87 (Kinsman Road) 1.8 miles to the park entrance on the right. Enter the park and drive straight 0.3 mile to the nature center on the right. From the nature center parking area, cross the park road and pick up the Ansel's Cave Trail at the trailhead by a few parking spots. *DeLorme: Ohio Atlas & Gazetteer:* Page 41 A1. GPS: N41 27.46' / W81 18.19'.

▶ **Two other eastern forest trees are now experiencing blights: Unless a cure is found, flowering dogwood and eastern hemlock numbers will continue to diminish, if not disappear altogether.**

AMERICAN CHESTNUT *(CASTANEA DENTATA)*

Just when you start to feel that the world is coming to an end—global warming, clear-cuts, huge forest fires, massive road-building projects, suburbs—take a minute to think about what it must have been like to live through the American chestnut blight.

Until the beginning of the twentieth century, fully one in every four trees in the central Appalachians and the eastern half of Ohio was an American chestnut. This was the dominant tree species in more than 9 million acres in the East, most often found on dry ridgetops. These giants regularly grew to 5 feet in diameter and 100 feet tall, and many were bigger than that.

The American chestnut was easily the most important tree species in the forest. Wild animals, domesticated animals, and people near and far feasted on the large, meaty nuts. The lumber from the American chestnut was also very important. The trees grew tall and straight, and often the first branches were 50 feet from the ground (think of a mature tulip poplar in today's forest). Straight-grained and fairly easy to work, the wood was used for just about everything—from furniture to musical instruments to railroad ties to pulp.

In 1904 an Asian fungus was discovered in New York that would turn out to be the American chestnut blight. Less than fifty years later, virtually every American chestnut tree was dead. Dying trees were cut and milled for their usual lumber uses (check out the shelters and picnic tables at Fort Hill State Memorial, for example). You can sometimes see fallen chestnut logs along the trail today, long ago stripped of their bark. In fact, you can even see some American chestnuts growing in the forest, but these are mostly young stump sprouts that will succumb to the blight within a couple of decades, before producing nuts.

Researchers are now working on bringing back the American chestnut, mostly by breeding it with Asian chestnut varieties in an attempt to produce a blight-resistant strain. For more information, contact the American Chestnut Foundation at (802) 447-0110; chestnut.acf.org.

Central Ohio

C entral Ohio is often overlooked as a hiking destination, but a handful of very nice trails are within an hour or two of the state's largest (by area and population) city. When Columbus was designated state capital of Ohio in 1812, it was not yet a city at all. In fact, it was pretty much a wilderness

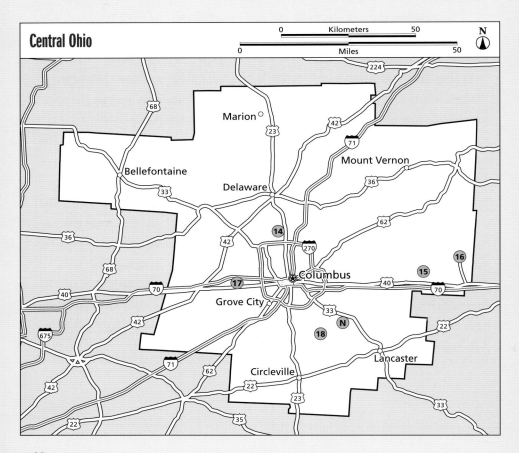

Central Ohio

area. Several landowners donated the property near the confluence of the Olentangy and Scioto Rivers to the relatively new state, and by 1816 the capital was relocated from Chillicothe, a former Shawnee Indian settlement that lay farther south along the Scioto River. The Scioto Trail, a Native American north–south thoroughfare running between Lake Erie and the Ohio River, ran right through present-day Columbus.

Many public lands that have been preserved in this region center around Native American sites. Flint Ridge is one of the most important sites in Ohio's human history. Native Americans and, to a lesser extent, European settlers converged here to quarry flint, a highly prized and useful stone. Blackhand Gorge, located along the Licking River near Flint Ridge, served as a byway along another major Native American thoroughfare, this one east–west. Closer to Columbus, Highbanks Metro Park is home to a Cole Indian earthen embankment and an Adena Indian burial mound. The park overlooks the Olentangy, a state scenic river.

Slate Run, Battelle Darby, and Clear Creek, other featured Columbus Metro Parks, are just part of the sixteen parks operated by the Metro Parks System, which was established in 1945. Metro Parks operates 26,000 acres in seven central Ohio counties.

Prior to European settlement, the Till Plains region of Ohio was home to a vast beech–maple forest, with occasional prairie openings. The Till Plains are so called due to the thick layer of till, or debris, left by the Wisconsinan Glacier that retreated from Ohio about 12,000 years ago. Not only did the soils of these plains prove to be very fertile, but the flat landscape made the work of clearing and working the land easier than in Ohio's hill country. Today 95 percent of the land in the Till Plains is cultivated or urbanized, a ratio that makes parkland all the more valuable.

Central Ohio's state parks all surround reservoirs of varying sizes. Hiking trails complement water sports at these parks, and lakeside hikes are a common feature.

Overlook and Dripping Rock Trails

Highbanks Metro Park

Highbanks gets its name from the towering shale riverbanks that rise from the Olentangy, a state scenic river. Your best bet to see the unusual bowling ball–like rock concretions that jut out of the shale banks is in the park's nature center. Combine the Overlook and Dripping Rock Trails to get a 5.8-mile sampling of everything at this suburban park, including a fairly mature forest, prehistoric Native American earthworks, pioneer artifacts, a constructed wetland, and a river overlook.

Start: Oak Coves Picnic Area
Distance: 5.8-mile trail network, including spur trails
Hiking time: About 2 to 3 hours
Difficulty: Moderate due to length
Trail surface: Dirt and gravel
Blaze: Overlook Trail, blue arrowhead; Dripping Rock Trail, woodpecker silhouette
Best season: Apr through Oct
Other trail users: Pedestrian traffic only, but these trails are very popular with joggers, so expect to share the trail with them.

Canine compatibility: Leashed dogs permitted only on separate 3.7-mile Primitive Pet and Ski Trail
Water: Available in the picnic area
Land status: Columbus Metro Park
Nearest city: Columbus
Fees and permits: None
Schedule: Open from 6:30 a.m. to 10 p.m. in summer, 6:30 a.m. to 8 p.m. in winter
Maps: USGS quad: Powell
Trail contact: Columbus Metro Parks, Westerville; (614) 508-8000; www.metroparks.net

Finding the trailhead: From I-270 on the north side of Columbus, turn north onto US 23 (exit 23). Drive 3 miles to the park entrance on the left. Past the nature center on the right, continue to the second left into the Oak Coves Picnic Area. Park at the first lot, in front of the trailhead kiosk. *DeLorme: Ohio Atlas & Gazetteer:* Page 58 C1. GPS: N40 08.93' / W83 01.87'.

The Hike

Before you start hiking, stop by the attractive and informative nature center. There you'll find information on the park's natural features, including unusual rock "concretions," bowling ball–looking rocks that formed around organic materials 300 to 350 million years ago during the Devonian period. These concretions now protrude out of the sedimentary shale banks. A large window in front of bird feeders allows you to watch some of the sixty species of forest birds found here, including woodpeckers, jays, and finches. The nature center also features interpretive exhibits about local Native American and early European settler history.

Start the hike with the Overlook Trail. Here you will walk by the Pool family gravestones, which were moved here from their original place. Next to the gravestones,

A rock concretion in shale near the Dripping Rock Trail COLUMBUS METRO PARKS/CHERYL BLAIR

notice the line of stately oaks that once served as a fencerow. Continuing on, you will walk beside a 1,500-foot horseshoe-shaped earthwork. An interpretive sign tells you that this earthwork, likely a fortification of an old village, was constructed by the Cole Indians of the Late Woodland period around AD 800 to 1300. This portion of the park is designated a National Natural Landmark.

Continue to an observation deck overlooking the Olentangy River, its high shale banks, sycamore trees, soaring birds, encroaching development, and a new feature—a bald eagle nest that has successfully fledged eaglets each year since 2010. Contact the park ranger for canoe-access information.

Soon you will come to the Wetland Spur Trail that takes you to a bird blind overlooking a pond. This is an excellent spot to see migrating ducks and geese. These constructed wetlands are important for wildlife, since Ohio has lost more than 95 percent of its original wetlands to agriculture and development.

After completing the Overlook Trail, return to the Dripping Rock Trail, where you should notice an abundance of spiny honey locust trees. Walking along streams that drain into the Olentangy, you will get a better view of the shale banks that prevail in the area. At several points, this trail skirts a forest–meadow edge area. Look here for wildlife, including birds and white-tailed deer.

Toward the end of the trail is a spur leading to an Adena mound. The Adena people settled the area around 800 BC to AD 100. They are best known as prehistoric mound builders. Some of these mounds were burial mounds; others are thought to have been constructed for ceremonial purposes. The Adena lived throughout what is now Ohio and in parts of Kentucky and West Virginia. Evidence shows that the Adena were primarily hunters and gatherers who practiced some agriculture. Shortly after the Adena mound, the trail returns to the trailhead.

Miles and Directions

0.0 Start at the Oak Coves Picnic Area. Looking at the trailhead kiosk from the parking area, walk left (east) to the edge of the asphalt. Follow the woodpecker blaze and walk the wide, gravel path that parallels the shale-bottomed streambed.

0.1 Come to a fork. Stay right, following the blue arrowhead blaze to begin the Overlook Trail.

0.4 Come to another fork, where the Overlook Trail loop begins. You can go either way, but staying right you will come to a spur in about 100 feet. To the left is a relocated pioneer cemetery.

0.8 Walk along a long, narrow earthwork to your right and come to a T-intersection. Take a right here and cross the earthwork.

1.0 Approach the observation deck overlooking the Olentangy River. Return the way you came to the junction at mile 1.1.

1.2 Come to the Wetland Spur Trail. Turn right; walk a few hundred feet and look for a sign to the right for the Wetland Trail. Don't continue to the open field.

1.6 The Wetland Trail ends at a bird blind overlooking a pond. Return the way you came to the main trail at mile 2.0.

2.4 Return to the original junction for the Overlook Trail. Continue straight.

2.7 Hit the Dripping Rock Trail again. Turn left.

2.8 Return to the parking area. To continue on the Dripping Rock Trail, simply keep walking past the parking on your right and back into the woods. **Option:** You can end your hike here or stop for lunch before continuing on the Dripping Rock Trail.

3.4 Approach the junction with the Big Meadows path on the left at mile 0.7. Continue straight, follow the woodpecker blaze, and cross a bridge.

3.5 Come to a second junction. This time follow the blaze to the right to stay on the Dripping Rock Trail.

4.2 Pass a short side trail on the left to an observation deck overlooking the meadow.

4.6 Come to another fork. To the left is the nature center. Continue along the trail to the right and cross the park road. After crossing the road, you will see a picnic area to the right before you reenter the woods.

4.8 Cross a wooden bridge and come to a spur trail to the left that takes you to an Adena burial mound.

5.2 Return to the main trail and take a left.

5.4 Pass a spur on the right that takes you to a parking lot.

5.6 Come to a T-intersection. Take a right.

5.8 Arrive back at the trailhead.

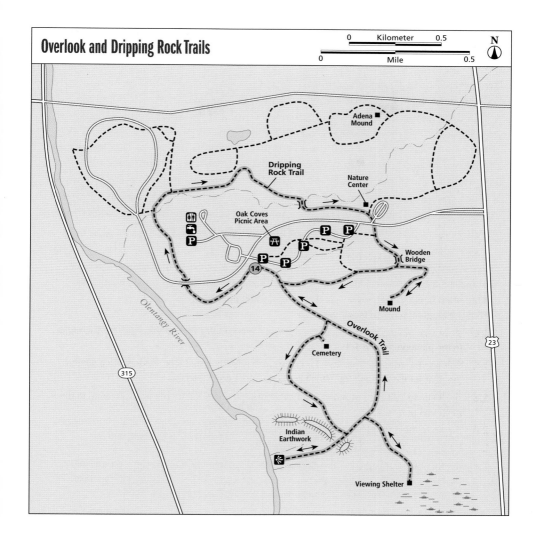

Overlook and Dripping Rock Trails

Adena Mound

Dripping Rock Trail

Nature Center

Oak Coves Picnic Area

Wooden Bridge

Mound

Olentangy River

Overlook Trail

Cemetery

23

315

Indian Earthwork

Viewing Shelter

Hike Information

Local information: City of Columbus, www.city ofcolumbus.org

Greater Columbus Convention and Visitors Bureau, (800) 354-COLS (2657), www.experiencecolumbus.com

Ohio Historical Society, (614) 297-2300, www.ohiohistory.org

Local events and attractions: Olentangy Indian Caverns are just north of the park; (740) 548-7917 or www.olentangyindiancaverns.com.

Accommodations: Alum Creek State Park campground, Delaware; (614) 548-4631; http://parks.ohiodnr.gov/alumcreek

The Wayfaring Buckeye Hostel, (614) 754-0945, sites.google.com/site/wayfaringbuckeye

Organizations: Columbus Outdoor Pursuits, (614) 442-7901, www.outdoor-pursuits.org

15 Lake Trail with Japanese Garden Spur

The Dawes Arboretum

On this 3.1-mile ramble through a human-manipulated landscape, the trees and shrubs along the path are identified for you. Highlights include a Japanese garden, prairie wildflowers, collections of exotic and unusual trees, magnificent older trees, views of the surrounding landscape, and a small cypress swamp. If you're looking for a more traditional trail through a forest (or more seclusion), check out the 3-mile Arboretum East Trail, which features a mature beech-maple forest, an Adena Indian mound, and an overlook of a glacial terminal moraine.

Start: Visitor center
Distance: 3.1-mile loop including spur loop
Hiking time: About 2 to 3 hours
Difficulty: Moderate due to length and sun exposure
Trail surface: Wide and clearly marked grass, mulch, dirt, cement, and gravel path
Blaze: No blazes, but there are signposts at every junction.
Best season: Mid-Apr through mid-Oct
Other trail users: Hikers only
Canine compatibility: Leashed dogs permitted, but owners are expected to clean up after their pets and prevent dogs from urinating on the plants.

Water: Available at the visitor center
Land status: Privately owned nonprofit arboretum
Nearest town: Newark
Fees and permits: None, but the arboretum does accept donations.
Schedule: Open daily from dawn to dusk except Thanksgiving, Christmas, New Year's Day, and during threatening weather
Maps: USGS quad: Thornville
Trail contact: The Dawes Arboretum, Newark; (800) 44-DAWES; www.dawesarb.org

Finding the trailhead: From I-70 about 30 miles east of Columbus, turn north on SR 13 (exit 132) and travel 2.6 miles to the Dawes Arboretum entrance on the left. Drive past the gate and continue straight past the visitor center to the parking lot. *DeLorme: Ohio Atlas & Gazetteer:* Page 69 A6. GPS: N39 58.81' / W82 24.79'.

The Hike

The trees and shrubs along the Lake Trail, compatible with central Ohio's climate zone, are identified for you. These identifications will help you better appreciate the forests you hike in afterward. This is an unusual Ohio hike in that it's not through a forest; rather it meanders through a human-manipulated landscape of many interesting plants and features.

The arboretum, a private not-for-profit enterprise, was established by Beman and Bertie Dawes in 1929. Beman Dawes was a successful businessman and an Ohio representative. His brother, Charles, vice president of the United States under Calvin Coolidge and recipient of the Nobel Peace Prize, also contributed to an endowment that set up a fund to operate the arboretum.

Wear a sun hat and head out on the Lake Trail. Begin by walking past mostly native trees that are identified along the path, such as serviceberry, shagbark hickory, hemlock, different maple species, and black walnut. Walk through some small patches of forest, both deciduous and evergreen. In about a half mile, take the Japanese Garden Trail on a cemented-grit loop path. Designed by Makoto Nakamura of Kyoto University, this traditional garden aspires to simplicity and harmony. Features include a "hide and reveal" element of landscape, a hill and pond, and a raked dry-landscape feature. Perhaps all the mowed grass is where the Japanese meets the American aesthetic. You can take a rest at a meditation house near the pond. No picnicking is allowed here.

After returning to the Lake Trail, continue on and skirt a meadow of native flowers, including wild sunflower, black-eyed Susan, and echinacea. Then walk through some woods again and out to Holly Hill, with an impressive collection of holly trees. Past Holly Hill are some of the most impressive trees in the arboretum, including a magnificent black maple. From this spot you get an expansive view of the landscape's rolling hills. Soon you will walk through a tunnel of trees and then circle around Dawes Lake, next to the 2,000-plus feet of hedge lettering. Much of the return trip is through a native forest. In late winter and early spring, enjoy the maple sugaring and the forest floor covered in ramps (wild leeks).

The last segment of the trail winds through the striking bald cypress swamp. Walk over the boardwalk and enjoy not only the beautiful deciduous trees with needlelike leaves but also the abundant wildlife that lives in the small swamp, including frogs, salamanders, and dragonflies.

The 3-mile Arboretum East Trail starts at the Cypress Swamp and continues through a maintained prairie ecosystem and then into a mature beech–maple forest. An Adena mound is located within the forest. The trail also skirts the edge of a glacial terminal moraine before returning along the edge of the forest and open meadow/farmland. If you plan to do the Arboretum East Trail, first stop by the visitor center to get directions and a free permit.

Miles and Directions

0.0   Start at the visitor center. Walk out of the visitor center and take a right. Walk to the gazebo-like "outpost" where most hikes in the arboretum originate. From the outpost walk west, following the sign for the hiking trails and Japanese Garden.

0.1   The trail forks. Take the right fork, following the blaze.

0.2   Cross the auto tour road and enter a pine forest.

Lake Trail with Japanese Garden Spur

Davis Drive Road

Cypress Swamp

Licking Trails

Japanese Garden

Sugarhouse

Beard-Green Cemetery

15

13

Ridgely Tract Road

N

0   Kilometer   0.5
0   Mile   0.5

0.3 Come to a four-way intersection with the Japanese Garden Trail. Take a left and walk a short loop trail through the Japanese Garden.

0.6 Return to the Lake Trail and take a left.

1.0 Come to a T-intersection at a gazebo. Take a right, following the blaze for the Lake Trail.

1.4 Cross the auto tour road.

1.6 Cross straight over a traffic circle and walk due south through a "tunnel" of various trees. Then circle around the south side of Dawes Lake. **FYI:** The benches around the lake might make a good lunch spot.

2.0 Pass a junction on the right for the tower overlook.

2.1 Come to a T-intersection next to the road. Take a right and cross the road.

2.5 Cross the auto tour road again.

2.6 Pass a side trail on the left and then a second side trail to the right for the cemetery. Continue straight.

2.7 Pass a side trail on the left that leads to an old log cabin/sugaring shack, and then pass another side trail coming in from the left. Emerge from the woods into a picnic area. Before the picnic shelter, turn right.

2.8 Cross the auto tour road again and enter the cypress swamp and a boardwalk trail. At the end of the boardwalk, turn right. Follow a mowed path that parallels the road.

3.0 Cross the road and head toward the visitor center.

3.1 Arrive back at the visitor center.

Hike Information

Local information: Licking County Convention and Visitors Bureau, (800) 589-8224, www.escapetolickingcounty.com

Local events and attractions: The Dawes Arboretum celebrates Arbor Day the last Sat in Apr. Flint Ridge State Memorial, Glenford; (800) 283-8707; www.ohiohistory.org/places/flint.

Longaberger Basket Company, Dresden; (740) 322-5900; www.longaberger.com

Accommodations: Dillon State Park campground, Nashport; call (866) 644-6727 for reservations; www.dnr.state.oh.us/dillon/tabid/730/Default.aspx.

Restaurants: Sunflower's Restaurant, Cherry Valley Lodge, Newark; (740) 788-1200

16 Blackhand to Quarry Rim Trail

Blackhand Gorge State Nature Preserve

Blackhand sandstone gets its name from an image of a large hand that was once carved into the sandstone walls of Blackhand Gorge. It's believed that this hand was engraved by Native Americans as a directional sign to the flint deposits at nearby Flint Ridge. At this spot the Licking River cuts a striking gorge through this sandstone, creating a scenic byway. Begin on the multiuse Blackhand Trail and then take the Quarry Rim Trail out of the river valley and around an old quarry. Return by walking through the Deep Cut and by the river's edge.

Start: Parking lot on Toboso Road (CR 278)
Distance: 1.9-mile lollipop
Hiking time: About 1 hour
Difficulty: Easy; short and well worn, with stairs to help you up and down steep parts
Trail surface: Begin and end on an asphalt path; dirt side trails with a few difficult footings
Blaze: None; Quarry Trail junctions are marked.
Best season: Mar through Oct and in winter after a snowfall
Other trail users: Bicyclists
Canine compatibility: Leashed dogs permitted on the Blackhand Trail only

Water: No potable water is available here; bring your own.
Land status: State nature preserve
Nearest towns: Zanesville, Newark
Fees and permits: None
Schedule: Open daily a half hour before sunrise to a half hour after sunset
Maps: USGS quad: Thornville
Trail contact: Blackhand Gorge State Nature Preserve, Newark; (614) 265-6453; http://ohiodnr.com/tabid/922/default.aspx

Finding the trailhead: From I-70 in Zanesville, take SR 146 west 17 miles to CR 273, marked with a green sign for Toboso and Blackhand Gorge State Nature Preserve. Turn left (south) and travel 1.8 miles to the parking lot on the right. *DeLorme: Ohio Atlas & Gazetteer:* Page 60 D1. GPS: N39 37.74' / W81 11.24'.

The Hike

The region around Blackhand Gorge and Flint Ridge is said to have once been neutral territory for all tribes coming to access the valuable flint deposits. Today you won't see the namesake engraved black hand; it was destroyed when the Ohio and Erie Canal was constructed through the gorge. But you will see fantastic outcroppings of the sandstone towering above the scenic Licking River.

This spot where the river cuts an east–west gorge has been used as a transportation route by humans for countless generations. Evidence of prehistoric Native American use includes petroglyphs and mounds. As is often the case with obvious

Blackhand Rock

transportation routes, European explorers continued to use this passageway. In the 1820s the Ohio and Erie Canal was constructed through the gorge. You can hop on the Canal Lock Trail on the river's north side to get a look at the long-dry sandstone locks. As railroads replaced the less efficient canal system, the Central Ohio Railroad was built through the gorge and carried steam-powered engines. A newer elevated rail line now crosses over the gorge. Also early in the twentieth century, an electric railroad (trolley) was built through the gorge, this time by blasting a tunnel for its right-of-way. (The tunnel is now on private property.)

Today most travelers through Blackhand Gorge are here for recreation rather than to get from one place to another. Running along the river is the Blackhand Trail, a

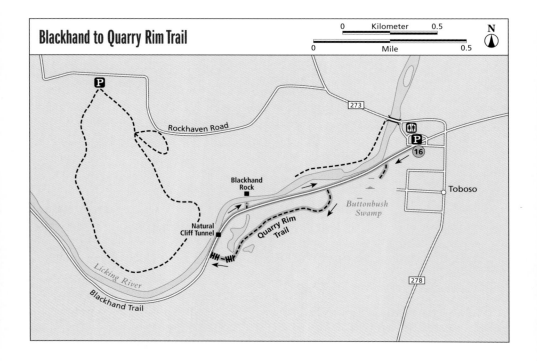

4.3-mile multiuse path. Two hiking trails are accessible from the Blackhand Trail, and two others are nearby.

A 1.9-mile loop beginning at the main parking lot on the east end of the preserve allows you to take in the main attractions of the preserve. Begin on the asphalt Blackhand Trail. Shortly you'll come to an overlook spur that lets you view the buttonbush swamp, named for the plant's round flowers. Return to the main trail and then hop on the Quarry Rim Trail, a 1-mile side path that, as the name implies, takes you around the lip of an old sandstone quarry that was in operation from the 1870s to the 1920s. From this trail you get good views of tall sandstone walls jutting out of the old quarry, now filled with water.

The Quarry Rim Trail ends farther down the Blackhand Trail. From here take a right and return by immediately walking through the "Deep Cut," blasted out by the Central Ohio Railroad in the winter of 1850–51. Reportedly the project consumed more than 1,200 kegs of gunpowder. The Deep Cut measures approximately 330 feet long, 65 feet deep, and 30 feet wide.

On your return trip be sure to take the Blackhand Stone Spur Trail to the river's edge, where you'll be across from sandstone outcroppings towering 100 feet over the meandering Licking River. Across the way are the sandstone block walls that were part of the Ohio and Erie Canal towpath. At the time, dams were also constructed at both ends of the gorge, creating a lake where the river now runs. Atop the rocks hemlocks grow, and out of the soil grow cottonwoods and sycamores. As you return to the trailhead, see the roots of yellow birch trees that extend like tendrils over the large sandstone rocks.

This short loop is just the beginning of all the hiking you can do at Blackhand Gorge. Continuing westward along the Blackhand Trail, hop on the 2.3-mile Chestnut Trail, another spur on the south side of the river. From there you can continue to the end of the multiuse path and return for a 10-mile round-trip walk. For a footpath that gets away from the crowds, hop on the Marie Hickey and Oak Knob Trail loop, above the gorge on its north side. This is a spectacular trail in springtime when the dogwoods are flowering.

All trails are excellent for wildflowers spring through fall. In the spring look for trillium, wild geranium, Solomon's seal, phlox, and Dutchman's-breeches on north-facing slopes near the Blackhand Trail. In the summer wingstem, sweet William, bouncing bet, and oxeye grow in sunny spots near the river. This is a great preserve to visit throughout the year for walking, wildflower viewing, canoeing, or fishing.

Miles and Directions

0.0 Start from the main parking lot off of Toboso Road. Walk past the latrines and hop on the asphalt Blackhand Trail.

0.2 Approach a spur trail on the left that leads to an overlook of the buttonbush swamp. Return to this spot and continue west along the Blackhand Trail.

0.4 Arrive at the junction with the Quarry Rim Trail. Take a left.

0.9 Take in good views of the quarry from a couple of overlook spots.

1.1 Return to the Blackhand Trail at a T-intersection. Take a right and walk through the narrows. **Option:** Turn left and take the Blackhand Trail to the Chestnut Trail.

1.3 Come to a sign for the Blackhand Rock. Take a left and walk on the short spur to the river's edge. Return to the Blackhand Trail and take a left (east) to head back to the trailhead.

1.9 Arrive back at the parking lot.

Hike Information

Local information: Licking County Convention and Visitors Bureau, (800) 589-8224, www.escapetolickingcounty.com

Local events and attractions: Flint Ridge State Memorial, Glenford; (800) 283-8707; www.ohiohistory.org/places/flint.

Dawes Arboretum, Newark; (800) 44-DAWES; www.dawesarb.org.

Longaberger Basket Company, Dresden; (740) 322-7800; www.longaberger.com.

Accommodations: Dillon State Park campground, Nashport; call (866) 644-6727 for reservations; http://parks.ohiodnr.gov/dillon.

Restaurants: Cottage Restaurant, Newark; (740) 763-3636

Organizations: Friends of Blackhand Gorge, www.friendsofblackhandgorge.org

17 Terrace to Ancient Trail Loop

Battelle Darby Creek Metro Park

Battelle Darby Creek Metro Park is a success story of conservation and restoration. Hike along Big Darby Creek, a protected state and national Wild and Scenic River and home to a hundred fish species, then walk through restored prairies and past a Native American mound. And where in Ohio can you visit reintroduced bison? You got it—right here at Battelle Darby Creek.

Start: Terrace Trail trailhead at the Indian Ridge Day Use Area
Distance: 3.9-mile double loop
Hiking time: About 2 hours
Difficulty: Easy to moderate, especially depending on time of day with sunlight
Trail surface: Gravel road
Blaze: Trails are not blazed but intersections are marked.
Best season: Year-round; prairies bloom in late summer.
Other trail users: Joggers and cross-country skiers (in season)

Canine compatibility: Dogs are not permitted on this trail. Dogs are allowed on selected trails in the park; check the trail map.
Water: There is a water pump in the parking lot.
Land status: Columbus Metro Park
Nearest town: West Jefferson
Fees and permits: None
Schedule: Open daily from 6:30 a.m. to 10 p.m. Apr through Sept and 6:30 a.m. to 8 p.m. Oct through Mar
Maps: Battelle Darby Creek Metro Park map; USGS quad: West Columbus
Trail contact: Metro Parks, Westerville; (614) 508-8000; www.metroparks.net

Finding the trailhead: From I-270 on the west side of Columbus, take exit 7B for US 40 West (West Broad Street) and travel 5.2 miles to Darby Creek Drive. Turn left (south) and travel 4.1 miles to the second park entrance, just past the railroad tracks. Turn right (west) into the Indian Ridge Day Use Area. Drive to the end of the third (last) parking area. *DeLorme: Ohio Atlas & Gazetteer:* Page 67 A7. GPS: N39 53.49' / W83 12.85'.

The Hike

The Nature Conservancy has labeled Big and Little Darby Creeks one of the "last great places" in the Western Hemisphere. The central feature of this metropark is, of course, Big Darby Creek. This state and national Wild and Scenic River is known for its intact, clean ecosystem that harbors healthy aquatic life, including several species of threatened or endangered mussels. In fact, 100 of the 166 fish species found in Ohio live in the Big Darby watershed, including 5 that are state endangered. But just because this metropark is known for its well-protected watershed doesn't mean it's a slouch when it comes to hiking—the park is home to 18 miles of trails.

A bison in the prairie at Battelle Darby Creek Metro Park Columbus Metro Parks/Tina Copeland

Before or after your hike, take a quick jaunt to the bison area, in the northern half of the 7,000-plus-acre park. In 2011 Columbus Metro Parks introduced six female bison to the park; in 2013 they introduced a male bison. There are two pastures on either side of the multiuse Darby Creek Greenway Trail. Both the prairies and the bison once existed in this Darby Plains area, and reintroduction of these animals helps to naturally maintain a portion of the 600 acres of prairie that have been restored here. Your best bet at seeing bison is morning or evening, as they are more active during these times of day.

The Terrace to Ancient Trail loop begins in a wooded area; look for silver maples and sycamores in the canopy near the creek. Along the first portion of the trail, look for signs leading you to the "natural play areas"—off-trail areas designated for children of all ages to turn over a few rocks and explore the forest and stream ecosystem up close. Several side trails also lead to Big Darby Creek. Take some time to enjoy bird-watching (great blue herons and kingfishers are common) and relaxation along this biodiverse waterway.

Join the Ancient Trail, and don't forget your sun hat. This trail skirts the edge of the forest and grassland and also the edge of a 1,000-year-old Fort Ancient earthwork, called the Voss Mound after the former property owner. It is known as the most northern of the Fort Ancient earthworks. Finally, walk through the prairie and enjoy the abundant flowers, like black-eyed Susan, echinacea (purple coneflower), prairie dock, and big bluestem. You will likely see birds (goldfinches, hummingbirds, and

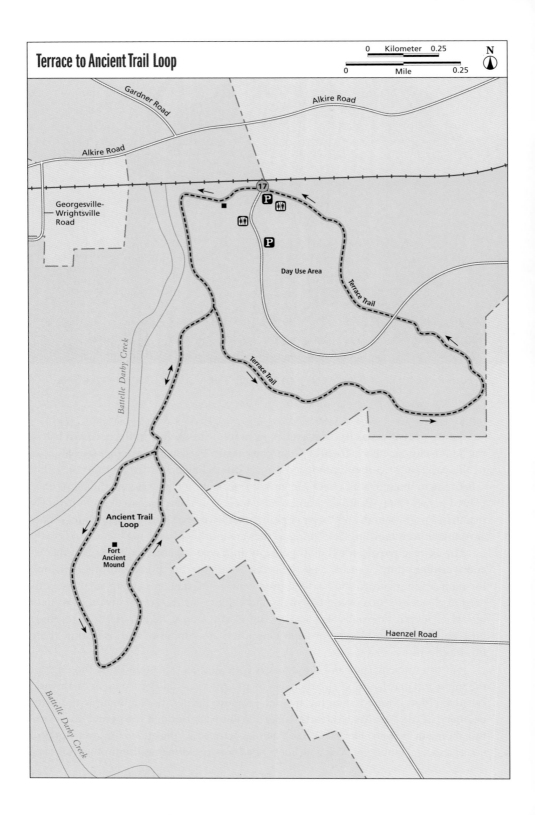

bluebirds, to name a few) and, if you look closely, many butterflies. White-tailed deer are also common here.

Interpretive signs help you see the results of retreating glaciers that left the landscape as it is today. Finish the hike back in the woods. There are plenty of other recreation opportunities at Battelle Darby, including paddling, cycling along the Darby Creek Greenway and Camp Chase Trails, fishing, and winter activities including sledding and skating.

Miles and Directions

0.0 Start at the Terrace Trail trailhead in the last parking lot in the Indian Ridge Day Use Area, past the swing set and picnic shelter. Walk about 20 feet past the trailhead sign to a junction. Take a left and begin the hike in a counterclockwise direction. **FYI:** There are three trailheads that originate from this parking area. All are marked with trailhead signs for the Terrace Trail.

0.1 Come to a junction and a post with directional arrows to parking areas. Take a left to continue on the Terrace Trail. You will pass several side trails on the right to the creek.

0.4 Come to a junction with the Ancient Trail on the right. Take a right and begin the Ancient Trail.

0.75 Come to a junction with an access road and the Ancient Trail loop. Take a right and continue straight for a counterclockwise loop. You will pass a few more dirt access roads from the right along this loop; stay on the main trail.

1.0 Pass the prehistoric Native American mound on the left.

1.4 The trail takes a sharp left. There are directional signs here.

1.9 End the loop portion of the Ancient Trail. Take a right in about 20 feet, then take a left and return to the Ancient Trail trailhead.

2.3 Return to the Terrace Trail. Take a right to complete the loop. **Option:** You can take a left and return the way you came to the trailhead for a 2.7-mile hike.

2.4 Pass an access trail on the left. Continue straight and ascend a small hill.

3.3 Cross a paved park road.

3.75 Come to a fork. To the left a spur leads you to the trailhead parking area. Go right to complete the loop.

3.8 Another spur on the left leads you to the trailhead parking area. Go straight to complete the loop.

3.9 End at the junction where you began the hike. Take a left to the parking area.

Hike Information

Local information: Greater Columbus Convention and Visitors Bureau, (866) EXP-COLS, www.experiencecolumbus.com

Local events and attractions: Battelle Darby Creek Metro Park offers a full schedule of events, including naturalist-led hikes. Events are listed on the park's website.

Accommodations: Deer Creek State Park is about 25 miles away; call (866) 644-6727 for campsite or cabin reservations; http://parks.ohiodnr.gov/deercreek.

Restaurants: Cattleman's Pizza, Grove City; (614) 877-4482

Organizations: Friends of Metro Parks, Westerville; www.metroparksfriends.org

18 Five Oaks to Kokomo Wetland Trail

Slate Run Metro Park

Slate Run Metro Park is an outstanding example of environmental restoration. Just twenty years ago, most of this park was a cornfield. Today it combines 6.6 miles' worth of park trails through an oak forest surrounding the shale-bottomed (and misnamed) Slate Run and a restored prairie that's home to a glacial outwash bank that provides an excellent view of the park's restored wetlands. This is a good bird-watching spot as well—the park is now home to some 200 bird species, including nesting sandhill cranes. While here visit Slate Run Living Historical Farm.

Start: Shady Grove Picnic Area
Distance: 6.6-mile trail system
Hiking time: About 2.5 to 3.5 hours
Difficulty: Moderate due to length and grassy/muddy trail conditions
Trail surface: Dirt, gravel, grass, wetlands, and boardwalks
Blaze: None, but trails are well worn. Look for blazes at junctions.
Best season: Apr through Oct
Other trail users: Hikers only

Canine compatibility: Leashed dogs allowed only on pet trails in the park (Covered Bridge and Shagbark Trails, 0.5 mile each)
Water: Available at Slate Run Living Historical Farm and Buzzard's Roost Picnic Area
Land status: Columbus Metro Park
Nearest towns: Lithopolis, Canal Winchester
Fees and permits: None
Schedule: Open daylight hours year-round
Maps: USGS quad: Canal Winchester
Trail contact: Metro Parks, Westerville; (614) 508-8000; www.metroparks.net

Finding the trailhead: From US 33 about 7 miles southeast of I-70, turn south onto SR 674 and follow signs 7 miles to the park's main entrance. Turn right (west) into the park and travel past the naturalist office on the right, taking the first left toward Shady Grove Picnic Area. Park at the picnic area and pick up the trailhead at the far west end of the area, next to the restrooms. *DeLorme: Ohio Atlas & Gazetteer:* Page 68 B3. GPS: N39 45.51' / W82 50.34'.

The Hike

Based on soil and groundwater conditions, park naturalists believe that the land now comprising Slate Run Metro Park was originally a meadowy wetland. In 1995 and 1996 the park reverted a portion of its lands to grasslands. Species you'll see growing here include Kentucky bluegrass, short fescue, ashy sunflower, purple bergamot, and butterfly milkweed. In 1999, with the help of the Wetlands Foundation, the park constructed an approximately 155-acre wetland. Since then more than thirty new species of birds have been observed as well as six new species of toads and frogs.

Restored wetlands

Begin hiking on the Five Oaks Trail, a wide, flat gravel path winding through young woods and paralleling Slate Run on the right. This shale-bottomed stream was misnamed by European settlers, who mistook the shale for similar-looking slate. The bedrock of the park is Ohio black shale, laid down some 400 million years ago during the Devonian period. You'll find yourself walking in a predominantly oak–hickory forest, but also look for beech, maple, pawpaw, buckeye, cherry, and hackberry. Keep an eye out for woodpeckers and hawks.

Begin the Bobolink Grassland Trail by entering into the grassland and following a mowed path. Look around for glacial erratics, pieces of granite left by retreating glaciers. This trail begins by paralleling an old fence-line marking the boundary for Slate Run Farm. This is a "living historical farm," operating as it did in the 1880s. Volunteers work the farm using period tools and equipment. Plan time to visit Slate Run Farm during your visit. As you walk in the grassland, keep an eye out for a resident herd of white-tailed deer.

Take the spur to the overlook for the Kokomo Wetland Trail. You'll be rewarded with an expansive view of the restored wetland and beyond. You'll also have the chance to get up close and personal with a hundred-year-old Osage orange tree. The spot you're standing on is a glacial outwash bank, made up of sediment deposited by a melting glacier.

Continuing on to the Kokomo Wetland Trail, walk along the boardwalks and through the wetlands. You might glimpse nesting and migrating birds, including pipe-billed grebes, American bitterns, and blue-winged teals. This trail

▶ **Five Oaks Trail is an understatement. The nine oak species found in Slate Run Metro Park include white, swamp white, red, black, chinquapin, burr, shingle, chestnut, and pin.**

Five Oaks to Kokomo Wetland Trail

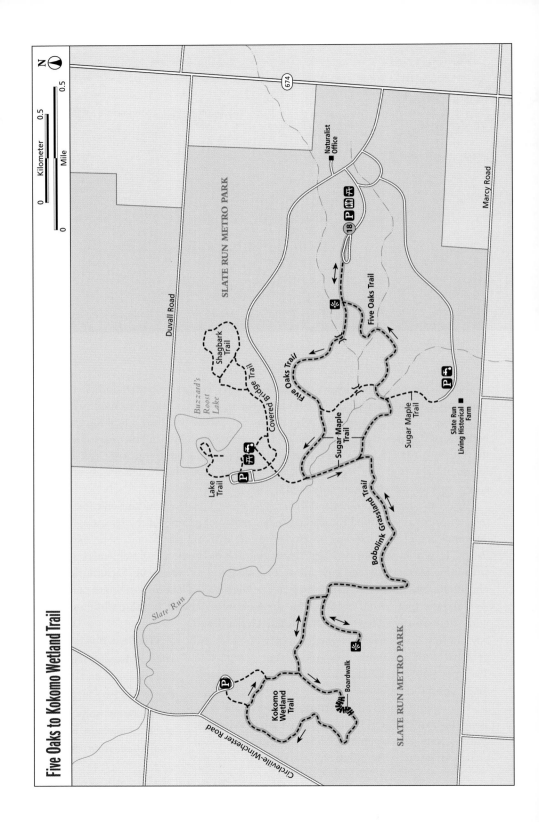

can be very muddy, so wear appropriate footwear. Return on the Bobolink Trail to the Sugar Maple Trail and the wooded section of the park. Complete the loop made by the Sugar Maple and Five Oaks Trails. Toward the end of the hike, you'll see some of the most mature trees in Slate Run, including several species of the trail's namesake oaks. Park gates are locked at dusk, so plan to return to your car by then.

Miles and Directions

0.0 Start at the Shady Grove Picnic Area.

0.1 Come to the first junction that begins the Five Oaks Trail loop. You can travel it in either direction, but staying right, pass the observation deck and descend to two bridges that cross the stream.

0.7 Come to the junction with the Sugar Maple Trail. Continue straight. **Option:** You can return directly on the Five Oaks Trail for a 1.5-mile hike by turning left.

1.0 Pass a spur trail to the right that takes you to another parking area and the trails around Buzzard's Roost Lake. The trail here turns south and crosses Slate Run again.

1.2 Arrive at the junction with the Bobolink Grassland Trail. Take a right. **Option:** You can continue straight and return directly for a 2.5-mile loop, but at least a short foray onto the Bobolink Trail is recommended.

2.1 Reach the junction with a spur trail to an overlook deck. Continue straight to the overlook. Return to this junction at mile 2.5 and take a left.

2.9 Come to the junction with the Kokomo Wetland Trail. Take a left.

3.1 Cross a lengthy boardwalk.

3.9 Pass a spur trail coming in from the left.

4.0 Pass another spur trail on the left.

4.2 Come back to the Bobolink Grassland Trail. Turn left, returning the way you came.

5.5 Return to the junction with the Sugar Maple Trail. Turn right.

5.9 Return to the junction with the Five Oaks Trail. Take another right.

6.4 Return to the first junction, by the viewing platform. Take a right.

6.6 Arrive back at the trailhead.

Hike Information

Local information: City of Columbus, www.cityofcolumbus.org

Greater Columbus Convention and Visitors Bureau, (800) 354-COLS (2657), www.experiencecolumbus.com

Ohio Historical Society, (614) 297-2300, www.ohiohistory.org/places/ohc

Local events and attractions: Slate Run Living Historical Farm is part of the metropark. Nearby Canal Winchester boasts one of the largest Labor Day parades in Ohio.

Accommodations: Four Seasons Farm Bed, Breakfast and Barn, Canal Winchester; (614) 499-5126

A. W. Marion State Park campground, Mount Sterling; (740) 869-3124; http://parks.ohiodnr.gov/awmarion

Organizations: Columbus Outdoor Pursuits, (614) 447-1006, www.outdoor-pursuits.org

Honorable Mention

Central Ohio

N Ridge to Meadows Trail Loop, Chestnut Ridge Metro Park

Only 15 miles outside of Columbus's outerbelt, Chestnut Ridge is one of the city's more rural Metro Park holdings. As the name suggests, the flat landscape of Columbus starts to give way to the ridges and hollows of Appalachian Ohio here. Once home to abundant American chestnut trees (wiped out by the chestnut blight), the forest is now successional mixed hardwoods. Start by the pond and wetland, where you are likely to see a wide variety of birds, including ducks and herons. Walk past a spring and an amphitheater built with locally quarried sandstone blocks and then begin a clockwise loop. The Meadows Trail takes you through woods and meadows and past an old homestead orchard near the junction with the Homesite Trail. Complete the 2-mile loop on the Ridge Trail, which ascends the ridge in the forest and includes an overlook where, on a clear day, you can see the downtown Columbus skyline.

Trail contact: Metro Parks, Westerville; (614) 508-8000; www.metroparks.net

Finding the trailhead: From I-270 in Columbus, take US 33 east 12 miles to Carroll. Turn right (southeast) on Winchester Road (there is a brown park sign here) and drive 2.7 miles to the park entrance on the left. Enter the park and go 0.4 mile to the second parking lot on the left, by the playground, toilets, and pond. Take the gravel trail past the amphitheater to the trailhead, marked with a sign and map. *DeLorme: Ohio Atlas & Gazetteer:* Page 68 B4. GPS: N39 48.38' / W82 45.18'.

Southwest Ohio

Southwest Ohio is an area defined by both physical and political features, and a label can only just begin to provide a description. Native Americans inhabited southwest Ohio long before Europeans came to North America and started drawing straight lines and right angles. North of the Ohio River and west of the Scioto River, prehistoric Native Americans lived and built earthen embankments that today serve as mysterious reminders of their presence on this land long ago. Most famous of these is Serpent Mound, a quarter-mile-long earthwork in the image of a snake opening its mouth around an egg-shaped object. Fort Ancient and Fort Hill are two other well-known sites where hiking trails take today's visitors around and through the earthen embankments. The Hopewell Indians are credited with most of the mound building, but other prehistoric peoples, such as the Adena, Cole, and Fort Ancient Indians, also inhabited and built up their cultures in southwest Ohio.

When Europeans arrived here, the Shawnee Indians claimed the southern portion of the state as their hunting grounds and, to a lesser extent, their permanent home. Lower Town, near the confluence of the Scioto and Ohio Rivers (today Portsmouth, Ohio), was the home of a Shawnee settlement. Now just west of Portsmouth lies Shawnee State Park and Forest. By far the state's largest state forest, Shawnee is home to Ohio's only wilderness area, and the park and forest combined host 60 miles of hiking trails. Southwest Ohio was also home to the Miami Indians at the time of European settlement.

Downstream on the Ohio River, Cincinnati grew to become the state's most important river city. In the midst of rapid industrialization, the Cincinnati Park Board in 1911 had the foresight to embark on the country's first urban reforestation project. Today Mount Airy Forest lies at the heart of Cincinnati's popular metropolitan park system. Cincinnati's Eden Park hosts the southern terminus of the statewide Buckeye Trail.

While Native American paths were becoming roads wide enough to haul Conestoga wagons, a young nation embarked on canal- and road-building projects. The

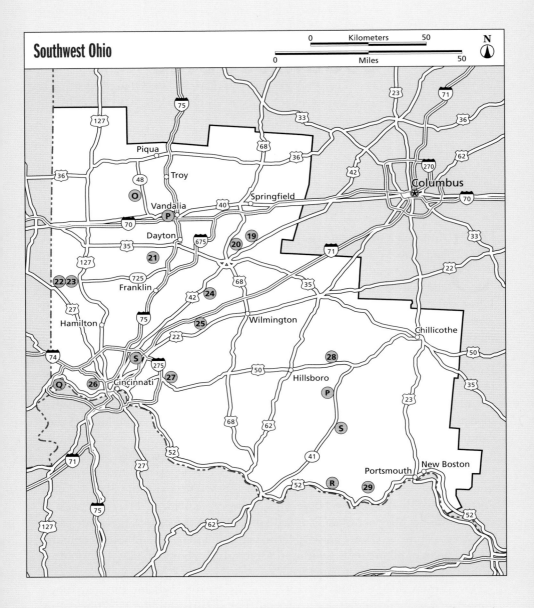

National Road, designed to link state capitals, continued west past Columbus and bypassed Dayton by just a few miles to the north. Dayton's leaders and citizens pulled together to make possible the construction of the Dayton Cutoff, an alternate spur that became the preferred route for travelers and settlers moving west. The city of Dayton grew, and when the largest recorded flood hit the Great Miami River in 1913, hundreds were killed and thousands were displaced from their homes. In the process of building flood-control dams, the city of Dayton set aside the river and creek valleys for metropolitan parks. Today's Five Rivers MetroParks provide ample quality hiking opportunities.

More or less paralleling the Great Miami River to the east, the Little Miami River became the first state and national Wild and Scenic River in Ohio, designated in 1969. Running alongside the river from Springfield to Milford is the Little Miami Scenic Trail, a 75-mile shared-use asphalt path. The Little Miami River Valley serves as a natural greenway that connects excellent hikes in John Bryan State Park, Clifton Gorge State Nature Preserve, Glen Helen Preserve, Caesar Creek State Park, and Fort Ancient State Memorial, among others.

Ecologically, most of southwest Ohio lies in the Till Plains region, atop rich soils left by the last glacier. The original forests were cleared for today's landscape of agriculture and cities. Hueston Woods State Nature Preserve, however, is home to a footpath exploring nearly 200 acres of virgin and near-virgin beech-maple forest. Surrounding that is the popular Hueston Woods State Park, with full amenities and many more miles of hiking trails. Jutting up from Kentucky across the Ohio River and into Brown and Adams County is the state's smallest ecoregion—the Interior Low Plateau, or Bluegrass region. The Nature Conservancy's Edge of Appalachia Preserve contains a few public-access hiking trails that allow you to check out globally rare plant and animal communities.

19 Little Miami River Loop and Spur Trail

Clifton Gorge State Nature Preserve and John Bryan State Park

When you hike along this portion of the Little Miami Scenic River, the strong forces of natural and human history make themselves known. Clifton Gorge is best known for its rushing waters through a striking narrow gorge that was cut by glacial melt-waters some 10,000 years ago. Its geologic history is largely the reason this 269-acre preserve is home to 347 plant species and 105 tree species. Start from John Bryan State Park and walk upstream 4.1 miles and then back down for a 7.8-mile loop along the Little Miami in a gorge with dolomite walls, slump blocks with stands of cedar, and an upland chinquapin oak forest. Visit the adjoining preserve and learn about the natural and human history of the gorge from interpretive signs.

Start: Clifton Gorge Trail trailhead in John Bryan State Park

Distance: 4.1 miles one way or 7.8-mile loop with spur

Hiking time: About 2 to 5 hours

Difficulty: Moderate to difficult due to length and the climb out of the gorge

Trail surface: Dirt, with some boardwalks

Blaze: None

Best season: Mid-Apr through mid-Oct and after a winter snowfall

Other trail users: Hikers only

Canine compatibility: Leashed dogs permitted in the state park but not in the state nature preserve. It's easy to make a 4.2-mile loop hike with pets.

Water: Available at the campground

Land status: State park and state nature preserve

Nearest town: Yellow Springs

Fees and permits: None

Schedule: Open daylight hours year-round

Maps: USGS quad: Clifton

Trail contacts: John Bryan State Park, Yellow Springs; (937) 767-1274; http://parks .ohiodnr.gov/johnbryan. Clifton Gorge State Nature Preserve, Yellow Springs; (937) 767-7947; http://ohiodnr.com/location/clifton/ tabid/882/Default.aspx.

Finding the trailhead: From I-70 in Springfield, turn south onto SR 72 (exit 54) and drive 6.6 miles to SR 343. Turn right (west) and travel 2.3 miles to SR 370. Turn left (south) and drive 1 mile to the entrance to John Bryan State Park on the left. Turn into the park and drive 0.5 mile to the Clifton Gorge Trail parking lot. *DeLorme: Ohio Atlas & Gazetteer:* Page 66 B2. GPS: N39 47.09' / W83 51.84'.

To shuttle: From I-70 in Springfield, turn south onto SR 72 (exit 54) and drive 6.6 miles to SR 343. Take a right onto SR 343 and in 0.1 mile take a left onto Jackson Street. On the right is the parking lot for Clifton Gorge State Nature Preserve. GPS: N39 47.66 / W83 49.73.

Water rushing through Clifton Gorge

The Hike

One of the most famous incidents at Clifton Gorge occurred between the Shawnee and European frontiersmen. As the story goes, Daniel Boone and members of his party, including Cornelius Darnell, were captured by Shawnee Chief Black Fish in 1799. During their escape, Darnell outpaced his Shawnee pursuers by leaping 22 feet across the upper gorge to safety. More detailed accounts say that Darnell didn't quite make it across, but he was able to grab hold of tree branches and still make his way to the other side. You probably don't want to try anything this risky while visiting John Bryan State Park and Clifton Gorge, but you can still have fun.

Begin the hike downstream from Clifton Gorge. As you walk upstream, notice the way the water has carved out layers of rock. The uppermost layer of rock in the gorge is Cedarville dolomite, which is resistant to weathering. Below that are two thin layers of other dolomites and then a thick layer of Massie shale. This shale weathers easily, and eventually its undercutting leads to "slump blocks," where the upper layers of rock have tumbled down into the gorge, sometimes into the middle of the

JOHN BRYAN

John Bryan, inventor and conservationist, bequeathed 500 acres of his Riverside Farm to the state of Ohio in 1924. His offer had been previously rejected by three governors because he required that no religious worship could take place on the land. He also took matters into his own hands to ensure that the trees in the campground would never be cut—he reportedly spiked them!

river. Below the layer of shale is Brassfield limestone, also weather-resistant, and then Elkhorn shale. Due to the types of rock present, the river is now mostly widening rather than deepening the gorge.

The relatively unusual geology of Clifton Gorge has contributed to its biodiversity. Naturalists have identified 347 species of wildflowers and 105 species of trees and shrubs within the 269-acre preserve. Along the river, water-loving sycamore and cottonwood trees thrive. Maple grows abundantly in the gorge, and a chinquapin oak forest dominates the upland area. Growing on the slump blocks is white cedar. In the spring, look for such wildflowers as spring beauty, trillium, hepatica, and jack-in-the-pulpit. Some rare species that grow here include the mountain maple, identifiable by its striped bark, as well as red-berried elder and Canada yew.

This area has long been inhabited by humans. Nearby earthworks provide evidence that prehistoric peoples, probably the Hopewell culture, lived here. More recently the Shawnee Indians made this region their home.

As Europeans continued to settle the area, gristmills, a textile mill, and a sawmill popped up along the gorge, all using the natural power of the rushing waters. The Clifton Mill, built in 1802, is still in operation today. Plan time to visit the mill on your trip. Clifton was home to more than 300 people in the mid-1800s. A railroad was never built here, but the Pittsburgh-Cincinnati Stagecoach Road was, and you will walk along this old road on your return trip downstream.

The preservation of this area has a history of nearly missed opportunities and narrowly avoided development. In 1924 the state of Ohio accepted 500 acres of land around the river, bequeathed by John Bryan. Hugh Taylor Birch later donated another 161 acres. But the upper portion of Clifton Gorge was still in private hands. In 1963 the Ohio chapter of the Nature Conservancy raised enough money to buy some of the upper gorge area, saving it from private recreation development. In 1968 the Nature Conservancy came through again and bought the rest of today's preserve land before a private housing development could be built.

The hike begins and ends downstream in John Bryan State Park. A 4.2-mile loop takes you up the south bank and down the north bank of the Little Miami Scenic River. If you have pets, you can do this loop. But the most spectacular part of the trail, overlooking the narrow gorge, is the 4-mile out-and-back spur that begins at the turnaround for the loop hike. Plan accordingly.

Little Miami River Loop and Spur Trail

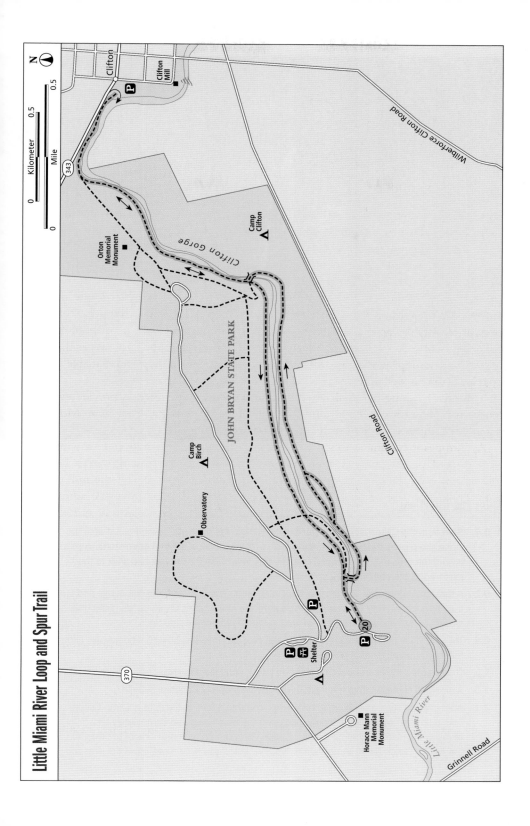

The Little Miami River

Miles and Directions

0.0 Start from the Clifton Gorge Trail parking lot. Walk to the trailhead bulletin board near the stone shelter. The trailhead sign reads TO RIVER/TO TRAILS. Follow the trail down stone steps toward the river. In a few hundred feet, the trail forks. Take the left fork and walk to the river's edge, then begin hiking upstream.

0.2 Approach a footbridge that crosses the Little Miami Scenic River. Cross the bridge and then turn left, walking upstream on the south side of the water. Continue along the trail closest to the river whenever you encounter formal or informal side trails.

0.6 The trail forks; the left branch stays near the river and the right crosses a boardwalk. Either fork ends up in the same place.

1.3 The two forks rejoin and become one trail again. Continue straight.

1.5 A side trail comes in from the right. This is private property. Continue straight.

2.1 After passing some tall dolomite rock faces, come to a fork. To the right is Camp Clifton. Take a left and cross the footbridge back over the river. Cross and immediately hit a four-way intersection. Turn right and continue upstream on the north side of the river. You are now in Clifton Gorge State Nature Preserve. **FYI:** If you have a pet, cross the river and turn left, as pets are not allowed in the preserve. This is also a good spot for lunch, since picnicking isn't allowed in the preserve either.

2.7 Come to a pool in the river, marked as the Blue Hole.

3.1 Pass Amphitheater Falls on the left and then Steamboat Rock (a slump block in the river) on the right.

3.4 Climb out of the gorge by way of steep wooden stairs. Take a right onto a crushed gravel path.

3.5 Cross a footbridge over a side waterfall and continue to a sidewalk along a roadway bridge. Cross the bridge and then continue along the trail, stopping at a number of overlooks along the way.

4.1 Approach a three-way intersection; to the left is a parking lot. Take a right to the final gorge overlook. Return the way you came. **Option:** If you shuttled, end here.

6.1 Arrive back at the footbridge at the edge of the preserve and a four-way intersection. Continue straight, picking up the old Pittsburgh-Cincinnati Stagecoach Road, marked with a sign.

7.2 Cross a stream over stepping-stones. Check out the top of the falls and an overlook for the river.

7.4 Come to a fork with an unmarked side trail to the left. Take this to rejoin the river's edge. You've passed this side trail if you see a fading orange arrow spray-painted on a tree.

7.6 Rejoin the stagecoach road (see another orange arrow), and in about 200 feet pass the footbridge you crossed toward the beginning of the hike. About 20 feet past the footbridge, take a left and return the way you came to the trailhead.

7.8 Arrive back at the trailhead.

Hike Information

Local information: Greene County Convention and Visitors Bureau, (800) 733-9109, www .greenecountyohio.org

Local events and attractions: In John Bryan State Park, go rock climbing or check out the observatory, a decommissioned US Air Force satellite tracking station. Nearby attractions include the shared-use Little Miami Scenic Trail (www.miamivalleytrails.org) and Antioch College's Glen Helen Preserve (937-769-1902 or http://glen.antiochcollege.org).

Restaurants: Eat pancakes from locally milled flour at the Clifton Mill's Millrace Restaurant; (937) 767-5501 or www.cliftonmill.com.

Accommodations: John Bryan State Park campground; call (866) 644-6727 for reservations.

Hike tours: Ranger-led hikes are offered between Memorial Day and Labor Day. Get the specifics from the park bulletin board.

20 Glen Helen Loop Trail

Glen Helen Nature Preserve

Glen Helen is Antioch College's very own land laboratory. Like nearby Clifton Gorge, the glen was created by glacial meltwaters 10,000 years ago. On a 4.4-mile loop that takes you downstream along Yellow Springs Creek and then back up the other side, take in some of Glen Helen's most well-known attractions: the Yellow Spring, after which the town is named; dolomite cliffs and Pompey's Pillar; a beautiful waterfall known as the Cascades; excellent wildflowers; a relocated covered bridge; mature trees; and glacial erratic rocks strewn throughout the preserve.

Start: The museum
Distance: 4.4-mile loop with a short spur
Hiking time: About 2 hours
Difficulty: Easy; mostly flat and fairly short
Trail surface: Dirt
Blaze: None
Best season: Apr through Oct and after a winter snowfall
Other trail users: Hikers only
Canine compatibility: Leashed dogs permitted
Water: Available at the museum when it's open
Land status: Privately owned by Antioch College, open to the public

Nearest town: Yellow Springs
Fees and permits: There is a suggested donation for parking and for the trail map. Groups of more than 10 persons are asked to make a small per-person donation for a self-guided hike or for a guided hike with a naturalist.
Schedule: Open daily from dawn to dusk
Maps: Glen Helen trail map; USGS quad: Yellow Springs
Trail contact: Glen Helen Nature Ecology Institute, Antioch College, Yellow Springs; (937) 769-1902; http://glen.antiochcollege.org

Finding the trailhead: From SR 68 in Yellow Springs, turn east onto Corry Street (on the north side of town) and travel 0.4 mile to the parking area on the left, marked with a sign. Park and then walk past the parking lot kiosk about 50 feet to the museum. *DeLorme: Ohio Atlas & Gazetteer:* Page 66 B2. GPS: N39 48.05' / W83 53.08'.

The Hike

Glen Helen Nature Preserve is a 1,000-acre land lab for Antioch College, replete with a state and national scenic river, rock formations, waterfalls, and a pine forest. The land was donated by Antioch alumnus Hugh Taylor Birch in 1929 and has been managed for ecological restoration.

Like nearby John Bryan State Park and Clifton Gorge Nature Preserve, the valleys here were cut by glacial meltwaters. Begin the hike by stopping at the museum to learn more about the natural features of Glen Helen. Then descend into the Yellow Springs Creek Valley and walk upstream. This upstream portion of the preserve

The Yellow Spring

features a large collection of attractions in the glen. Walk past Pompey's Pillar, a solitary column of dolomite. Then arrive at the famous Yellow Spring, from which the town gets its name. Flowing at a rate of 60 to 100 gallons per minute, the spring looks more orange than yellow, due to high concentrations of iron. The glen was home to a nineteenth-century resort that drew visitors to the believed healing qualities of the spring.

Past the Yellow Spring is the Cascades, one of the most scenic and well-known spots in the glen. A waterfall pours into a large pool, which then feeds a series of cascading waterfalls. After checking out the Cascades, head downstream along Birch Creek. The creek is small and attractive, bordered in some spots by dolomite cliffs and a forest that includes chinquapin oak, hickory, ash, tulip poplar, and maple. Underfoot, look for the many species of flowering plants, including broad waterleaf, phlox, twinleaf, trillium, jack-in-the-pulpit, giant bellwort, and Solomon's seal. By now you may have noticed a number of invasive exotics taking hold, including garlic mustard and honeysuckle. Glen Helen, with the

▶ **Legend has it that if you drink from the Yellow Spring, you will always return.**

A barred owl at the raptor center

support of the Nature Conservancy, has been tackling this problem with an invasive species removal project.

As you walk streamside, you'll see a number of side trails. These lead to upland portions of the preserve, including the pine forest, planted in the 1920s by the Ohio Division of Forestry. The turnaround point on the hike is at Grinnell Road. It's worthwhile, however, to continue downstream a couple hundred feet and explore a relocated covered bridge, more than a hundred years old. Past the bridge, come to the confluence of Yellow Springs Creek and the Little Miami Scenic River. This is a nice spot to rest and wait to see some of the usual inhabitants, including ducks, geese, great blue herons, and kingfishers. Preserve property and trails continue downstream on either side of the river if you're looking to add a few more miles to your hike.

Then walk up the trail along the water's edge, taking in new views along the same stretch of creek. Pass the tallest dolomite rock cliffs in the preserve just before returning to the trailhead by the museum.

Miles and Directions

0.0 Start at the museum. Walk down a few stairs to a junction. Continue straight down the stone steps.

0.1 Cross a footbridge over Yellow Springs Creek; in about 150 feet come to a T-intersection. Take a left.

0.2 A side trail to the right takes you to Pompey's Pillar. Continue straight.

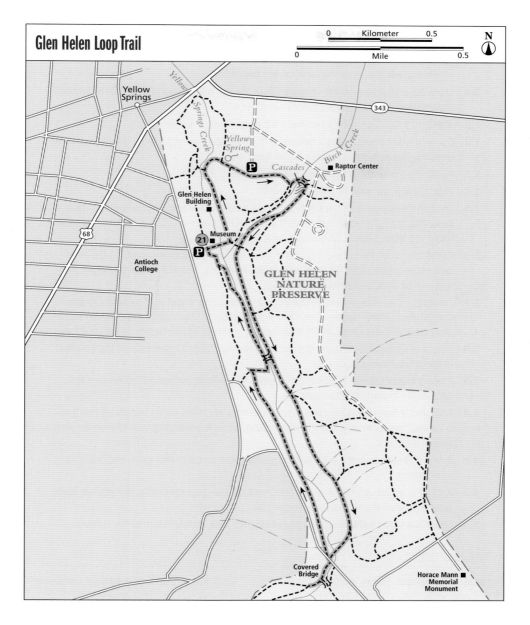

Glen Helen Loop Trail

0   Kilometer   0.5

0   Mile   0.5

N

Yellow Springs

Yellow Springs Creek

343

Yellow Spring

Cascades

Birch Creek

Raptor Center

P

Glen Helen Building

68

Museum

21

P

Antioch College

GLEN HELEN NATURE PRESERVE

Covered Bridge

Horace Mann Memorial Monument

0.3   Pass a footbridge on the left and approach an old cement bridge foundation, also on the left. A waterfall is on the right. Continue straight.

0.5   An access trail comes in from the left. Continue straight to the famous Yellow Spring. About 100 feet past the spring, come to a junction. Continue straight, passing a side trail on the right.

0.7 Pass a side trail to a somewhat obscured monument on the left (a plaque affixed to a glacial erratic stone) and come to a fork. Look left and see the footbridge you will cross. But first take a short side trip to the right and down the stairs to check out the Cascades on Birch Creek. Return to this junction and take a right.

0.8 Cross the footbridge over the Cascades. Take the first trail off to the right. Slowly descend toward the creek, crossing a tributary along the way.

1.0 Come to a fork. Take a right and finish the descent into the valley.

1.2 Come to a four-way junction. Continue straight. **Option:** Turn right and cross the creek over stepping-stones to return directly to the museum.

1.5 A side trail comes in from the left. Continue straight.

1.7 Pass a footbridge over the creek on the right.

1.8 The trail turns away from the creek, crosses a tributary over stepping-stones, and then forks. Take the right fork, staying near the creek. Over the next 0.5 mile, various formal and informal trails crisscross. Stay always near the creek.

2.5 Come to Grinnell Road. Take a right and cross over the creek on the road. On the other side of the bridge, cross the road, heading downstream, and pick up the trail again. The trail may be faint or overgrown here.

2.7 Come to an old covered bridge. Continue downstream for about 200 more feet to the confluence of Yellow Springs Creek and the Little Miami Scenic River. **FYI:** You can explore more trails and dirt roads on either side of the river here before beginning the return trip.

3.0 Return to Grinnell Road. Cross the road and pick up the trail again, now on the west side of the creek, heading upstream.

3.5 Cross a footbridge over a cascading tributary, then almost immediately come to a fork. Take a right to stay near the creek.

3.8 Approach a fork. Take a right and descend to the creek. Walk over a boardwalk and then a bridge, then come to a four-way intersection. Turn left, continuing upstream on the west side of the creek.

4.1 A side trail joins from the left. Look across the creek for cascading water and dolomite rock shelves.

4.3 Ascend to a T-intersection. Take a right. Check out the dolomite cliffs to the left, but keep generally below the rocks to stay on the trail.

4.4 Reach the stone stairs where you began the hike. Walk up and return to the museum.

Hike Information

Local information: Yellow Springs Chamber of Commerce, (937) 767-2686, http://yellowspringsohio.org

Greene County Convention and Visitors Bureau, (800) 733-9109, www.greenecountyohio.org

Local events and attractions: John Bryan State Park, (937) 767-1274, http://parks.ohiodnr.gov/johnbryan

Little Miami Scenic Trail (shared use), www.miamivalleytrails.org/little-miami-scenic-trail

Accommodations: John Bryan State Park campground; call (866) 644-6727 for reservations.

Restaurants: The Winds, Yellow Springs; (937) 767-1144; www.windscafe.com

Sunrise Cafe, Yellow Springs; (937) 767-7211; www.sunrisecafe-ys.com

Organizations: The Glen Helen Association, (937) 769-1902, http://glen.antiochcollege.org

21 Orange Trail

Twin Creek MetroPark

Grab your sun hat and binoculars, then head out to Twin Creek MetroPark, whose restored meadows allow expansive views of the Twin Valley and beyond. This varied hike takes you through these meadows, into woods, past a Hopewell earthwork, and down to Twin Creek, one of the cleanest waterways in the state.

Start: Eby Road/High View parking lot
Distance: 5.8-mile loop
Hiking time: About 2 to 3 hours
Difficulty: Moderate due to length and some ascents
Trail surface: Mowed grass and dirt trail
Blaze: Orange, marked only at junctions
Best season: Year-round; the meadow blooms in late summer.
Other trail users: Hikers only
Canine compatibility: Leashed dogs permitted
Water: Available at the Chamberlain Road parking and picnic area, 3.4 miles into the trail

Land status: Five Rivers MetroPark (Montgomery County)
Nearest town: Germantown
Fees and permits: None
Schedule: Open from 8 a.m. to 10 p.m. Apr through Oct, 8 a.m. to 8 p.m. Nov through Mar; closed Christmas and New Year's Day
Maps: Twin Creek MetroPark trail map available at trailhead; USGS quad: Miamisburg
Trail contact: Five Rivers MetroParks, Dayton; (937) 275-PARK; www.metroparks.org

Finding the trailhead: From the junction of SR 123 and SR 4 in Germantown, take SR 4 south 0.3 mile to Eby Road. Turn south and go 0.1 mile to the parking lot on the left. *DeLorme: Ohio Atlas & Gazetteer:* Page 65 D5. GPS: N39 36.33' / W84 21.75'.

The Hike

Begin your hike at the Eby Road/High View parking area, where you immediately get expansive views of the Twin Valley below. The hilltop here is maintained as a meadow, allowing not only these views but up-close "views" of meadow flowers including echinacea (purple coneflower), black-eyed Susan, and Queen Anne's lace. Five Rivers MetroParks mows and conducts controlled burning as needed to maintain these grasslands and the habitat they provide for bird and other species. This was farmland before it became a park, and some cedar trees as well as autumn olive dot the landscape. As you hike, look around for the occasional "glacial erratic" rocks that were deposited here by a glacier more than 12,000 years ago.

▶ **The Great Miami, Mad, and Stillwater Rivers plus Twin and Wolf Creeks inspire the Five Rivers MetroParks name.**

Orange Trail in Twin Creek MetroPark

At mile 1.3 come to Dogwood Pond. This is a good spot to take a break. If you hike this trail in the morning or evening (recommended), sit quietly here and observe birds, dragonflies, and deer. Reenter the woods after Dogwood Pond and at about mile 2.5, look closely and you will see a former "fall line" trail (one that goes straight up and down the slope) rehabilitated into an ecologically friendly trail with switchbacks. Five Rivers MetroParks' commitment to ecological stewardship reaches far beyond trail maintenance. Efforts include habitat and wildlife management, invasive species control, and a sustainability committee. Five Rivers has a strong commitment to land protection, requiring since 2010 that 90 percent of its total land holdings (more than 15,000 acres) be managed as "natural area."

Come to the second parking area/trailhead for the Orange Trail at the Chamberlain Road parking lot and picnic area. There is potable water here. The Orange Trail turns north and begins its return trip here, but Twin Creek MetroPark extends south of Chamberlain Road. The southern section was Boy Scout Camp Hook since the 1920s. The Boy Scouts closed the camp in the early 1990s, and Five Rivers purchased the property in 1997.

At mile 3.8 walk by an old Hopewell earthwork, an earthen hilltop enclosure some 2,000 years old. It can be easy to miss, but an interpretive sign helps you understand what you're looking at. After this the trail begins a descent to Twin Creek, one of the cleanest waterways in Ohio. There is a spot where you have a clear view of the creek from the trail. Shortly after this a side trail leads to the creek's edge. Swimming and wading are prohibited, which seems pretty unjust after you've hiked all the way here.

The trail continues to parallel the creek before turning west and ascending to the trailhead and parking. In the meantime, you will pass by the connector trail for the Twin Valley Backpacking Trail (see In Addition: Selected Ohio Backpack Trails),

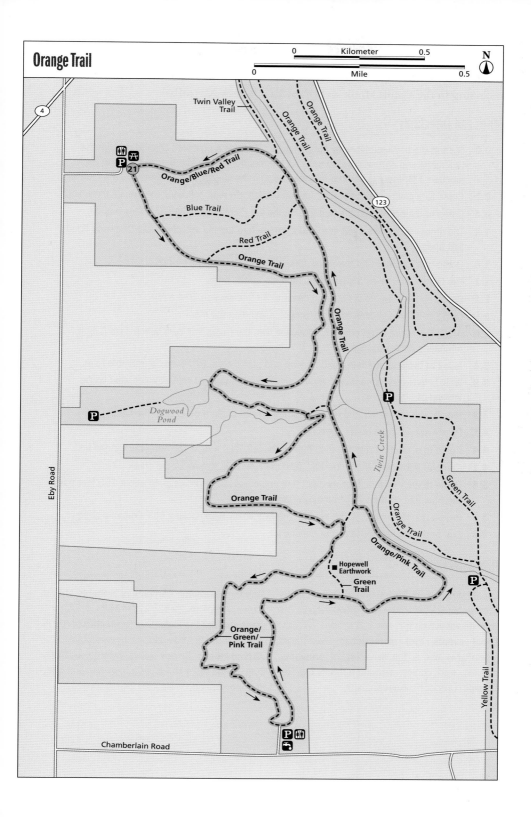

Orange Trail

Kilometer
0   0.5

Mile
0   0.5

N

4

Twin Valley
Trail

Orange Trail

Orange Trail

123

21

Orange/Blue/Red Trail

Blue Trail

Red Trail

Orange Trail

Orange Trail

P

Dogwood
Pond

Twin Creek

P

Orange Trail

Orange Trail

Orange/Pink Trail

Green Trail

Hopewell
Earthwork

Green
Trail

P

Orange/
Green/
Pink Trail

Eby Road

Yellow Trail

Chamberlain Road

P

which connects Twin Creek and Germantown MetroParks. The Orange Trail is part of the Twin Valley Backpacking Trail, and the trail has several backcountry campsites, including in the Camp Hook section of Twin Creek MetroPark.

Miles and Directions

0.0 Start at the trailhead kiosk by the parking lot. There is a post with colored dots for the trailheads and a mowed swath entering the meadow. Follow the orange blazes at each junction. **FYI:** There is another trailhead beyond the shelter; this is where you will return.

0.2 Come to a junction with the Blue Trail on the left. Go right, following the orange blaze.

0.4 Come to a junction with the Red Trail on the left. Continue straight, following orange.

1.3 The orange trail takes a left at this junction. Before turning left, check out Dogwood Pond just ahead.

1.6 Come to a junction with the Yellow Trail. Take a right, following orange.

1.7 The Orange Trail takes a sharp right, heading up the ridge.

2.1 Pass through a livestock gate and come to a T-intersection. Take a left.

2.5 Come to a T-intersection and take a right, ascending the hill.

2.6 At the top of the ridge, come to a junction with the Green Trail by a bench. Take a right, remaining on the Orange Trail.

3.4 Arrive at the Chamberlain Road parking and picnic area. **FYI:** Water is available here.

3.8 Walk by a Hopewell earthwork on the right. An informational sign explains what you're looking at.

3.9 Pass a trail on the left and continue straight, then begin a descent to the creek.

4.1 Pass a service road on the right.

4.4 Come to a junction with the Pink Trail on the left. Take a right, following the Orange Trail.

4.7 Come to a fork with the Yellow Trail. Take the right fork, staying by the creek.

5.4 Come to another fork. Take the right fork and cross over a drainage. In about 150 feet pass the Blue Trail on the left, continuing straight.

5.5 Pass a connector trail on the right for the Twin Valley Backpacking Trail. Continue straight.

5.8 End at the shelter house by the parking lot.

Hike Information

Local information: Dayton/Montgomery County Convention & Visitors Bureau, (800) 221-8235, www.daytoncvb.com
Local events and attractions: Five Rivers MetroParks has a full schedule of programs, classes, and clinics; www.metroparks.org/Get Outside/OutdoorRecreation.aspx.

Accommodations: Camping is available at Twin Creek MetroPark; (937) 277-4374.
Restaurants: The Florentine, Germantown; (937) 855-7759; www.florentine-restaurant.com
Organizations: Dayton Hikers, www.daytonhikers .org; Miami Valley Outdoor Club, www.miamivalley outdoorclub.org

22 Big Woods and Sugar Bush Trails

Hueston Woods State Nature Preserve

It's said that when Europeans first set foot on North American soil, a squirrel could climb into the forest canopy at the Atlantic Ocean and not touch the ground again until it hit the Mississippi River. The ensuing years have seen great change in the natural landscape. Today almost every tree that was growing in Ohio when Europeans arrived has been cut. Not so at Hueston Woods. Hike the 2.3-mile Big Woods and Sugar Bush trail system to see a virgin beech–maple forest. The Hueston family homesteaded this spot and farmed most of it but kept some woods for maple sugaring. Thanks to that and the work of conservationists, you can now hike a trail through this spectacular bit of forest.

Start: Trailhead located off the nature preserve parking lot
Distance: 2.3-mile lollipop
Hiking time: About 1 to 1.5 hours
Difficulty: Easy; short and flat
Trail surface: Dirt trail, with a short section on the road
Blaze: None
Best season: Apr through Oct
Other trail users: Hikers only in the nature preserve
Canine compatibility: Dogs not permitted in the state nature preserve

Water: Available at Scenic 1 Picnic Area, north of the trailhead on Main Loop Road
Land status: State nature preserve, surrounded by state park
Nearest town: Oxford
Fees and permits: None
Schedule: Open daily from dawn to dusk
Maps: Nature preserve brochure map; USGS quad: College Corner
Trail contact: Hueston Woods State Nature Preserve; (513) 524-4250, ext. 27; http://ohiodnr.com/location/hueston_woods/tabid/894/Default.aspx

Finding the trailhead: From SR 177 north of Oxford, turn south onto SR 732 and travel 0.5 mile to the Hueston Woods State Park entrance on the right. Follow Loop Road for 5 miles to the Hueston Woods State Nature Preserve parking lot on the left, marked with a preserve sign. *DeLorme: Ohio Atlas & Gazetteer:* Page 64 D1. GPS: N39 34.47' / W84 45.69'.

The Hike

Hueston Woods contains a 200-acre tract of virgin and "near virgin" (lightly and selectively timbered) forest, a rarity in Ohio's western Till Plains region, where 95 percent of the original forests are now agricultural fields or urban areas. Enjoy this short hike along the Big Woods Trail for both a respite from modern-day life and a look into the former landscape of this region.

Beech trees along the Big Woods Trail

The ancient history of this area begins, geologically, more than 400 million years ago, during the Ordovician era. What is now Ohio was under a sea that laid down many layers of sediment containing marine invertebrates such as corals, clams, snails, trilobites, and brachiopods. The remains of these sea creatures are seen today as fossils. In fact, there's now a designated fossil collection area in Hueston Woods State Park. The seas drained away about 200 million years ago and the erosion process began. Then a series of four major glaciers advanced over this region beginning two million years ago and continuing until only about 15,000 years ago, leaving behind the rich soils on which vast beech-maple forests grew.

The history of the park and preserve is somewhat shorter. Matthew Hueston came to this region in the last years of the eighteenth century as a soldier under the leadership of American General "Mad Anthony" Wayne. He later bought land for a farm but also preserved a forested portion of his homestead. He and his descendants tapped the maple trees to make syrup—probably a major reason the woods were spared the saw. When the last of the Hueston descendants passed away in the 1930s, a local conservationist purchased the land and held it in trust until the state of Ohio was able to buy it in 1941. Preble County Legislator Cloyd Acton proposed the purchase to the state legislature. The Oxford Honor Camp was established in 1952, and Acton Lake was created with the completion of an earthen dam in 1957.

Today Hueston Woods State Park is an expansive compound with recreational opportunities for all tastes. Hiking, equestrian, and mountain biking trails surround Acton Lake, a popular fishing and boating destination. The park also features a lodge, cottages, a campground, and an eighteen-hole golf course. Before your hike, check out the nature center to learn more about the natural history of the area. The Big Woods and Sugar Maple Trails are located within Hueston Woods State Nature Preserve, which is within the state park.

The Big Woods Trail begins by winding through virgin beech-maple forest. The beech trees (which could be called "graffiti trees"—please don't add to their scars) tower above, casting shade on the understory. Naturally hollow beech trees provide habitat and food for such critters as squirrel, deer, and large birds, including turkey, bobwhite, pheasant, and ruffed grouse. Listen and look for the pileated woodpecker (North America's largest), which thrives in these forest conditions. Understory trees and shrubs are mostly pawpaw and spicebush. On the fairly clear forest floor, look for lots of fungi (able to thrive on the many logs left here to rot) and a variety of fern species, including the black-stemmed maidenhair. Cross a number of streams and drainages over footbridges, and look for fossils in the streams. If you see some, it's because folks who were here before you did not collect any. You should do the same. (There is an official fossil collection area in adjacent Hueston Woods State Park.)

At the end of the Big Woods Trail, pick up the Sugar Bush Trail. This is also a magnificent forest, and in late winter/early spring, you'll see buckets hanging from the maple trees to collect sap. If you're not hiking during sugaring season, look on the trunks of the sugar maples along the trail. You'll see the telltale holes in the bark drilled to access the sap. This loop returns in part along the banks of Lake Acton before rejoining the Big Woods Trail.

Miles and Directions

0.0 Start the Big Woods Trail at the trailhead kiosk. Walk straight into the woods (on the other side of the parking lot, a portion the Big Woods Trail heads into the state park). You'll walk over a couple of footbridges within the first half mile of trail.

0.5 Come to a junction with an informal side trail just before the stream. Cross over the stream and pick up the trail, which switches back downstream. Look for the American Discovery Trail blaze.

0.7 Come to Brown Road. Take a left and walk along the road. (**FYI:** Water is available here.) The American Discovery Trail branches off. **Option:** You can turn back here for a 1.4-mile out-and-back hike.

0.8 Pass another trailhead on the left and follow the road as it curves to the right. In about 75 feet, hop onto the Sugar Bush Trail to the right, marked with a sign.

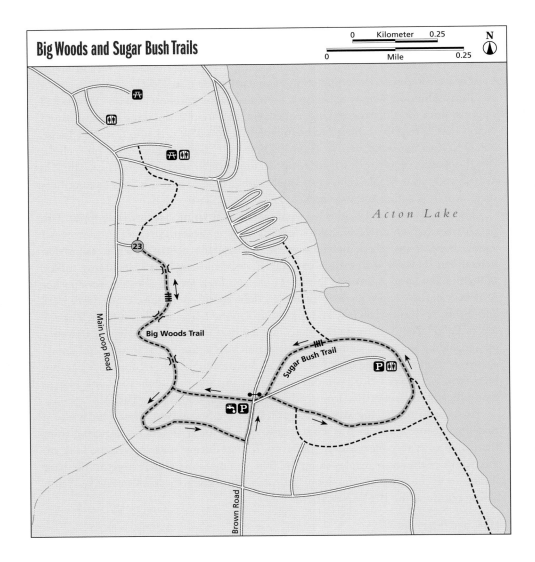

Kilometer

Mile

Acton Lake

Main Loop Road

Big Woods Trail

Sugar Bush Trail

Brown Road

0.9   Reach a junction with the Blue Heron Trail. Continue straight.

1.2   Come to a fork. Take the left fork.

1.3   Approach the Sugar Camp parking lot. Walk to the other side of the parking lot and pick up the trail again, marked with a sign for the Sugar Bush and West Shore Trails.

1.4   Reach an unmarked four-way intersection. Take a left to return on the Sugar Bush Trail.

1.5   Come to a fork. Again, stay to the left.

1.6   Come to another fork. Again, stay left.

1.7   Return to Sugar Camp Road. Take a right and in about 75 feet come to a trailhead kiosk for the Big Woods Trail. Walk straight past the trailhead and back into the woods.

1.8 Cross the stream and come to a T-intersection with the original trail. Take a right and return the way you came.

2.3 Arrive back at the trailhead.

Hike Information

Local information: Oxford Visitors and Convention Bureau, (513) 523-8687, www.enjoyoxford .org

Local events and attractions: Hueston Woods State Park, College Corner; (513) 523-6347; http://parks.ohiodnr.gov/huestonwoods. The park is host to 10 miles of hiking trails, a fossil collection area, horse rentals, mountain biking trails, an 18-hole golf course, and a paintball range. Boating, fishing, and swimming are popular on the 625-acre Acton Lake. Nearby Oxford is home to Miami University and the McGuffey House and Museum of William McGuffey of McGuffey Readers fame.

Accommodations: Hueston Woods State Park campground; call (513) 523-1060 for information or (866) 644-6727 for reservations.

Hueston Woods Lodge; call (513) 664-3500.

Restaurants: Hueston Woods Lodge dining room; (513) 664-3527

Bagel and Deli, Oxford; (513) 523-2131; www.bagelanddeli.com

Hike tours: Naturalist-led hikes are offered year-round; contact the park for up-to-date information at (513) 524-4250, ext. 27.

Organizations: Friends of Hueston Woods State Park, Inc., www.friendsofhuestonwoods.com

23 Harkers Run to Bachelor Preserve East Loop

Miami University Natural Areas

You don't have to go back to school to make the most of Miami University's campus. This walk in the woods is literally within walking distance of uptown Oxford, and part of the campus's "greenbelt." After checking out the student-built bird blind and the historic DeWitt log cabin, walk along Harkers Run and cross it twice, once on stepping pads and again on a suspension footbridge. End your day with a good meal and a brew at any number of restaurants nearby.

Start: Trailhead off of SR 73
Distance: 2.8-mile lollipop
Hiking time: About 1 to 2 hours
Difficulty: Easy
Trail surface: Dirt trail
Blaze: No blazes; all junctions have a trail map.
Best season: Spring
Other trail users: Hikers only
Canine compatibility: Leashed dogs permitted
Water: Available at the bird blind and on the east side of the parking lot

Land status: Miami University-owned land
Nearest town: Oxford
Fees and permits: None
Schedule: Open daily from dawn to dusk
Maps: Miami University Natural Areas Hiking Trails map; USGS quad: Oxford
Trail contact: Miami University Natural Areas, Oxford; (513) 524-2197; www.muohio.edu/naturalareas

Finding the trailhead: From the junction of SR 27 and SR 73 in Oxford, take SR 73 east 0.7 mile to a gravel parking lot on the left (north). It's just past the creek crossing, and there is a sign for the DeWitt Log Homestead. *DeLorme: Ohio Atlas & Gazetteer:* Page 64 D2. GPS: N39 30.51' / W84 42.98'.

The Hike

When Zachariah Price DeWitt built his log cabin near Harkers Run around 1805, this area was truly wilderness. Miami University was not yet established, the town of Oxford did not exist, and black bears roamed the forest. Needless to say, a lot has changed since then. The wilderness was cleared for agriculture, and cities sprang up, large and small.

Joseph M. Bachelor was an English professor at Miami University (and a gentleman farmer) from the late 1920s until his death in 1947. He owned the land that is today the Bachelor Preserve, which he bequeathed to the university. This original

Swinging bridge over Harkers Run ▶

One of some twenty geocaches in the Miami University Natural Areas

400 acres, the Bachelor Wildlife and Game Reserve, has been augmented by other land donations, and today the Miami University Natural Areas consist of 1,000 acres of contiguous or near-contiguous parcels. These lands are protected and open to the public and university researchers for recreation, education, and research. There are more than 15 miles of trails here.

Before starting at the trailhead by Harkers Run, take some time to visit the DeWitt Cabin, which was listed on the National Register of Historic Places in 1973 and restored in 2003 by the Oxford Museum Association. Adjacent to the cabin is a bird blind built in 2010 by Miami University architecture students. You can sit or stand inside the wooden blind and peer out at bird activity among the feeders and plants that surround the blind. More than 120 bird species have been recorded on these lands,

▶ **Miami University Natural Areas are home to nineteen geocaches, all placed by Natural Areas staff. Go to www.geocaching.com to find coordinates.**

Harkers Run to Bachelor Preserve East Loop

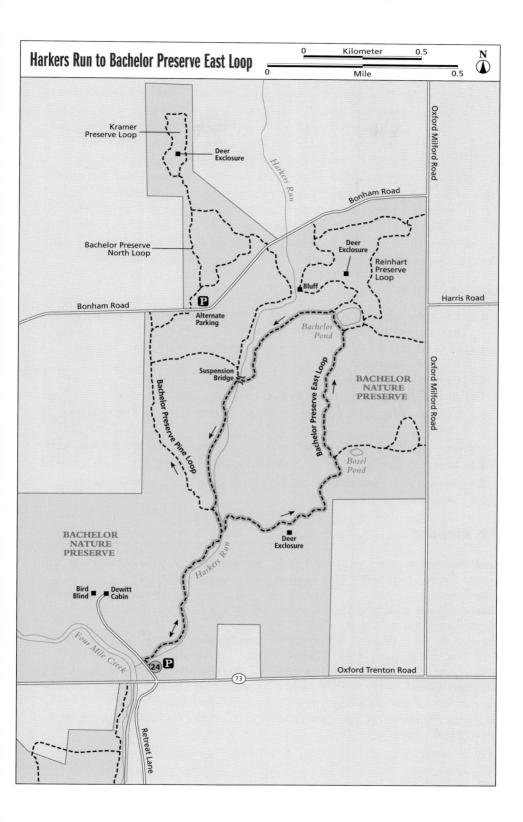

Kramer Preserve Loop

Deer Exclosure

Harkers Run

Bonham Road

Deer Exclosure

Reinhart Preserve Loop

Bachelor Preserve North Loop

Bluff

Harris Road

Bonham Road

P

Alternate Parking

Bachelor Pond

Oxford Milford Road

Suspension Bridge

Bachelor Preserve East Loop

BACHELOR NATURE PRESERVE

Bachelor Preserve Pine Loop

Bosel Pond

BACHELOR NATURE PRESERVE

Deer Exclosure

Bird Blind

Dewitt Cabin

Harkers Run

Four Mile Creek

24 P

73

Oxford Trenton Road

Retreat Lane

and some 60 nest here as well. Common birds include cardinals, bluebirds, goldfinches, and ruby-throated hummingbirds.

Begin the hike by paralleling Harkers Run upstream. Along this first section of trail, look for some mature trees, including sycamores with diameters up to 8 feet. In the understory you'll see a lot of Amur honeysuckle, an invasive plant that's quite prolific in southwest Ohio. Cross Harkers Run to the east over a series of stepping pads—concrete posts that allow you to cross the run in high water. Continuing on the other side of the run, the trail winds through former pasture land. You can see some of the early succession trees that grow here, predominantly cedar.

At the halfway point, arrive at Bachelor Pond. There is a bench here where you can relax and observe wildlife, including birds and beavers (wildlife is more active around dawn and dusk). The trail returns to Harkers Run and crosses it again, this time on a pedestrian suspension bridge. Walk downstream back to the trailhead.

Miles and Directions

0.0 Start at the trailhead kiosk in the parking lot. Cross the bridge over Harkers Run and take an immediate right, paralleling the creek upstream.

0.4 Come to a fork. Take the right fork and cross Harkers Run on stepping pads, then take a left, continuing upstream.

1.0 The trail forks. Take the left fork.

1.4 Come to a T-intersection in front of Bachelor Pond. Take a left.

1.5 Come to two forks. Take a left at the first fork, away from the pond. Take a left again at the second fork.

1.8 Cross a suspension bridge over Harkers Run and then take a left, returning downstream.

2.2 Arrive at a T-intersection. Take a left, back onto the Harkers Run Trail.

2.3 Return to the first junction by the stepping pads. Continue straight, paralleling the run.

2.8 Arrive back at the trailhead.

Hike Information

Local information: Oxford Visitors and Convention Bureau, (513) 523-8687, www.enjoyoxford.org

Local events and attractions: Miami University Natural Areas sponsors a free Hike-A-Thon every fall; check the website for details. Hueston Woods State Park, College Corner; (513) 523-6347; www.dnr.state.oh.us/tabid/745/default.aspx.

Accommodations: Hueston Woods State Park has camping, cottages, and a lodge; call (888) 711-4725 for reservations; http://parks.ohiodnr.gov/huestonwoods.

Restaurants: Kona Bistro, Oxford; (513) 523-0686; www.konabistro.com

Quarter Barrel Brewery and Pub, Oxford; (513) 523-4911; http://quarterbrewpub.webs.com

Organizations: Audubon Miami Valley, Oxford; http://amvohio.org

Avian Research Education Institute, College Corner; (513) 382-4889 or (513) 218-7228; www.avianinstitute.com

Orienteering Cincinnati, http://ocin.org

24 Flat Fork Ridge Trail to Pioneer Village

Caesar Creek State Park

More than 50 miles of developed trails circle 10,000-acre Caesar Creek Lake. The 6-mile out-and-back segment from Flat Fork Picnic Area to Pioneer Village offers a little bit of everything at Caesar Creek: fossil hunting, lake views, forest, a rocky-bottomed river, shale cliffs, a small waterfall, and a restored pioneer village. Stop by the visitor center to learn more about the natural and human history of this area before hitting the trail.

Start: Flat Fork Picnic Area
Distance: 6-mile out-and-back or 3-mile point-to-point
Hiking time: About 2 to 3 hours
Difficulty: Moderate due to length
Trail surface: Dirt, grass, and gravel trail
Blaze: Yellow
Best season: Apr through Oct
Other trail users: Hunters (in season)
Canine compatibility: Leashed dogs permitted
Water: Available at the picnic area
Land status: US Army Corps of Engineers and state park
Nearest town: Waynesville

Fees and permits: None for hiking; a free permit is required for fossil collection. The Pioneer Village suggests a donation.
Schedule: Open daylight hours year-round
Maps: An excellent Friends of Caesar Creek map and guide is available at the visitor center for a small fee. USGS quads: Oregonia, Waynesville.
Trail contacts: Caesar Creek Lake Visitor Center, Waynesville; (513) 897-1050. Caesar Creek State Park Nature Center, Waynesville; (513) 897-2437; http://parks.ohiodnr.gov/caesarcreek.

Finding the trailhead: From I-71 north of Wilmington, turn west onto SR 73 (exit 45) and drive 7.7 miles to Clarksville Road, past Caesar Creek Lake. Turn left (south) onto Clarksville Road and drive 2.9 miles to the Flat Fork Picnic Area on the left, past the visitor center and the dam. *DeLorme: Ohio Atlas & Gazetteer:* Page 75 A7. GPS: N39 29.02' / W84 03.29'.

The Hike

Trails in the park surround Caesar Creek Lake, which was home to the towns of Harveysburg and New Burlington until 1978, when the Army Corps of Engineers created the 10,550-acre lake as part of an overall Miami Valley flood-control project. Caesar Creek flows into the Little Miami River just downstream from the dam.

Caesar Creek gets its name from a slave who was adopted by the Shawnee Indians after his party's capture in 1776. A contemporary of Shawnee War Chief Blue Jacket, Caesar often hunted along the banks of the creek that eventually bore his name. At

A small waterfall at Caesar Creek State Park PHOTO OHIO DEPARTMENT OF NATURAL RESOURCES

that time the west side of the Little Miami River served as a portion of the Bullskin Trace (Native American) Trail, along which many Shawnee villages existed. The valley was home to other cultures before the Shawnee, including the Fort Ancient culture around 600 BC and, before that, prehistoric Mound Builders.

From the Flat Fork Picnic Area, you'll walk through some forest along the edge of Caesar Creek Lake and then into the spillway, whose construction essentially excavated a long escarpment of shale in front of you. Everywhere you look (if you look closely), there are fossils. Caesar Creek is home to one of the world's most renowned fossil beds. These fossils were created during the Ordovician period, roughly 445 to 510 million years ago, when a sea existed here. The prehistoric sea animals were laid down on the sea floor and materials accumulated into what is today's sedimentary rock. The ones that most resemble seashells are brachiopods. The ice cream cone–shaped fossils are horn coral, and the ones that look like coral are byrozoa. Thistle favor this rocky area near the lake, and swallows dart around overhead.

The trail soon enters the woods, where it then stays. First walk above the Flat Fork Valley, with occasional views overlooking this rocky-bottomed creek. Sycamores grow up from the valley; upslope the forest is mainly deciduous, but the fragrant cedars have a strong foothold. Underfoot, look for a wide array of spring wildflowers, including spring beauty, trillium, ginger, and jack-in-the-pulpit. Also look for spleenwort on the forest floor and fruit-bearing pawpaw trees in the understory. The trail then descends to the creek, which you should cross only when the water is low enough to make it safely passable. A thick stand of willow grows here. This is a spot where you may find some of the many reptiles and amphibians that call the area home, including salamanders, toads, and turtles.

▶ **The trilobite is the official Ohio state fossil.**

Be sure to take the spur loop trail past the footbridge, which takes you to the river's edge near a small waterfall and tall shale cliffs. After returning to the main trail, continue hiking in the forest, crossing other tributaries that feed Caesar Creek Lake, until you reach the Pioneer Village. The Pioneer Village is a collection of relocated log homes and shops built between 1797 and 1860, now in a circle around a village green. Explore the village (an interpretive guide is available at the visitor center) and then return to the Flat Fork Picnic Area the way you came. You can continue past the Pioneer Village for as long as you want if you'd like to tack on some more miles.

Miles and Directions

0.0 Start from the Flat Fork Picnic Area. Pick up the trailhead at the east end of the parking lot, marked with a hiker sign and two yellow blazes. Descend the stairs and in about 70 feet reach a junction. Continue straight over the footbridge and hit a fork in about another 50 feet. Take the left fork, following the yellow blaze.

0.2 Come out of the woods into a rocky prairie area. Follow the well-worn path that parallels the lakeshore.

0.5 Where the exposed shale seam and the water meet, the trail forks. Take the right fork and walk up the stairs.

0.7 The trail forks. Take the right fork, following the yellow blazes.

1.1 A short spur on the left leads to an overlook of the rocky-bottomed Flat Fork. Continue straight.

1.3 Cross Flat Fork and take a left at the other side. **Note:** Do not cross Flat Fork if the water is high. Use caution here.

1.4 The trail forks, with the Flat Fork Ridge Trail continuing to the right. Take the left fork and pick up the spur trail.

1.5 After passing a couple of side trails to the creek on the left, come to a T-intersection. The trail turns right here and continues to parallel the creek. In a couple hundred feet, reach an overlook boardwalk. Take the stairs up to the right.

1.6 Pass a faint side trail to the right with a faint yellow blaze. Continue straight.

1.7 Come to a junction with a footbridge on the right. Cross over the footbridge, then take an immediate left at a fork. Climb to the top of the stairs and reach a T-intersection with the Flat Fork Ridge Trail. Take a left.

2.0 Pass a side trail and footbridge on the left and continue straight, following the yellow blaze.

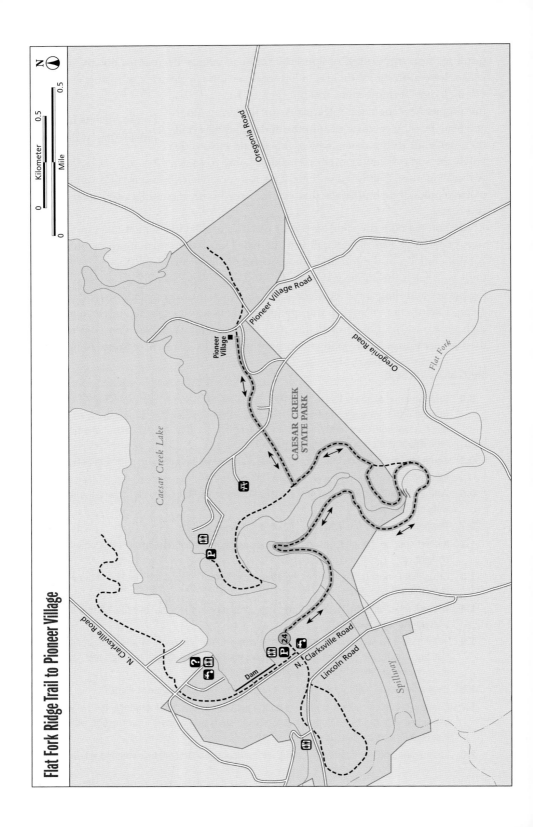

Flat Fork Ridge Trail to Pioneer Village

Pioneer Village

Pioneer Village Road

Oregonia Road

Oregonia Road

Flat Fork

CAESAR CREEK
STATE PARK

Caesar Creek Lake

N. Clarksville Road

N. Clarksville Road

Lincoln Road

Spillway

Dam

24

N

Kilometer

Mile

0   0.5

0   0.5

2.2 Come to a junction. Take a right and walk through a stand of cedar trees, following the yellow blaze.

2.4 Cross Wellman Meadows Road.

2.6 Pass an access trail to a picnic area on the left.

2.8 Come to a junction with a footbridge to the left. Either direction takes you out to an open field and then the two trails converge.

3.0 This section of the trail ends at the Pioneer Village. Turn around and return the way you came.

6.0 Arrive back at the trailhead.

Hike Information

Local information: Warren County Convention and Visitors Bureau, (800) 791-4FUN, www.ohios largestplayground.com

Local events and attractions: The park offers a "stargazer campout" on the beach about once a year during a major meteor shower; contact the park for up-to-date information.

Caesar's Creek Pioneer Village, (513) 897-1120, www.caesarscreekpioneervillage.org

Little Miami Scenic Trail (shared use), www.miamivalleytrails.org

Accommodations: Caesar Creek State Park campground; call (937) 488-4595 for information or (866) 644-6727 for reservations.

Restaurants: Cobblestone Cafe, Waynesville; (513) 897-0021

Hike tours: Ranger-led walks are available in-season; contact the park for up-to-date information.

Organizations: Friends of Caesar Creek, (513) 897-1050, www.facebook.com/FOCaesarCreek

NATIVE AMERICAN TRAILS

Roads existed in Ohio long before the Ohio Department of Transportation was formed. The first roads were broad trails beat by Native Americans and their animal brethren, including rather imposing species such as the wood bison. These transportation routes were often the most practical way of getting from one place to another and usually followed water routes in order to stay on relatively flat terrain and to access the water. Today highways and roads have replaced most Native American trails (think US 50 and US 23). Generally, today's hiking trails exist to take you away from these roads. The result is that you are most often not hiking along ancient Native American trails.

25 Earthworks Trail to Sun Serpent Effigy

Fort Ancient State Memorial and YMCA Camp Kern

Take a 3.4-mile out-and-back trail beginning at the earthworks constructed by the prehistoric Hopewell Indians. Follow the earthworks and then descend a forested slope to the Little Miami Scenic Trail, a 70-mile multiuse path. Continue across the Little Miami Scenic River and along a farm field to the Sun Serpent Effigy, built by Native Americans to mark the summer solstice. Don't forget to stop by the excellent museum that will help you interpret what you see along the trail.

Start: Earthworks trailhead

Distance: 3.4-mile out-and-back

Hiking time: About 1.5 to 2 hours

Difficulty: Moderate due to a steep ascent on the return trip

Trail surface: Mostly dirt, with a section on the asphalt bike path and then the road. There is a steep descent and then ascent out of the river valley.

Blaze: None for Fort Ancient trails, but junctions are marked. The Buckeye Trail is blue blazed.

Best season: Mid-Apr through mid-Oct

Other trail users: Only hikers on footpaths. The Little Miami Scenic Trail is a multiuse trail.

Canine compatibility: Leashed dogs permitted

Water: Available at the museum when it's open; otherwise, bring your own.

Land status: State memorial and private camp

Nearest town: Lebanon

Fees and permits: There is an admission to Fort Ancient State Memorial; stop at the museum to pay and pick up a trail map. You must get permission from YMCA Camp Kern to take the spur trail to the effigy. Since it is a youth camp, trespassing laws are strictly enforced. For permission call (513) 932-3756.

Schedule: Fort Ancient State Memorial is open Tues through Sat 10 a.m. to 5 p.m. and Sun noon to 5 p.m. Apr through Nov; open Sat 10 a.m. to 5 p.m. and Sun noon to 5 p.m. Dec through Mar. The gate is locked at all other times.

Maps: Buckeye Trail Association section map: Loveland; USGS quad: Oregonia

Trail contacts: Fort Ancient State Memorial, Oregonia; (800) 283-8904; www.fortancient .org. YMCA Camp Kern, Oregonia; (513) 932-3756; www.CampKern.org.

Finding the trailhead: From I-71 east of Lebanon, turn east onto Wilmington Road (exit 36) and take an immediate right onto Middleboro Road. Drive 1.9 miles to a stop sign at SR 350. Turn right (west) and drive 0.7 mile to the entrance on the left. Drive past the guard shack and take the first left to the museum.

To get to the trailhead, drive straight (south) 0.5 mile past the guard shack to a large parking lot. Pick up the trailhead at the southern end of the parking lot. *DeLorme: Ohio Atlas & Gazetteer:* Page 75 A7. GPS: N39 23.91' / W84 05.66'.

The Hike

Situated on a wooded ridgetop 235 feet above the Little Miami Scenic River in Warren County is an earthen embankment that snakes around for 3.5 miles, enclosing the hilltop with walls from 4 to 23 feet in height. Built by the prehistoric Hopewell culture, the earthwork retains for the most part the same form it had when it was constructed some 2,000 years ago. But as time undeniably marched on, the Hopewell culture and later the Fort Ancient culture ceased to exist as the mound builders and traders they once were. Some of these peoples eventually became known as the Shawnee Indians, who were hunting and growing crops here when European settlers arrived. Today contemporary Ohioans drive to the site and stare, impressed at the achievements of people who conducted a large earth-moving project with little more than hand tools.

Before hitting the trail, stop at the impressive Fort Ancient museum that raises and then answers just about any question you could have about the region's human history. It even takes a look at the discipline of archaeology and the scientific method. Archaeologists figure that the first humans to reach the Ohio Valley were Paleo-Indian hunters and gatherers about 15,000 years ago. The Hopewells added horticulture to their hunting and gathering lifestyle. This non–nomadic life allowed the Hopewells to construct their now-famous mounds and earthworks. They inhabited the Ohio Valley from approximately 100 BC to AD 400, and no one knows exactly what happened to their culture after that.

▶ **By some estimates, there were once more than 10,000 Native American mounds in the Ohio Valley.**

The Fort Ancient culture then occupied this region from about AD 900 to the time of "historic" contact. The site was named after the Fort Ancient Indians because it was originally thought that they built the earthworks. The Fort Ancient people did inhabit the site sometime between AD 1200 and 1600. They practiced full-fledged agriculture, and behind the museum today is a nice demonstration garden that features heirloom varieties of the "three sisters" common to Native American agriculture: corn, beans, and squash.

When Europeans arrived here by 1700, they found 400- to 600-year-old trees growing out of the earthworks. Excavations have turned up innumerable artifacts, mainly tools and implements such as arrowheads, drills, and knives. Today younger trees grow atop the still recognizable earthworks.

Begin your hike on the Earthworks Trail, following along the inside of the enclosure. Interpretive signs tell you that the embankment was originally thought to be a fort. Archaeologists today, however, believe this theory is false. They cite the fact that sixty-four openings in the walls would have been difficult to defend, and that most of the domestic sites excavated are outside the earthworks, not inside. This has led archaeologists to theorize that the enclosed earthwork was built primarily for social and/or ceremonial purposes.

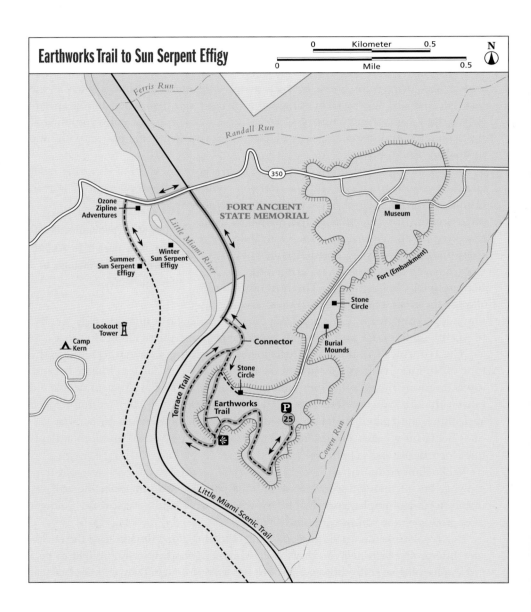

Earthworks Trail to Sun Serpent Effigy

Kilometer
0   0.5

0   Mile   0.5

N

Ferris Run

Randall Run

350

Ozone
Zipline
Adventures

**FORT ANCIENT
STATE MEMORIAL**

Museum

Little Miami River

Winter
Sun Serpent
Effigy

Summer
Sun Serpent
Effigy

Fort (Embankment)

Stone
Circle

Lookout
Tower

Connector

Burial
Mounds

Camp
Kern

Stone
Circle

Terrace Trail

Earthworks
Trail

P
25

Cowen Run

Little Miami Scenic Trail

Continue from the Earthworks Trail to the Terrace and then Connector Trails. Walk down the steep slope in a forest of oak, hickory, maple, tulip poplar, and cherry in the canopy with understory species such as pawpaw, redbud, and spicebush. In the springtime, look for ramps (wild leeks) and wildflowers. Descend all the way to the Little Miami Scenic Trail, a 70-mile all-purpose asphalt path stretching from Milford in Hamilton County to Springfield in Clark County. This also serves as a portion of the statewide Buckeye Trail.

Get permission from YMCA Camp Kern to walk as far as the Sun Serpent Effigy (also known as the Kern Effigy), a snake-shaped collection of flagstones with a tall wooden pole at one end. Archaeologists have studied several of these effigies around the site and conclude that they were constructed to mark solar solstices. From here you can return basically the way you came to the trailhead. If you like, when you hop on the Little Miami Scenic Trail, you can add a few more miles in either direction.

Miles and Directions

0.0 Start at the trailhead off of the southernmost parking lot. It's marked with a sign that reads To South Overlook. This is the Earthworks Trail. Walk along the edge where the field meets the woods.

0.1 Reach a fork on a mowed path. Take the right fork, staying on the edge of the field.

0.2 Come to the overlook. Take the stairs to the overlook patio, then continue clockwise around the edge of the field.

0.3 Come to a junction. Take a left and walk into the woods.

0.4 Hit a junction just before wooden steps. Continue straight and over the steps to walk the Terrace Trail.

0.9 Arrive at the junction with the Earthworks and Connector Trails. Take a left and descend the steps on the Connector Trail.

1.0 Reach a T-intersection with the Little Miami Scenic Trail (bike trail). Take a right and walk north.

1.4 Come to SR 350. Turn left (west) and cross the Little Miami River. You will pick up white blazes for the Silver Moccasin Trail.

1.5 On the other side of the bridge, look left for a farm lane that follows the edge of a field. Turn left onto the lane.

1.7 Arrive at the Sun Serpent Effigy on the right. Turn around and return to the Terrace Trail.

2.5 Arrive at a T-intersection with the Terrace Trail. Take a left to finish the Terrace Trail.

2.6 Approach a wooden overlook platform that provides a nice view of the Little Miami Valley below. Walk down the steps on the other side of the platform and back onto the Earthworks Trail. In about 50 feet the trail forks. Take a right and walk back into the woods.

2.8 Walk straight through a four-way intersection underneath a magnificent white oak tree.

2.9 Reach a fork just before the steps where you began the Terrace Trail. Take a left and return the way you came on the Earthworks Trail.

3.4 Arrive back at the trailhead.

Hike Information

Local information: Warren County Convention and Visitors Bureau, (800) 791-4FUN, www.ohios largestplayground.com

Local events and attractions: The annual Fort Ancient Celebration is held the second weekend in June, and Archaeology Day takes place the third weekend in July; (800) 283-8904.

Ozone Zipline Adventures; (513) 932-3756; http://campkern.org/ozone

Morgan's Canoe Livery offers trips down the Little Miami Scenic River; (800) WE-CANOE; www.morganscanoe.com.

Accommodations: Morgan's Fort Ancient Canoe Livery and Riverside Campground, (513) 932-7568 or (800) WE-CANOE, www .morganscanoe.com

Restaurants: The Golden Lamb Inn, at more than 200 years old, is Ohio's oldest restaurant and inn, Lebanon; (513) 932-5065; www .goldenlamb.com.

The Corwin Peddler rents bikes but also has a restaurant and tearoom; (513) 897-3536; www.thecorwinpeddler.com.

Other resources: *Fort Ancient: Citadel, Cemetery, Cathedral, or Calendar?* by Jack Blosser and Robert Glotzhober (Ohio Historical Society, 1995)

Organizations: Ohio Historical Society, Columbus; (614) 297-2300; www.ohiohistory.org/ index.html

Buckeye Trail Association, Worthington; (740) 832-1BTA; www.buckeyetrail.org

26 Beechwood to Red Oak Trail Loop

Mount Airy Forest

One of the few hikes in Ohio accessible by public transportation, Mount Airy Forest is an oasis of greenspace within the heart of greater Cincinnati. Combine several trails to make a 3.6-mile loop around the oval picnic shelter. A flat, well-worn footpath makes its way around the ridge in a maturing deciduous forest—all thanks to the Cincinnati Park Board, which embarked on the first municipal reforestation project in the United States, beginning in 1911.

Start: Oval Open Shelter
Distance: 3.6-mile loop
Hiking time: About 1.5 to 2.5 hours
Difficulty: Easy; fairly short, flat, and well-maintained
Trail surface: Mostly flat dirt trail with many intersections
Blaze: An occasional white blaze; an E blaze for most of the trail; some junctions are marked.
Best season: Apr through Oct
Other trail users: Cross-country skiers (in season); park bridle trails are separate but you may run into an errant equestrian.

Canine compatibility: Leashed dogs permitted
Water: Available next to the shelter house
Land status: Cincinnati park
Nearest city: Cincinnati
Fees and permits: None
Schedule: Open daily from 6 a.m. to 10 p.m.
Maps: USGS quad: Cincinnati West
Trail contact: Cincinnati Parks, (513) 352-4080, www.cincinnatiparks.com

Finding the trailhead: From the junction of I-74 and I-75 in Cincinnati, take I-74 west to Colerain Avenue (one-way only) and drive 1.5 miles to the Mount Airy entrance on the left. Take the first left onto Trail Ridge Road and drive 0.5 mile to the oval. *DeLorme: Ohio Atlas & Gazetteer:* Page 74 C3. GPS: N39 10 39' / W84 34 15'.
   For public transportation, use Metro Route 19.

The Hike

Take a break from the noise and crowds of the city, step onto a trail, and find solitude within minutes in Mount Airy Forest. This is possible due to the forethought of the Cincinnati Park Board, which in 1911 bought 168 acres of abused farmland around the top of Colerain Hill and embarked on the first municipal reforestation project in the United States.

As the Queen City became more urbanized and industrialized, the Cincinnati Park Board continued planting trees and acquiring more land. In the 1930s African-American crews employed by the Civilian Conservation Corps (CCC) planted more

Everybody's Treehouse in Mount Airy Forest is wheelchair accessible.

than a million trees and built the shelters that are still in use. Today's Mount Airy Forest comprises nearly 1,500 acres of native hardwoods, evergreens, open space, a popular arboretum, and even a wheelchair-accessible tree house.

Begin your hike from the Oval Open Shelter, which was built in 1931 and has the telltale characteristics of the structures erected during that period: stone floor and foundation, cedar-log framing, and wooden roof shingles. From the shelter, located on Trail Ridge Road, pick up the Beechwood Trail, toward Sunset Ridge. Begin a counter-clockwise loop that takes you around Trail Ridge on a flat, even footpath. Soon you will cross the first of many attractive drainages while hiking in a forest of maple, beech, and hemlock. The understory is full of spicebush and fruiting pawpaw trees. In springtime look for such flowers as trillium, jack-in-the-pulpit, and common blue violet.

The trail crosses many side paths to and from picnic shelters, but as long as you stay straight and level, you should remain on course, where you will soon pick up the Furnas Trail and an E blaze for La Trainee de L'Explorateur Boy Scout Trail—aka the E Trail—which joins for a while. You may also notice orange boxes on some trees. These are orienteering geocaches, used by groups who put together recreational orienteering courses. You may also notice some small fenced-in areas in the park. These are deer exclosures, designed to keep deer out of small patches of the forest. The use of exclosures allows the park to monitor the damage deer are doing to the forest understory; the park sometimes uses these exclosures to protect patches of wildflowers.

As the trail curves around to the south side of the ridge, note the change in the forest. Oak and hickory trees dominate on these drier slopes. Some of the trees along this stretch are quite mature—they were probably growing here when the Cincinnati Park Board bought the land. Shortly after the E Trail branches off, return to the oval by ascending alongside the drainage up the Red Oak Trail.

The classic hike at Mount Airy is the entire length of La Trainee L'Explorateur for a 5-mile one-way or 10-mile out-and-back walk. It will take some route-finding skills and perhaps some luck to complete it. La Trainee L'Explorateur was built and maintained by Boy Scout Troop 83, and you may notice the old metal blazes in addition to the new painted ones. This trail takes you through nearly the entire length of Mount Airy Forest. Access it at McFarlan Woods, on Westwood Northern Boulevard. Near the Maple Ridge Lodge, look for a trailhead sign and the trademark E blazes. The other trailhead is located on West Fork Road below Lingo Woods.

Miles and Directions

0.0 Start on the north side of the oval, to the right of a stone restroom building. The trailhead is marked with a Beechwood Trail sign. Enter the woods and descend slightly.

0.1 Come to a footbridge. Take a left down a few stairs, following the drainage downstream. Do not cross the footbridge.

0.4 Arrive at a junction with a post for H and G Trails and take a right. In about 75 feet take a left at a junction marked with a green F for the Furnas Trail. In another 100 feet, reach another fork. Take a left to continue on the Furnas Trail.

0.8 After walking over a couple of footbridges, pass a side trail on the right that leads down the hill. Continue straight.

0.9 After walking over a couple more footbridges, pass a marked side trail on the left that leads to the Area 21 picnic shelter. Continue straight on the Furnas Trail.

1.3 Cross a footbridge and come to a marked junction with an access trail to the Area 23 picnic shelter. Continue straight.

1.4 Pass another side trail to the picnic area.

1.6 Pass the D Trail (Quarry Trail) on the right. Continue straight and come to a grassy field and a picnic shelter to the right of the trail. Cross the grass and pick up the Ponderosa Trail (B) on the other side, reentering the woods.

1.8 Come to a three-way junction and a sign for Trail Ridge Road and the Ponderosa Trail. Take a right, following the spray-painted blue arrows.

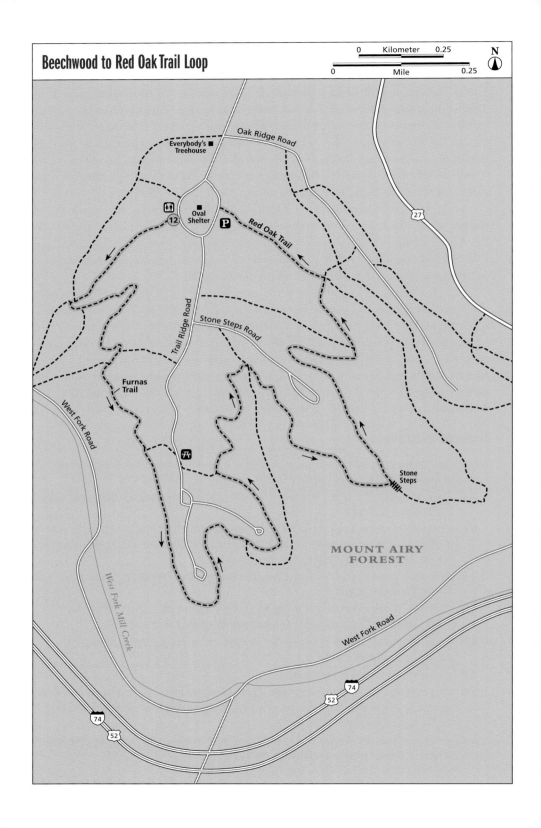

Beechwood to Red Oak Trail Loop

Oak Ridge Road

Everybody's
Treehouse

27

Oval
Shelter

12

P

Red Oak Trail

Trail Ridge Road

Stone Steps Road

Furnas
Trail

West Fork Road

Stone
Steps

MOUNT AIRY
FOREST

West Fork Mill Creek

West Fork Road

74

52

74

52

N

0   Kilometer   0.25

0   Mile   0.25

2.1 Come to a junction marked with a B (Ponderosa Trail) post. Take a right and in about 25 feet come to the junction with the Quarry Trail (D) on the right. Continue straight, ascending slightly. There are faded white, blue, and E blazes.

2.2 Walk past a side trail on the left. Continue straight.

2.5 Come to a signed four-way intersection. To the right are the stone steps that lead down from Stone Steps Ridge. Continue straight.

3.0 Approach a fork. Take a right and walk over the footbridge.

3.2 Approach a fork marked with a B post (Ponderosa Trail). Take a right.

3.4 Come to a fork with a post for the B and C (Red Oak) Trails. Take the left fork and walk uphill on the Red Oak Trail toward the oval.

3.6 Arrive back at the oval.

Hike Information

Local information: Cincinnati USA Convention & Visitors Bureau, (800) 543-2613, www.cincy usa.com

Local events and attractions: Mount Airy Arboretum, (513) 352-4080; disc golf course, (513) 541-7305. A full list of Cincinnati Parks events is online at www.cincinnatiparks.com/explore-nature.

Restaurants: Myra's Dionysus, Cincinnati; (513) 961-1578; www.myrasrestaurant.com

Accommodations: Winton Woods Campground (Hamilton County Park District), Greenhills; (513) 851-CAMP; http://greatparks.org/recreation/camping/winton-woods-campground.html

Parker House Bed-and-Breakfast, Cincinnati; (513) 579-8236; www.parkerhousecinci.com

Hike tours: Cincinnati Parks offer regular naturalist-led nature walks in the park system; call (513) 321-6070 for information.

Organizations: Cincinnati Parks Foundation, (513) 357-2618, www.cincinnatiparksfoundation.org

Tri-State Hiking Club, www.tristatehikingclub.com

Cincinnati Parks Hiking Club, www.facebook.com/CincinnatiParksHikingClub

JOHN JAMES AUDUBON

For most of us, the name Audubon is synonymous with birds and birding. Of course, this is because the Audubon Society and Audubon field guides bear the name of the first person to put together an exhaustive catalog of North American birds, complete with detailed paintings. Less known is John James Audubon's connection to Cincinnati. Born in the French colony Santo Domingo (now Haiti) in 1785, Audubon was raised and educated in France. He left for the United States in 1803 to escape conscription in Napoleon's army. The itinerant Audubon lived first on the East Coast and then in Kentucky, where he was jailed for debt in 1819. In 1820 he moved his family to Cincinnati, where he took a job as a taxidermist at the Western Museum while also working as a portrait artist and teacher. It was during this time that he began in earnest to catalog and paint North American birds. *Birds of America* was published in 1827.

27 Lookout to Geology Trail Loop

Rowe Woods, Cincinnati Nature Center

When young Carl Krippendorf came down with typhoid in the late 1800s, his family doctor recommended that Carl get out of Cincinnati and recuperate in the fresh air of the countryside. Carl's well-to-do father, founder and president of the Krippendorf-Dittman shoe company, sent him to live with a doctor east of the city. Carl grew to love the land so much that he bought 97 acres of it in 1898. What was then known as Lob's Woods is today known as Rowe Woods, operated by the Cincinnati Nature Center and open to the public with 16 miles of trails. Now you, too, can get out of the city and recuperate in the fresh air of the countryside.

Start: Rowe Visitor Center

Distance: 3.5-mile loop with spur

Hiking time: About 1.5 to 2.5 hours

Difficulty: Moderate due to some steep ascents

Trail surface: Well-maintained gravel, wood chip, and dirt trail system

Blaze: Only junctions are marked with trail blazes: Upland Trail, blue butterfly; Lookout Trail, brown hawk; Edge Trail, green turtle; Geology Trail, purple fossil.

Best season: Apr through Oct

Other trail users: Hikers only

Canine compatibility: Dogs permitted on a 6-foot leash; pet owners are expected to pick up after them.

Water: Available at Rowe Visitor Center when it's open; also available at restrooms, which are open year-round

Land status: Private, nonprofit nature preserve

Nearest town: Milford

Fees and permits: Daily admission fee. Annual memberships are available.

Schedule: Grounds open daily from sunrise to sunset except Thanksgiving, Christmas, and New Year's Day. Rowe Visitor Center open daily from 9 a.m. to 5 p.m.

Maps: A large map of all trails is available at the visitor center. USGS quad: Batavia.

Trail contact: Cincinnati Nature Center, Rowe Woods, Milford; (513) 831-1711; www.cincy nature.org

Finding the trailhead: From I-275 on the east side of Cincinnati, take exit 59B east to a T-intersection with US 50 east. Turn right and drive 2 miles to Roundbottom Road. Take a right (south) and drive 0.4 mile to Tealtown Road. Turn left and continue 0.6 mile to the entrance to Rowe Woods on the right. Stop at the guard shack and then continue on the paved road to the visitor center parking lot on the left. *DeLorme: Ohio Atlas & Gazetteer:* Page 75 C6. GPS: N39 7.53' / W84 14.75'.

The Hike

Home to 14 miles of trails, Rowe Woods can satisfy those looking for both quantity and quality of hikes. In the 1950s and 1960s, there was a small but significant trend

Naked lady lilies bloom at the Cincinnati Nature Center.

toward preserving the diminishing wild places in Ohio. A series of nature preserves were founded at this time, including the Cincinnati Nature Center's original site in 1965. Stanley Rowe Sr. was part of a group of environmentalists who established Rowe Woods on the Krippendorf land.

A good starting point for any hike in the preserve is the Rowe Visitor Center. This is home to the CNC's nonprofit educational center and hosts lots of programs, mostly for children but there are ample programs for adults as well, including nature, bird, and full moon hikes. Permanent and revolving exhibits feature nature interpretation as well as photography and art shows.

From the visitor center, walk north toward the butterfly garden, where you will see butterflies such as the eastern swallowtail and the plants that attract them, like the appropriately named butterfly bush. After walking past a couple of parking lots, join the Lookout Trail, where you will walk in young woods and fields. This is a great morning or evening hike, when you are more likely to see bird and deer activity along this edge habitat. In late summer the field is full of ironweed and goldenrod.

The Lookout Trail ends at the junction with the Edge Trail. Walk halfway around Powel Crosley Lake in a clockwise direction. You can stop at a shelter and a boardwalk to observe wildlife or to just relax.

Soon join the Geology Trail, which is named for the fossils from some 450 million years ago that exist in the limestone and shale here. Take a few minutes to turn over some stones in Avey's Run (but please replace them). Cross Avey's Run and go as far as Fox Rock—a side trip worth the exertion of climbing to this outcropping that overlooks the forest and stream valley below.

From the Geology Trail, take the limestone steps back up to the Rowe Visitor Center, walking through an area that is full of wildflowers spring, summer, and fall and through an herb garden.

Miles and Directions

0.0 Start at the Rowe Visitor Center. Walk out the front doors and look for a post with a blue butterfly icon in about 50 feet. This is the Upland Trail. The trail is paved here and takes you through the butterfly garden. Then skirt the (still paved) trail along the edge of the parking lot. A sign here reads BOULDER WALK.

0.1 Cross the road you drove in on and come to a fork. Take the right fork and cross the corner of a gravel parking lot, then pick up the trail again in the woods on the other side. In about 100 feet come to a T-intersection and take a right.

0.2 Come to another fork. Take a right to begin the Lookout Trail, blazed with a brown hawk.

0.5 Cross Tealtown Road and come to a T-intersection. Take a left to stay on the Lookout Trail.

0.6 Come to a three-way intersection. Continue straight. In about 200 feet come to a T-intersection. Take a right and immediately come to another T-intersection. Take a left to continue to the lookout. **Option:** A shortcut to the right shaves off 0.5 mile.

1.1 Come to a junction with a trail from the right. Continue straight to a bench and a bit of an overlook.

1.4 Return to the junction with the shortcut trail on the right. Continue straight.

1.6 Cross Tealtown Road at the entrance of the Cincinnati Nature Center. Walk along the entrance road about 50 feet, then take a left off of the road and back onto the trail.

PASSENGER PIGEON *(ECTOPISTES MIGRATORIUS)*

Cincinnati, the state of Ohio, and much of the eastern United States were home to one of the most tragic events in North American natural history. In the early to mid-1800s, passenger pigeon flocks were measured in miles and in billions. The flocks would reportedly darken the sky for hours, and a single arrow or gunshot skyward would guarantee a successful hunt. No one could have predicted that by September 1, 1914, the last passenger pigeon in the world, named Martha, would die at the Cincinnati Zoo.

How did this happen? Many factors contributed to the extinction of what had been one of the most abundant bird species in the world. The primary culprit, however, was unregulated overhunting. Passenger pigeons bred in colonies where a mating pair would both care for the single egg. Tens of thousands were killed at a time at their nesting sites. Also, since passenger pigeons did not always return to the same nesting place every year, most people didn't worry when they didn't see the birds each year, nor were they aware of how rapidly the numbers were declining. Captive breeding programs were generally unsuccessful, and soon the numbers of passenger pigeons fell below recoverable levels.

Lookout to Geology Trail Loop

1.75 Come to the end of the Lookout Trail at a T-intersection. Take a left and begin the Edge Trail, marked with a green turtle.

1.9 Come to a junction with the Whitetail Trail on the left. Continue straight.

2.1 At another junction with the Whitetail Trail, again continue straight.

2.2 Come to the junction with the Geology Trail on the left, marked with a purple fossil. Take the left.

2.25 The Geology Trail splits. Continue straight (don't take the bridge over the creek). Soon you will pass a maintenance access road on the right.

2.5 Pass the old pump house on the left and then stone steps on the right. Continue straight. **Option:** You can take a right and ascend the stone steps for a 2.8-mile option.

2.6 Descend to a T-intersection before the creek. Take a right and cross the creek over stepping stones. **FYI:** Look for fossils here. Leave any you find.

2.75 Come to a four-way junction with the Wildflower Trail. Make a U-turn and cross the creek again.

Jack-in-the-pulpit gone to seed

2.9 Take a long set of wooden stairs up to Fox Rock. Just before the gazebo, take the wooden stairs to the right to the rock. Turn around and cross the river again, returning the way you came to the stone steps. **FYI:** Look for a fernlike plant growing from the rock called purple cliffbrake.

3.2 At the stone steps, take a left and ascend out of the valley. Where the trail splits, take a left (the right is an unofficial shortcut).

3.3 Come to a junction by a bench. You are now rejoining the Upland Trail. Go straight.

3.4 Cross a stone bridge and continue straight. You can explore side trails here in the herb garden. When you come to a junction with more stone steps to the left and a concrete bench down to the right, take this left to a T-intersection marked with a trail sign. Take a right and walk back to the Rowe Visitor Center.

3.5 Arrive back at the Rowe Visitor Center.

Hike Information

Local information: Clermont County Convention and Visitors Bureau, (513) 732-3600, www.visitclermontohio.com

City of Milford, (513) 831-4192, www.milfordohio.org

Restaurants: 20 Brix, Milford; (513) 831-BRIX (2749); www.20brix.com

Miami Market, Milford; (513) 831-8646; www.miami-market.com

Accommodations: East Fork State Park, Bethel; (513) 734-4323; http://parks.ohiodnr.gov/east fork

Hike tours: Occasionally full moon and other guided hikes are offered; call the Rowe Visitor Center for up-to-date information at (513) 831-1711.

Other resources: You can download self-guided trail brochures at www.cincynature.org/self-guided-opportunities.html. The Rowe Visitor Center is home to the William Whitaker Memorial Library.

28 Fort to Gorge Trail Loop

Fort Hill State Memorial

Fort Hill is the site of an ancient stone-and-earth embankment that encloses the top of the hill and was likely built by the prehistoric Hopewell Indians. But for a nature lover, this is a secondary attraction. Walk in a healthy, beautiful (and in places virgin) forest while skirting the edge of Baker Fork, an attractive rippling creek that has undercut the dolomite rock faces that line its edge. Spring wildflowers are incredible, especially when complemented by numerous rock features, including a natural bridge and a cascading waterfall. Take a 4.5-mile loop that climbs the hilltop enclosure and then parallels Baker Fork.

Start: Parking lot
Distance: 4.5-mile loop
Hiking time: About 2 hours
Difficulty: Moderate due to ups and downs
Trail surface: Dirt path with some close drop-offs
Blaze: The trails are mostly unblazed; signs mark each junction.
Best season: Mid-Apr through mid-Oct
Other trail users: Hikers only
Canine compatibility: Leashed dogs permitted
Water: Available at the museum when open

Land status: State memorial, managed by the private Arc of Appalachia Preserve System
Nearest town: Hillsboro
Fees and permits: None
Schedule: Trails open daily from dawn to dusk; museum open noon to 5 p.m. on weekends May through Oct
Maps: State memorial brochure; Buckeye Trail Association section map: Sinking Spring; USGS quad: Sinking Spring
Trail contact: Arc of Appalachia Preserve, Bainbridge; (937) 365-1935; http://arcof appalachia.org/visit/fort-hill.html

Finding the trailhead: From US 32 at Peebles, turn north on SR 41 and drive 14.6 miles to Fort Hill Road. Turn left and drive 0.7 mile to the entrance on the left.

From SR 50 east of Hillsboro, turn south on SR 753 and drive 7 miles to SR 41. Turn right (south) onto SR 41 and continue 0.6 mile to Fort Hill Road. Turn right (west) and drive 0.7 mile to the entrance on the left.

From the entrance road, the museum is on the right and the parking lot is straight ahead, past the museum. *DeLorme: Ohio Atlas & Gazetteer:* Page 77 D5. GPS: N39 6.2' / W83 21.73'.

The Hike

Fort Hill State Memorial is a place rich in both archaeological and natural history. The name comes from the memorial's central feature, a prehistoric Native American hilltop enclosure that covers 40 acres. All trails encircle Fort Hill, and the Fort Trail takes you over and into the ancient stone and earthen embankment, now largely

The trail goes through an old log cabin.

overgrown but still recognizable. The wall ranges from 6 to 15 feet tall and is 40 feet wide at its base. Burrow pits within the enclosure may have been dug for wall materials, and they are now hilltop ponds. It's not certain who built Fort Hill and for what purposes, but it was possibly the Hopewell Indians (100 BC to AD 400), who are also credited with building nearby Serpent Mound.

To the nature lover, the forest itself is the main attraction. Ecologically, Fort Hill is an exceptionally biodiverse region, situated along the edge of the Appalachian Plateau where it meets the glaciated plains of central Ohio. Due to this edge topography, Fort Hill is home to some locally rare and endangered species, including Sullivantia and Canada yew—plants that normally grow only in more northern climes. They likely migrated south more than 12,000 years ago, keeping ahead of the advancing glaciers.

Begin at the shared trailhead for the Gorge, Fort, Buckeye, and North Country Scenic Trails. These trails all eventually break off from one another. One of the first things to notice is a healthy, mature forest. In fact, some sections of this forest are virgin or nearly so. When the chestnut blight came through in the first half of the twentieth century, American chestnut trees were cut and the wood was used to construct some of the buildings, shelter houses, and picnic tables still in use today.

The forest canopy consists of large tulip, beech, and maple trees along the slopes and oaks and hickories on the ridgetop. Understory species include witch hazel, pawpaw, spicebush, and sourwood. On the forest floor there's no shortage of showy wildflowers, including trillium, wild ginger, Solomon's seal, wild yam, wild geranium, dwarf larkspur, celandine poppy, spiderwort, Canada violet, and wood sorrel, to name just a few. In springtime arguably no other trail in the state is more beautiful.

▶ The Hopewell were a prehistoric people, so we don't know what they called themselves. The name we use today for this culture comes from an 1893 excavation of twenty-eight mounds on Captain Mordecai Hopewell's Ross County farm.

E. LUCY BRAUN (1889–1971)

E. Lucy Braun reportedly logged 65,000 miles hiking, but this is not her claim to fame. Rather, she is probably Ohio's most accomplished plant ecologist. Braun spent her life in Cincinnati, growing up the daughter of schoolteachers. She earned a PhD in botany in 1914 from the University of Cincinnati and went on to become a full professor of plant ecology at her alma mater. She was a prolific researcher and writer, with 180 works to her credit. Her seminal piece is *Deciduous Forests of Eastern North America,* published in 1950. *The Woody Plants of Ohio* (1961) is used today as a textbook for aspiring plant ecologists.

Braun was the first woman president of the Ohio Academy of Science and the Ecological Society of America. Her work went beyond studying single plant species to studying the ecology of entire regions. Her research led her to identify some of the forests found in southeast Ohio and elsewhere in the Appalachian region as "mixed mesophytic." In a mixed mesophytic forest, twenty to twenty-five tree species are common, such as oak, hickory, tulip, buckeye, and maple, but no single species dominates the canopy. Most commonly found on north- and east-facing slopes, mixed mesophytic forests are also identified as highly biodiverse, made up of thousands of species of plant and animal life.

Devoted to conservation, Braun is credited with helping to preserve more than 10,000 acres of Ohio land. Two of her students, Richard and Lucile Durrell, helped lead the effort to create the Edge of Appalachia Preserve.

Lucy Braun was often accompanied by her sister, Annette, an entomologist. Old photos show the two women in the field wearing full-length skirts, as expected of them during the early years of the twentieth century.

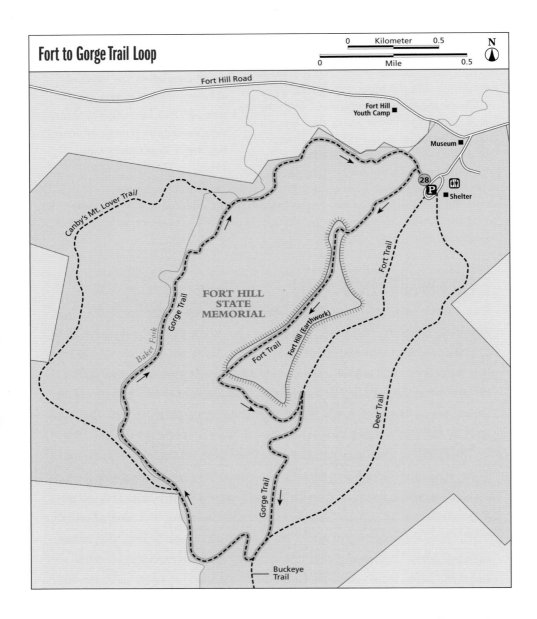

Fort to Gorge Trail Loop

FORT HILL
STATE
MEMORIAL

You will first hike to the top of the 400-foot-tall ridge. As you walk atop the ridge, look to your right for a long, distinctive embankment with occasional openings. After walking along the length of the fort, descend to the creek.

More than half the Gorge Trail runs alongside Baker Fork, a beautiful, winding creek that has undercut the dolomite rocks along its banks. You will walk right along the water's edge and under recessed overhangs and then climb atop columbine-covered rocky overlooks on this up-and-down trail. The scenery is ever unfolding and fantastic, including views of cascading waterfalls and a natural bridge. There are a number of rocky overlooks along the trail. Footing can be dangerous at times, so walk with care and keep an eye on children. At one point the trail even walks right through an old log cabin.

The trail eventually turns away from the creek and rejoins the Fort Trail shortly before returning to the parking lot.

Miles and Directions

0.0   Start at the trailhead kiosk on the west side of the parking lot. A sign is here for the Fort and Gorge Trails; a blue blaze marks the Buckeye Trail. In about 200 yards the Gorge Trail and the Buckeye Trail go off to the right. Take the left fork, ascending the ridge on the Fort Trail.

0.4   Reach the top of the ridge. There is a view to the north and the trail takes a sharp left turn. You will pass informal side trails taking you over the fort embankment on your right, which becomes more distinctive around the half-mile point.

1.0   Begin descending the ridge. The trail takes a sharp left turn.

1.4   Come to the junction with the Gorge Trail. Take a right, following the Gorge Trail sign.

1.7   Come to a junction with the Deer Trail. Take the right fork.

1.9   Come to a junction with the Buckeye Trail and a trail to the circular earthworks to the left. The Gorge Trail takes a sharp right here.

2.7   Come to a junction with Canby's Trail to the left. Continue straight on the Gorge Trail.

3.6   The trail passes through an old log cabin, then it comes to a fork. Take the right fork, walking down and over a footbridge.

4.5   Arrive at the original junction with the Fort Trail. Take a left and walk back to the parking lot.

Hike Information

Local information: Highland County Convention and Visitors Bureau, (937) 402-4347, www.highlandcouty.com

Local events and attractions: Serpent Mound, (937) 587-2796, www.ohiohistory.org/places/serpent/index.html

Organizations: Ohio Historical Society, Columbus; (614) 297-2300; www.ohiohistory.org

Buckeye Trail Association, Worthington; (740) 832-1BTA; www.buckeyetrail.org

North Country Scenic Trail; (866) 445-3628; www.northcountrytrail.org

29 Day Hike Trail

Shawnee State Forest

Within the 60-mile backpack loop in Shawnee State Forest lies a 7.2-mile loop that's a perfect day-hike option. Here in the "Little Smokies" of Ohio, ascend steeply to ridgetops of oak-hickory forest and then walk in cool beech-maple hollows. If you're lucky, you might see the overly harvested ginseng on the forest floor or even the elusive timber rattlesnake. Spring wildflowers and fall foliage draw hikers and photographers from all over the state.

Start: East Turkey Creek Lake boat ramp parking lot

Distance: 7.2-mile loop

Hiking time: 2.5 to 3.5 hours

Difficulty: Moderate to difficult due to length and steep ascents and descents over the ridges

Trail surface: Dirt footpath that is narrow but clear. Footing can be difficult when walking straight up and down the ridges.

Blaze: Blue

Best season: Spring, when the water is flowing and wildflowers are abundant

Other trail users: Hunters (in season) and equestrians on one portion of the trail

Canine compatibility: Leashed dogs permitted

Water: Available at the nature center and at backpack Camp 3

Land status: State forest

Nearest town: Portsmouth

Fees and permits: None. For backpacking, self-register at the backpack trail trailhead.

Schedule: Open daily from 6 a.m. to 11 p.m.

Maps: USGS quad: Pond Run

Trail contact: Shawnee State Forest, West Portsmouth; (740) 858-6685; http://ohiodnr.com/forests/shawnee/tabid/5166/Default.aspx

Finding the trailhead: From US 23 in Portsmouth, take SR 52 west 6.6 miles to SR 125 (past the state forest headquarters). Turn right (west) onto SR 125 and drive 5.8 miles to the boat ramp and nature center parking lot on the left. *DeLorme: Ohio Atlas & Gazetteer:* Page 84 C3. GPS: N38 43.99' / W83 11.21'.

The Hike

Shawnee State Forest is often called the Little Smokies of Ohio, in reference to the area's steep hills and narrow hollows. This 63,000-acre forest is by far the state's largest, and when you get an opportunity to peer into the distance, you will see gently undulating ridges unfold as far as the eye can see. Then when you get into the forest to explore it on foot, you'll soon recognize the biodiversity that this geography supports.

Hundreds of millions of years ago, an uplift created the Appalachian or Western Allegheny Plateau. In the time since, water has carved out the resulting landscape. Drainages flow into streams and creeks, and they all make their way to the mighty

Turkey Creek Lake in Shawnee State Forest

Ohio River, which borders Shawnee State Forest to the south. Across the way are Kentucky and more ridges unfolding into the distance.

Just east of the forest is the confluence of the Scioto and Ohio Rivers. Archaic Native Americans inhabited this fertile and accessible spot as far back as 15,000 years ago. By the time Europeans arrived, the Shawnee Indians lived here, hence the name of the state forest. This land was hotly contested in the eighteenth century as the Shawnees defended Lower Town and other settlements and hunting grounds in the Ohio River Valley. But soon enough the Shawnees were driven out.

In 1922 the state of Ohio purchased 5,000 acres of abused land and opened the Theodore Roosevelt State Game Preserve. In the 1930s the Civilian Conservation Corps (CCC) set up six work camps, and young men built roads and lakes in the forest. Over the years more acreage was acquired. Land oversight changed hands, but it stayed in state ownership—today as Shawnee State Forest and Shawnee State Park. Between state forest and state park lands, more than 60 miles of hiking trails exist for just about any hiking taste. The Shawnee State Forest Day Hike is a good 7.2-mile loop that takes you through much of what this landscape has to show.

Start at Turkey Creek Lake, one of five human-made lakes in the forest. (The Turkey Creek Lake earthen dam was built in the 1960s, not by the CCC.) From here you'll get your best views along the trail of the surrounding ridges. Enter the forest and begin walking up Williamson Hollow. Almost immediately you'll come upon a large beaver pond. The trail skirts around the beaver pond and then crosses the first of several drainages. Cross this drainage and shortly find yourself ascending a ridge. On this section of trail, look to your right for what appears to be a Native American signal tree. This oak, a couple hundred years old, was bent horizontally and then allowed to grow straight up from there. Signal trees served as directional markers on long-distance Native American trails, and quite a few remain standing today. Of course, the tree may have just grown this way for another reason as well.

As you'll soon find out, the trail doesn't cross over the ridges too often—but when it does, it goes straight up and then straight down. Be careful, especially when descending the ridges; erosion is a problem, and footing can be sketchy.

As you ascend to the drier ridgetops, especially on south-facing slopes, note the forest makeup. Oak and hickory as well as native pitch and shortleaf pines (look for three needles bundled together) are well adapted here. On the forest floor, look for blueberry bushes. Once you've ascended the ridge and descended back to the stream, especially on north-facing slopes, note how the forest makeup changes. Maple, beech, sycamore, ash, elm, hemlock, and even magnolia trees thrive here. Wildflowers are abundant, and goldenseal is growing everywhere. You'll be lucky to spot ginseng, another medicinal plant, since it has been so heavily poached by both humans and deer in Shawnee State Forest.

As you cross the rocky streambeds and drainages, turn over a few stones and look for fossils. Reptiles and amphibians are also well represented here, including the endangered timber rattlesnake. (You're probably less likely to see one of these than you are to see ginseng.) Common forest animals such as beaver, fox, white-tailed deer, and turkey are present, and occasional sightings of bobcat and black bear have been reported.

Walk along the sandy ridgetop trail shared with horses before making a final push toward the trailhead on a west-facing slope. Look here for numerous stump sprouts of the American chestnut. These small trees will succumb to the chestnut blight before they reach maturity. After descending to the streambed, walk through a young, dense stand of tulip poplar. This is an example of what the Division of Forestry calls "even-aged management"—otherwise known as a former clear-cut. Past that, look for an old sandstone chimney, evidence of a former homestead.

MEDICINAL PLANTS

Even in our technological age, most medicines are still derived from plants before they're copied in the laboratory. Most plants have medicinal characteristics, some more than others. Goldenseal, which grows abundantly in Shawnee State Forest, is used topically as an antibacterial and to treat inflammation. Ginseng, which once grew abundantly in Shawnee State Forest, is used as a general tonic. Wild ginseng is more lucrative than its domesticated relative, selling for as much as $500 a pound. Once there was a ginseng season in the Shawnee, but overcollection and poaching have led the forest to ban its collection altogether.

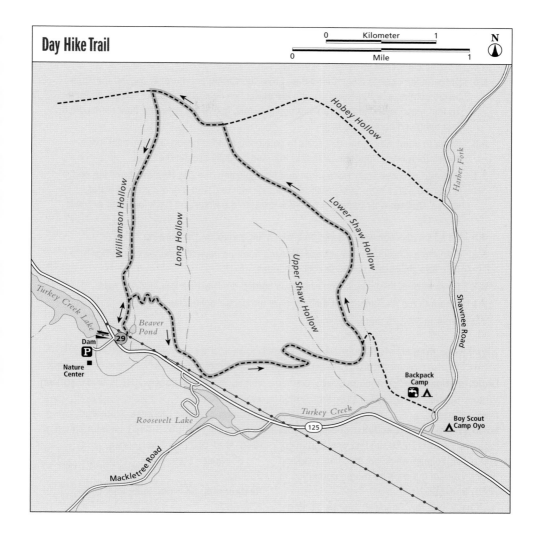

Day Hike Trail

0 — Kilometer — 1

0 — Mile — 1

N

Hobey Hollow

Harber Fork

Williamson Hollow

Long Hollow

Lower Shaw Hollow

Upper Shaw Hollow

Turkey Creek Lake

Beaver Pond

Dam

29

P

Nature Center

Shawnee Road

Backpack Camp

Boy Scout Camp Oyo

Roosevelt Lake

Turkey Creek

125

Mackletree Road

You can make this loop into an overnighter by staying in Camp 3. If you're ready for more miles, even days, hit the 40-mile Shawnee Backpack Trail. Try the south loop first—and come back in fifty years to hike the Wilderness Side Trail when the forest has had a chance to mature undisturbed. Shawnee State Park offers a few shorter day hikes. The best view of Ohio's Little Smokies can be found from the aptly named Lookout Trail.

Miles and Directions

0.0   Start from the Turkey Creek Lake boat ramp parking lot. Follow the driveway back to SR 125 and cross the road, looking for the wooden trailhead sign. **FYI:** The trailhead sign says this is a 6.5-mile trail; it's actually longer than that.

0.2 Come to a junction where the trail turns off to the left. Straight ahead is the beaver pond.

0.5 Hit a fork near the creek bed. Take a right to begin the loop, following the sign for the Day Hike Trail. Soon you will ascend the ridge.

1.5 Descend the ridge to Long Hollow Run. Cross the stream and partially ascend the ridge before coming to a T-intersection with the power line right-of-way. Take a left and in about 15 feet reach a junction with an informal side trail. Take a left, pass the power line pole on your right, and ascend the ridge.

2.6 Come to a fork, where the trail splits to go around a fallen beech tree. The right fork is easier. Then cross Upper Shaw Hollow Run and partially ascend the ridge.

3.1 Descend to Lower Shaw Hollow Run and hit a junction. The Day Hike Trail turns left and is marked with a sign. Straight ahead is a side trail to Camp 3 and a potable water source. **Option:** Walk through a hemlock forest to the water and back for about a 1-mile round-trip.

4.8 Hit a T-intersection with a bridle trail. Take a left and follow the ridgetop.

5.6 Come to a junction. Take a left and descend from the ridge to continue on the Day Hike Trail. Straight ahead, the bridle trail continues.

6.8 Arrive back at the first junction where you started the Day Hike Trail loop. Go right.

7.1 Return to the first junction of the trail, near the beaver pond. Take a right.

7.2 Arrive at SR 125 and the trailhead.

Hike Information

Local information: Portsmouth–Scioto County Visitors Bureau, (740) 353-1116, http://ohio rivertourism.org

Local events and attractions: Shawnee State Park hosts a Trout Derby the last weekend in Apr and a Fall Foliage Weekend the third weekend in Oct; contact the park for more information at (740) 858-6652.

Check out the floodwall murals in Portsmouth, which give a pictorial history of the area.

The Nature Conservancy's Edge of Appalachia Preserve is just west of Shawnee State Forest, in Adams County; (513) 544-2880 or www.nature.org.

Accommodations: Shawnee State Park campground; call (740) 858-4561 for information or (866) 644-6727 for reservations.

Shawnee State Park Lodge; call (800) 282-7275.

Restaurants: Shawnee State Park Lodge, (740) 858-6621

Organizations: Buckeye Trail Association, Worthington; (740) 832-1BTA; www.buckeye trail.org

Honorable Mentions

Southwest Ohio

○ Brukner Nature Center Trails

If you go for a hike at Brukner Nature Center, you're guaranteed to see a fox, a bald eagle, a great horned owl, or a bobcat. Okay, so maybe it's cheating to view them at the Interpretive Center, but these wildlife "ambassadors" reflect some of the wild animals that do inhabit nature center property. (They are injured animals that can no longer survive in the wild.) Brukner Nature Center is a nonprofit, privately funded preserve whose mission is to promote the appreciation and understanding of wildlife conservation through education, preservation, and rehabilitation. Combine the outer loop of trails at the preserve to make a 4.3-mile hike that takes you through pine forests, along an oak–hickory ridgetop, and into the Stillwater River Valley. Hang around the interpretive building, where you can check out wildlife exhibits, a treetop bird vista, a nineteenth-century log home, a totem pole, and an amphitheater around a small pond. There is an entrance fee.

Trail contact: Brukner Nature Center, Troy; (937) 698-6493; www.brukner naturecenter.com

Finding the trailhead: From I-75 in Troy, turn west onto SR 55 (exit 73) and drive 2.4 miles to Horseshoe Bend Road. Take a right and drive 2.2 miles to the preserve entrance on the right. Continue all the way to the end of the driveway at the interpretive building parking lot. Start at the Pinelands trailhead. *DeLorme: Ohio Atlas & Gazetteer:* Page 55 D5. GPS: N40 00.98' / W84 19.03'.

P Valley of the Ancients to Etawah Woods Trail, Highlands Nature Sanctuary

The folks at Highlands Nature Sanctuary are into sprawl—woodland sprawl, that is. The sanctuary is part of the Arc of Appalachia Preserve system, 4,000 acres (and growing) of land purchased to create a wilderness area in the East. Since purchasing the neighboring 7 Caves property, trails around the sanctuary's Appalachian Forest Museum take you along the scenic Rocky Fork with its dolomite cliffs and spring wildflowers that include wood columbine, jack-in-the-pulpit, shooting star, and even a pyramid of trillium (it looks like it sounds—visit the second or third weekend in April). These trails are open to the public on the weekends April through October, 9 a.m. to 5 p.m. If you become a member of this private nonprofit preservation and education organization, you gain access to the sanctuary's 14 miles of wilderness trails. Cabins are also available for rent.

Trail contact: Highlands Nature Sanctuary, Bainbridge; (937) 365-1935; www
.arcofappalachia.org/visit/highlands-nature-sanctuary.html

Finding the trailhead: From US 50 4.3 miles west of Bainbridge, turn south
onto Cave Road and travel 1 mile to the museum on the right. *DeLorme: Ohio Atlas
& Gazetteer:* Page 77 C6. GPS: N39 13.23' / W83 21.98'.

Q Little Turtle and Blue Jacket Trails, Shawnee Lookout Park

Combine the Little Turtle and Blue Jacket Trails for a 3.3-mile hike to overlooks of
the Great Miami and Ohio Rivers. The trails are named after two Native American
war chiefs who fought against American federal troops in eighteenth-century battles
over the Ohio Valley territories. Little Turtle was a Miami Indian and Blue Jacket
was a Shawnee. Human history at this spot dates back a lot further, however, to
14,000 years ago. The earth mound hilltop and the burial mounds found here have
been thoroughly excavated by archaeologists, who have turned up countless artifacts,
including projectile points, tools, pottery, jewelry, and mortars and pestles. The park is
also home to the 1.5-mile Miami Fort Trail, which also affords a hilltop vista.

Trail contact: Hamilton County Park District, Cincinnati; (513) 521-7275;
www.greatparks.org

Finding the trailhead: From SR 50 in Elizabethtown, turn south onto Lawrenceburg Road and drive 0.7 mile to a T-intersection. Turn right (south), still on
Lawrenceburg Road, and drive 1.5 miles to the park entrance on the left, marked
with a sign. Drive 0.7 mile to the trailhead parking on the right for both the Blue
Jacket and Little Turtle Trails. *DeLorme: Ohio Atlas & Gazetteer:* Page 74 C1. GPS: N39
07.54' / W84 47.37'.

R Trail to Buzzardroost Rock, Edge of Appalachia Preserve

Atop Buzzardroost Rock, you're more than 300 feet above Ohio Brush Creek, with
an expansive view of the creek valley and the ridges beyond. This is a must-do hike
for southern Ohio. It's listed here as an honorable mention due to a rerouting of the
trail at press time; beginning in 2013, the 3.5-mile out-and-back trail to Buzzardroost
Rock was being rerouted. Contact the Nature Conservancy before heading out to
make sure you have up-to-date information on the hike. This hike is a prominent feature in this 13,000-acre preserve, which is also characterized by barrens and glades—
small patches (up to 10 acres) of prairie communities. These mini prairies are found
in only a few places in the US Midwest and are globally rare. The Edge of Appalachia
Preserve, operated by the Nature Conservancy and the Cincinnati Museum Center,
is home to more than 135 species of rare plants and animals. Globally rare plant species include ear-leafed foxglove and juniper sedge. Endangered animals found here
include the green salamander and eastern woodrat.

Trail contact: The Nature Conservancy in Ohio; (937) 544-2188; www.nature
.org/ourinitiatives/regions/northamerica/unitedstates/ohio

OHIO'S LEGENDARY SHAWNEE LEADERS

In the decades leading up to the American Revolution, European-American explorers, trappers, and then settlers made substantial inroads into the territory north of the Ohio River. At the time a handful of Native American nations called this region home or used it for hunting grounds. Clashes soon grew violent between the Native Americans and the homesteaders. The place names we're left with today—Chillicothe, Defiance, Shawnee Lookout—reflect these war-torn times. Many capable leaders emerged on both sides, and two of the most legendary were Shawnees Blue Jacket and Tecumseh.

Blue Jacket was born around 1743 and grew up in a time of treaties ceding the Ohio lands to American and British rule, broken promises, skirmishes, and still more suspect treaties. His origins are a point of contention: Although he is widely known as a white man who grew up a Shawnee, his descendants contradict this claim and maintain that Blue Jacket was born a Shawnee. He was an important player in the defeat of US forces in battles with General Josiah Harmar in 1790 and Arthur St. Clair in 1791 (St. Clair would later become Ohio's first governor). In 1794 Blue Jacket was the leading war chief at the Battle of Fallen Timbers in northwest Ohio, where his forces were defeated by those of General "Mad Anthony" Wayne. This defeat was the beginning of the end for Ohio's Native Americans. Also present at that battle was a young Shawnee warrior named Tecumseh.

Tecumseh means "panther crossing the sky" and refers to the accounts of his birth in 1768: When the Shawnee chief's wife gave birth to this future legend, a shooting star crossed the sky with such brightness and longevity that people were called out of their homes to see it. Tecumseh grew into something of a golden boy, with outstanding skills in hunting, warfare, leadership, and prophecy. His brother, Tenskatawa, was known as "the prophet," but it may have actually been Tecumseh's predictions that Tenskatawa put forth. Tecumseh became best known as an advocate of unity among the many Native American tribes so that they could build a force strong enough to defeat the increasingly invasive federal army. He traveled far and wide to drum up support for this massive effort while his support back home waned, especially after William Henry Harrison's troops destroyed Prophetstown while Tecumseh was away.

To close friends, Tecumseh predicted his own death in the Battle of Thames in Ontario, Canada. He reportedly went into battle in disguise in an effort to avoid having his dead body mutilated by American troops. Tecumseh was killed in the battle, but it's unclear whether his body was mutilated, as the American version goes, or if his body was taken away by Shawnees and buried, perhaps in Clark County, as the Shawnee version tells it.

Finding the trailhead: Check in with the Edge of Appalachia Preserve for trailhead directions. To find the nearby preserve offices, start at the junction of SR 41 and SR 125 in West Union. Take SR 125 east 5.8 miles to Waggoner Riffle Road. Turn right (south) and go 2.3 miles to the preserve office on the right. *DeLorme: Ohio Atlas & Gazetteer:* Page 84 B1. GPS: N38 44.99' / W83 27.88'.

S Gorge Trail, Sharon Woods

Get some bang for your buck on the Gorge Trail at Sharon Woods, a Hamilton County park located within Cincinnati's outerbelt. In just 0.6 mile one-way, walk to two waterfalls that cascade into pools. As the name suggests, this trail takes you through a small gorge made up of limestone and shale that, combined, create the horizontal layers you can see quite clearly on the gorge walls. Aside from the waterfalls, this area is perhaps best known for its fossil collection. Take some time to look closely for fossils, including brachiopods and trilobites. But remember, just look. Leave the fossils where you find them so other visitors can enjoy this resource long into the future. The forest is quite mature and diverse, with tree species including oak, maple, cherry, and ash. In the spring, look for an abundance of wildflowers, including common waterleaf and pipevine, a climbing vine with pipe-shaped flowers. This plant is food for the pipevine swallowtail butterfly; look for both in late spring and early summer.

Trail contact: Sharon Centre (visitor center), (513) 563-4513, http://greatparks .org/parks/sharon-woods.html

Finding the trailhead: From the junction of I-275 and US 42 on the north side of Cincinnati, take US 42 south 0.7 mile to the park entrance. Take a left (east) and go 0.1 mile to Buckeye Falls Drive. Take a left and go 1 mile to the parking lot on the right. Backtrack on the road about 150 feet to the trailhead. *DeLorme: Ohio Atlas & Gazetteer:* Page 75 B5. GPS: N39 16.94' / W84 23.34'.

Southeast Ohio

The least populated and least trampled part of Ohio is the southeast. This is also the most rugged section of the state, with narrow hollows and steep ridges supporting a mostly forested landscape. The Ohio River serves as a geographical as well as political boundary on one side. As the region bleeds north and west, the other boundary is also clear to the eye: The edge of the Appalachian Plateau gives way to the glacier-flattened landscape that most of Ohio is known for.

The forests here are very biodiverse. Oak-hickory forests dominate the ridgetops, although maple and beech are well represented in the lowlands. Mixed mesophytic forests abound in southeast Ohio, where a large number of tree species are common, but no single species dominates the canopy. Dysart Woods, Ohio's largest tract of virgin forest, is located here.

Southeast Ohio was home to Native Americans as far back as 15,000 years ago, evidenced by Adena mounds that occasionally dot the landscape. This region was primarily used as hunting grounds for Shawnee Indians when Europeans arrived, and great clashes ensued between Native Americans and European settlers during much of the eighteenth century.

As Native Americans were driven out and settlers proceeded west of the Appalachian Mountains, Ohio River cities served as gateways. Marietta, Ohio's first city, was one of these. Resource-based communities popped up around timber and coal-mining operations. Today many of these are ghost towns or shadows of their former selves. The "Hanging Rock" region of southeast Ohio provided much of the growing nation's iron, extracted from sandstone and smelted on-site, using wood-fired blast furnaces. By the turn of the twentieth century, southeast Ohio's landscape was denuded.

In the 1930s Wayne National Forest began acquiring land, and the Depression-era Civilian Conservation Corps (CCC) began work in earnest. They planted trees and built roads, dams, and many of the shelters and buildings still in use today. The Wayne National Forest has a somewhat unusual configuration in that it is divided into three noncontiguous units—Athens, Marietta, and Ironton. The Wayne, like all national forests, is a multiple-use public land where timbering and gas development occur, but hiking is accessible in all districts. The Ironton Ranger District contains Lake Vesuvius Recreation Area, where hiking and other outdoor sports do not share space with extraction, hunting, or other activities allowed elsewhere in the Wayne.

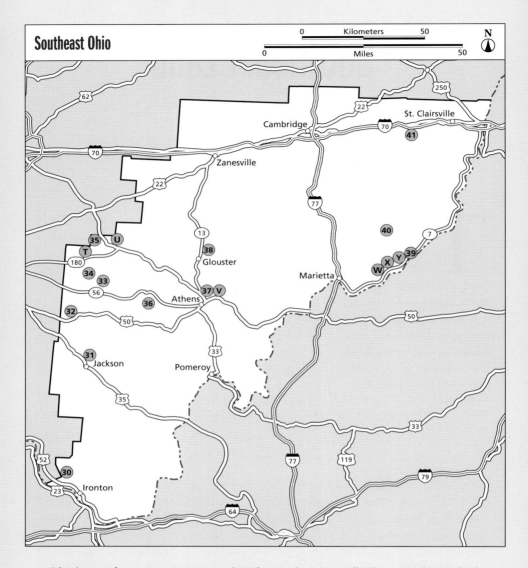

Southeast Ohio

Ohio's state forests are concentrated in the southeast as well. These are also multiple-use lands managed largely for timber, but they also afford ample hiking opportunities. Between national and state forest lands, a number of lengthy day hikes and backpacking options are available.

Some of Ohio's most popular state parks are here in the southeast region. Hocking Hills State Park is home to such well-known attractions as Old Man's Cave, Cedar Falls, and Ash Cave. Burr Oak State Park hosts a lodge and nearly 50 miles of hiking trails in the park and surrounding national forest. Many state parks are anchored by salamander-shaped lakes. No natural lakes exist in this Appalachian Plateau region, so dammed reservoirs take on the shape of the hollows they fill.

30 Lake Vesuvius Lakeshore Trail

Wayne National Forest–Ironton Ranger District

Take the 7.8-mile Lake Vesuvius Lakeshore Trail all the way around the reservoir, beginning and ending at the Vesuvius Furnace. This sandstone blast furnace was used to smelt iron ore in the nineteenth and early twentieth centuries. Walk in a deciduous forest along the shore, with water on one side of you and rock outcroppings on the other side. Look for a good lunch spot overlooking the lake, and jump in at the beach when it gets hot.

Start: Parking lot at the dam, across from the iron furnace
Distance: 7.8-mile loop
Hiking time: About 3 to 5 hours
Difficulty: Moderate due to length
Trail surface: Dirt
Blaze: White diamond with a blue dot
Best season: Apr through Oct
Other trail users: Hikers only
Canine compatibility: Leashed dogs permitted
Water: Available at the boat dock, the beach, and near the dam Apr through Oct
Land status: National forest recreation area
Nearest town: Ironton

Fees and permits: None
Schedule: Trails in the Wayne National Forest are open 24 hours a day, 365 days a year. The safest time to hike, however, is between dawn and dusk.
Maps: A brochure with topo maps of all hiking and backpacking trails in the Wayne is available for purchase at Wayne National Forest offices. USGS quad: Kitts Hills.
Trail contact: Wayne National Forest, Ironton Ranger District, Pedro; (740) 534-6500; www .fs.usda.gov/wayne

Finding the trailhead: From Ironton, travel north on SR 93 for 6.5 miles and turn right (east) onto CR 29 (if you come to the headquarters office you've passed CR 29). Follow the signs 0.9 mile to the parking lot, across from the furnace on the left. *DeLorme: Ohio Atlas & Gazetteer:* Page 85 D7. GPS: N38 35.04' / W82 38.22'.

The Hike

Lake Vesuvius Recreation Area lies in the heart of the Hanging Rock iron furnace region, named for the outcroppings of ferriferous limestone mined to fuel the iron furnaces that, in turn, fueled the economy of this region between 1818 and 1916. The Vesuvius Furnace (yes, named after the Italian volcano) was built in 1833 to smelt iron ore and was in use until 1906. At its peak the Vesuvius Furnace produced 8 to 12 tons of iron each day. Iron munitions from these furnaces were critical to the Union effort during the Civil War.

A boardwalk over Lake Vesuvius

The Lake Vesuvius Lakeshore Trail begins and ends near the furnace. This rock chimney, built without mortar, is all that remains of a larger blast furnace as well as a storage yard, casting house, scale house, and carpenter and blacksmith shops. Furnace workers, much like coal miners, lived in company towns and were paid in goods or scrip. The furnaces consumed 300 to 350 acres of timber each year for fuel, so when the industry died, it left behind a denuded landscape.

Enter the Wayne National Forest and Civilian Conservation Corps in the 1930s. The Wayne began purchasing land in 1935, and in 1943 the CCC built an earthen dam near the furnace, creating Lake Vesuvius, a salamander-shaped reservoir. One of the features that makes this hike interesting is how often the trail is pinched between the water and rock outcroppings. There are several choice lunch spots atop the rocks overlooking the lake. When you walk by these outcroppings, look for little bits of iron, noticeably darker and harder than the surrounding sandstone and limestone.

THE UNDERGROUND RAILROAD

Iron furnaces weren't the only things burning in this part of the country during the nineteenth century. Antebellum politics were boiling over between the North and South. Several areas in what is now Wayne National Forest were stops along the Underground Railroad, where people risked their own lives and livelihoods to help escaped slaves on the path to freedom. Underground Railroad routes ran from the slave-holding Southern states to the North (Ohio was part of the Union) and into Canada.

For obvious reasons, the routes were unpublished, requiring escaped slaves to rely mostly on the help of sympathetic people from one stop to the next. Human contact was kept to a minimum, but clues were sometimes otherwise available, such as coded quilts hanging on clotheslines. The former loose-knit community of Pokepatch, Ohio, north of where Lake Vesuvius is today, seemed to exist solely as a stop along the Underground Railroad between 1820 and 1870. Pokepatch was home to freed slaves, whites, Native Americans, and people of mixed race. Some of their descendants live in nearby Blackfork today. Learn more about underground railroad and freedom trails in the national forests at www.fs.usda.gov.

Beginning from the dam, hike the trail clockwise to get the early sun and counterclockwise to try to stay in the shade. The trail generally hugs the lakeside in an oak-hickory forest and through occasional pine plantations. Walking clockwise, look across the lake for views of the dam and a large rock outcropping. Be prepared, however, for the trail often recedes from the lakeshore and moves up and down the ridges. Pass a swimming beach while continuing upstream. As you approach the turnaround point, you will cross over Storms Creek, which feeds the lake. This is a nice area in a creek valley lined by hemlock-dotted rock outcroppings and water-loving sycamore trees. A decent water hole awaits the few who venture this far along the trail. This is also the spot where the Vesuvius Backpack Trail momentarily converges. The backpack trail continues farther into the forest.

On the return trip, the views are ever-changing and you get a chance to see how far you've come. Look for signs of beaver activity, and keep an eye open for a good rocky lunch spot if you haven't stopped yet. Toward the end of the loop is the largest rock outcropping, more than 30 feet high. This is a popular spot among hikers, picnickers, and rock climbers.

End the walk back at the dam, about 0.5 mile past this point. For a longer hike opt for the Vesuvius Backpack Trail, which shares part of its length with the Lakeshore Trail but continues past the lake and into the forest for a 16-mile loop.

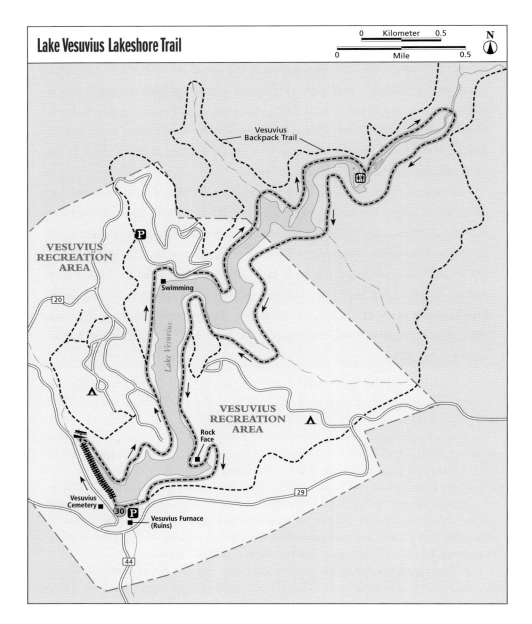

Lake Vesuvius Lakeshore Trail

Vesuvius
Backpack Trail

VESUVIUS
RECREATION
AREA

Swimming

Lake Vesuvius

20

Rock
Face

VESUVIUS
RECREATION
AREA

Vesuvius
Cemetery

30

Vesuvius Furnace
(Ruins)

29

44

Miles and Directions

0.0 From the parking lot, look toward the dam and a trailhead kiosk. Start at the dam. Take the stairs past the spillway to the top of the dam and cross it. Pick up the boardwalk and walk along it over the water.

0.3 The boardwalk ends at the boat launch. Cross the boat launch and see a trailhead sign for the Lakeview Trail and the Vesuvius Backpack Trail. Enter the woods here.

0.4 Pass a red-blazed junction for the Rock House Trail to the left. Continue straight, paralleling the lakeside. You will soon find yourself directly across from the dam.

0.7 Pass a stand of cedars and cross a long footbridge. Soon a large rock face will come into view across the lake.

1.2 An old doubletrack joins the trail from behind. In a few hundred feet, another doubletrack comes in from the side.

1.3 A wooden post indicates a junction. The backpack trail, blazed with a yellow dot, heads off to the left. Continue straight, along the Lakeshore Trail, blazed with the blue dot.

1.7 The trail comes out at the beach area and restroom/concession building. Water should be available here during summer. Walk past the beach and concession building and pick up the trail again behind the chain-link fence. Look to the trees for blazes.

2.0 The trail rounds a bend and ascends the ridge, now overlooking the lake and heading north. In another 0.5 mile the trail begins to descend again to the lake.

2.7 Cross a footbridge and enter a more mature forest, including a nice stand of cedars. The trail zigzags back and forth to cross side drainages. Ascend again to the top of a rock outcropping, which could serve as a nice lunch rock.

3.4 The trail descends to a fork. Although the right fork is well worn, don't take it. Look for the blazes along the left fork and descend to the bottomlands. **FYI:** In another 0.5 mile, look for a good water hole.

4.0 Come to a junction. Straight ahead is the backpack trail. Take a right and cross Storms Creek to remain on the Lakeshore Trail. Begin the return trip now, walking south and west, on the east side of the lake.

4.3 Come to another junction marked with wooden signposts and blazes. Follow the blazes out of the floodplain and up the ridge. Pass hemlocks on the right, then slowly descend the ridge back down to a couple of stream crossings.

5.8 Reach another rock outcropping that could serve as a nice lunch spot.

6.5 Pass the Whiskey Run Loop Trail on the left (blazed red) and keep walking until the swimming area comes into view across the lake. In a few hundred feet, you will see a side trail to the right, which leads to a bench.

6.7 The other end of the Whiskey Run Trail comes in from the left. Cross the footbridge and stay lakeside.

7.2 A series of large rock outcroppings culminate in a large, protruding rock face, a popular spot for recreation area users. Round the corner to begin the last leg of the hike.

7.7 Arrive at the top of the earthen dam. Follow the stairs down.

7.8 Arrive back at the Vesuvius Furnace parking lot.

Hike Information

Local information: Lawrence County Convention and Visitors Bureau, South Point; (800) 408-1334; www.lawrencecountyohio.org/convention

Accommodations: Lake Vesuvius Recreation Area has 2 campgrounds, Oak Hill and Iron Ridge; (740) 534-6500 or www.reservation.gov. Back-country camping is allowed in the national forest, but only outside the recreation area boundaries.

Lake Katharine State Nature Preserve

The beautiful 5.4-mile trail system in Lake Katharine Preserve is unparalleled in springtime. Home to the northernmost range of umbrella and bigleaf magnolia trees, it can look as though the forest itself is one big bloom. That also includes the native mountain laurel, dogwood, redbud, and tulip trees. And as if that's not enough, look underfoot for the hundreds of wildflower species. Walk over the earthen dam that creates Lake Katharine on your way to a cascading waterfall and a hemlock forest. Then find yourself pinched between Little Salt Lick on one side and Sharon conglomerate outcroppings on the other.

Start: Calico Bush and Salt Creek trailhead next to the parking lot

Distance: 5.4-mile trail system

Hiking time: About 2 to 3 hours

Difficulty: Moderate due to length and several ascents and descents, including stairways

Trail surface: Dirt trail with some boardwalks and stairs

Blaze: None

Best season: Flowering trees are showy in May and June.

Other trail users: Hikers only

Canine compatibility: Dogs not permitted

Water: No potable water is available along the hike; bring your own.

Land status: State nature preserve

Nearest town: Jackson

Fees and permits: None

Schedule: Open daylight hours year-round

Maps: USGS quad: Jackson

Trail contact: Lake Katharine Nature Preserve, Jackson; (740) 380-8919; http://ohiodnr.com/location/lake_katharine/tabid/904/Default.aspx

Finding the trailhead: From SR 93 on the north side of Jackson, turn west on Bridge Street (SR 93 turns to the east). Stay to the right where the road curves at the old-fashioned traffic light and Bridge Street becomes State Street. In about 1.5 miles you will cross two sets of railroad tracks. Just past the second set of tracks, turn right onto Lake Katharine Road, marked by a brown sign. Follow the road 2 miles to the parking area. *DeLorme: Ohio Atlas & Gazetteer:* Page 79 D4. GPS: N39 5.17' / W82 40.17'.

The Hike

The forest in Lake Katharine State Nature Preserve seems like one giant bloom in the spring. Go then and link all three trails in the preserve to take in all the preserve's highlights, including a cascading waterfall, a quiet lake, towering rock walls, wildflowers, and flowering shrubs and trees—including three species of native magnolia trees.

Start at the parking area next to the former Camp Arrowhead lodge. Take a nature trail brochure from the trailhead kiosk, then walk past the Calico Bush and Salt Creek trailhead sign and through a young successional forest. When you branch off to the

A waterfall downstream of Lake Katharine

left onto the Calico Bush Trail, stop to take in the self-guided nature trail. Calico bush is a less common name for mountain laurel, a woody shrub that lines a portion of the trail and blooms from May to June. The midsize trees you see blooming in June are umbrella magnolias. This area is at the uppermost portion of the bigleaf magnolia's range, so these trees are quite rare in Ohio. Their blooms are large and beautiful, and their leaves grow up to 3 feet in length.

By the time you come to the junction with the Pine Ridge Trail, you will have already recognized more of the natural features Lake Katharine has to offer: stands of hemlock and Sharon conglomerate outcroppings. If you look closely at the rock, you can see that it's made up of rounded quartz pebbles embedded in sandstone. This rock is evidence of both many years of sedimentation and the fact that moving water shaped the quartz into its smooth, rounded condition. The trail then takes you across the earthen dam that creates Lake Katharine, named after the wife of Edwin A. Jones, who (along with James J. McKitterick) purchased and later donated the land for a preserve. The preserve purchased more land with federal land and water conservation money in 1976. Canoeing and fishing on Lake Katharine are available by permit only.

Cardinal flower

Just past the dam is a beautiful spot where water cascades down the rocky bottom of Rock Run Creek. Continue upland among the hemlocks, oaks, and hickories. The trail eventually works its way back down to Little Salt Lick. Spend nearly the rest of the hike walking between rock outcroppings and the creek. Wildflowers are abundant here. In fact, Jackson County is reported to be the most biologically diverse of all Ohio counties. Look for common flowering plants such as spring beauty, Solomon's seal, and trillium. You might also get a glimpse of less common species as well, such as the stemless lady's slipper. Tulip trees dominate the canopy here.

The trail is in good shape and is only marked at junctions. Boardwalks and stairs allow you to walk the trails in all types of weather.

Miles and Directions

0.0 Start the hike next to the parking lot at the trailhead sign for the Calico Bush and Salt Creek Trails.

0.3 Come to a staggered junction for all three trails. Turn left, following the sign for the Calico Bush Trail.

0.9 Come to a junction with the Pine Ridge Trail. Continue straight.

1.1 Cross the earthen dam and then cross the stream over a footbridge.

2.0 Take a short spur to the right for an overlook.

2.3 The trail descends to the creek by way of switchbacks.

3.3 Arrive again at the staggered junction of all three trails. Keep walking straight ahead, following the signs for the Salt Creek Trail. **Option:** Return directly to the parking lot by taking a right.

4.0 Come to the junction for the short and long loops. Take a left and cross the boardwalk to take the long loop. (**FYI:** At the end of the boardwalk, look for a very large old sweetgum tree.) **Option:** Take the short loop to return to the parking lot.

4.5 Approach a recess cave on the right. The somewhat faint trail turns left here, away from the cave.

5.0 The trail turns right, away from the creek, and ascends to an old road.

5.1 A sign indicates a right turn, off the road and over the drainage.

5.3 Come to a junction with the short loop. Turn left to finish the hike.

5.4 Arrive back at the parking lot.

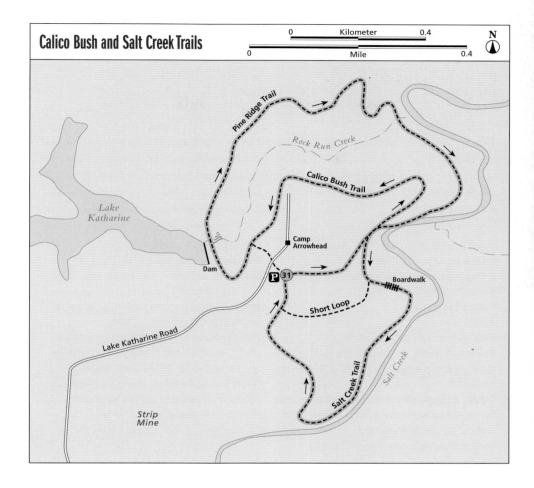

Calico Bush and Salt Creek Trails

Pine Ridge Trail

Rock Run Creek

Calico Bush Trail

Lake Katharine

Camp Arrowhead

Dam

P 31

Short Loop

Boardwalk

Lake Katharine Road

Salt Creek Trail

Salt Creek

Strip Mine

Hike Information

Local information: Jackson Area Chamber, (740) 286-2722, www.jacksonohio.org/tourism.html

Local events and attractions: Leo Petroglyph is about 5 miles northwest of Jackson; contact the Ohio Historical Society at (800) 686-1535 or visit www.ohiohistory.org/places/leopetro/index.html.

The Jackson County Apple Festival is held the third full week of Sept; www.jacksonapplefestival.com.

Accommodations: Lake Alma State Park, Wellston; (740) 384-4474 or (866) 644-6727 for reservations; http://parks.ohiodnr.gov/lake alma

Restaurants: Michael's ice cream shop on Main Street in Jackson has been in business more than 100 years; (740) 288-7577.

Hike tours: Ranger-led hikes are offered; contact the preserve for up-to-date information.

Organizations: Columbus Audubon, (614) 545-5497, www.columbusaudubon.org

32 Logan Trail–North Loop

Tar Hollow State Forest and State Park

The 12.1-mile north loop of the Logan Trail begins and ends at a fire tower that you can climb to get a view of the deciduous forest unfolding in all directions. But the beauty is in the details. Look for wild irises and other spring wildflowers as well as edible plants such as mushrooms, berries, and pawpaws. Hike this well-constructed trail through mature forest, clear-cuts, and successional (growing back) woods.

Start: Fire tower off FR 3
Distance: 12.1-mile loop
Hiking time: About 4 to 6 hours
Difficulty: Difficult due to length and hills
Trail surface: Dirt
Blaze: Red
Best season: Apr through Oct
Other trail users: Hunters (in season); watch out for the errant mountain biker or horse-back rider.
Canine compatibility: Leashed dogs permitted
Water: Available at Sheep Pasture Picnic Area, north of the fire tower on FR 3
Land status: State forest and state park

Nearest town: Adelphi
Fees and permits: None
Schedule: Tar Hollow State Forest open daily from 6:30 a.m. to 11 p.m.
Maps: Buckeye Trail Association section map: Scioto Trail; USGS quad: Hallsville
Trail contacts: Tar Hollow State Park, Laurel-ville; (740) 887-4818; http://parks.ohiodnr .gov/tarhollow. Tar Hollow State Forest, c/o Scioto Trail State Forest, Waverly; (740) 663-2538; http://ohiodnr.com/forests/tarhollow/ tabid/5168/Default.aspx.

Finding the trailhead: From SR 327 about halfway between SR 56 and US 50, turn west onto FR 10, marked with a park entrance sign. Travel 3.7 miles to a fork. Turn left (south) onto FR 3 and travel another 1.5 miles to the fire tower. Park on the grass or along the pullout. *DeLorme: Ohio Atlas & Gazetteer:* Page 78 A4. GPS: N39 22.51' / W82 45.76'.

The Hike

The Tar Hollow region was named for the pine tar that settlers extracted from native pitch pine trees. The tar was used for balms and as a lubricant for machinery. When you start your hike at Tar Hollow from the fire tower, you will immediately see pine trees. But climb up to the top of the tower and get a view of a deciduous forest stretching in all directions. From here you can get an idea of the terrain that lies ahead.

You can spend as much time as you desire hiking Tar Hollow State Forest's 50-plus miles of trails. One of the nicest is the north loop of the Logan Trail, which is off-limits to equestrians and mountain bikers. The trail is a narrow footpath for its entire length and generally has a backcountry feel. The Logan Trail was constructed by Boy

Dwarf iris

Scouts in the 1950s and is still maintained by Boy Scouts today. It's named after Chief Logan, who was the leader of the Mingo Nation in the late eighteenth century.

This particular hike is also a lesson in forest ecology and the politics of multiple use. Since Ohio's state forests are managed for timber, you will begin the hike by walking in a mature forest but will later skirt a former clear-cut and then walk through a successional forest.

Begin from the fire tower at the top of the ridge and gradually descend to the lowlands. This oak-hickory forest has some mature trees and a brilliant understory. In springtime wild irises are particularly showy, as are other wildflowers such as trillium, wild geranium, and fire pink. A wide variety of ferns help blanket the forest floor as well, including the black-stemmed maidenhair fern. Mushroom hunting is a popular activity in Tar Hollow, where the edible morel and chicken-of-the-woods grow.

The trail is well built, staying along ridgetops and along streambeds for the most part, reducing the number of ascents and descents on this long loop. When exploring along the streams, look for salamanders—several species live here. You may even get a glimpse of the conspicuous five-lined skink, identifiable by its bright blue tail. Don't expect to see the timber rattlesnake, however. Although it is known to inhabit Tar Hollow State Forest, this elusive reptile is on the federal endangered species list.

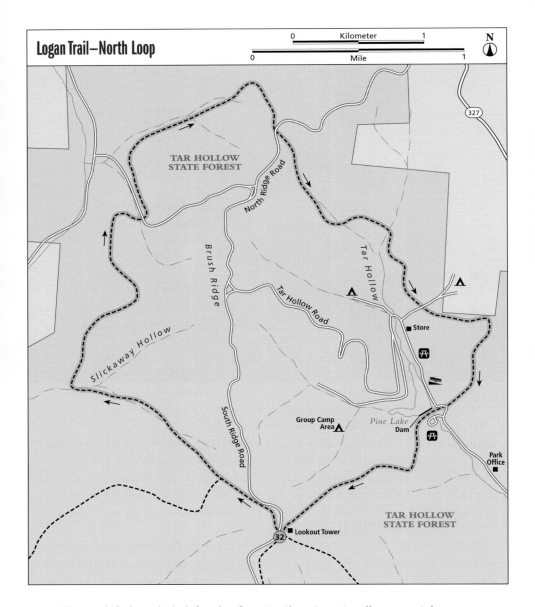

0   Kilometer   1

0   Mile   1

N

TAR HOLLOW
STATE FOREST

327

North Ridge Road

Brush Ridge

Tar Hollow

Tar Hollow Road

Slickaway Hollow

■ Store

South Ridge Road

Group Camp
Area

Pine Lake
Dam

Park
Office
■

TAR HOLLOW
STATE FOREST

32   ■ Lookout Tower

The trail feels secluded for the first 5 miles. Occasionally you might see some evidence of former land use. For example, look to see old logging roads, recognizable by flat grades along the slopes. About a mile after crossing FR 16, you will encounter a former clear-cut just off of the trail. These 19 acres were cut in November 2001. About a mile after that, you will be walking in a successional forest, which was clear-cut in sections totaling 126 acres from 1992 to 1994. Note the young trees and a lot of sunlight. There is more than one cache of black raspberries along this section of trail. Also notice the invasive Japanese honeysuckle and poison ivy.

The trail then cuts through Tar Hollow State Park, where you are most likely to run into other hikers along the trail. Walk past a campground and along the earthen dam that creates Pine Lake before reentering the state forest. The last section of the trail, between the park and the fire tower, is joined by the Buckeye Trail, marked with its trademark blue blazes.

A long hike like the Logan Trail is perhaps most comfortable, weather-wise, in spring or fall. Contact the state forest, however, to learn the dates of deer rifle season, since hiking during that time would be ill-advised.

Miles and Directions

0.0 Start at the fire tower. Look across FR 3 for the red trailhead sign.

0.2 Come to a fork. Follow the sign to the right to stay on the Logan Trail. To the left, the trail eventually peters out.

0.4 Walk straight through a four-way intersection, keeping an eye on the red blazes.

0.6 Come to the fork where the north and south loops of the Logan Trail diverge. Take a right.

2.9 A side trail joins from the right. Continue straight.

4.3 Cross FR 16.

6.3 Pass an orange gate and come to FR 4. There are no blazes here. Turn right and walk on the road for about 200 feet. Look for a red blaze and the trail across the road.

7.4 Approach a fork. Take the left fork, following the blazes. To the right is a side trail to a campground.

7.6 Pass another side trail on the right, leading to the campground.

7.7 Come to a four-way intersection. Continue straight, crossing the stream.

8.0 Just before you walk into a campsite, the trail turns sharply left.

10.0 Cross FR 10. Look to your right for the earthen dam that creates Pine Lake. Walk alongside the dam, crossing to the other side. Then cross the footbridge over the spillway and pick up the trail again.

10.1 Hit a fork, marked with a red post. Turn right, ascending the ridge. In about 20 feet cross a doubletrack dirt road.

11.3 The Buckeye Trail joins from the left. Continue straight, following red and blue blazes.

11.6 Walk straight past an old trail and sign for the group campground.

12.0 Pass a trail on the right that leads out to the road.

12.1 Arrive back at the fire tower.

Hike Information

Local information: Ross-Chillicothe Convention and Visitors Bureau, (800) 413-4118, http://visitchillicotheohio.com

Local events and attractions: Horse rentals and mountain bike trails are available in the park. The *Tecumseh!* outdoor drama is presented in Chillicothe; (866) 775-0700 or tecumsehdrama.com.

Accommodations: Tar Hollow State Park campground; call (866) 644-6727 for reservations.

Hocking Hills State Park

Begin walking the 5 miles from Old Man's Cave to Ash Cave and it won't take long to see why this is one of the state's most popular trails. Descend into Old Man's Creek Gorge and walk by rock features with such names as the Devil's Bathtub and the Sphinx Head. Explore Old Man's Cave, a large recess cave of Blackhand sandstone, before continuing downstream in the gorge all the way to Cedar Falls, the area's highest-volume waterfall. Then continue on in an upland forest to Ash Cave, the state's largest recess cave, complete with another waterfall and a forest of old-growth hemlocks.

Start: Old Man's Cave Visitor Center

Distance: 10.6-mile out-and-back or 5.5-mile point-to-point

Hiking time: About 5 to 7 hours

Difficulty: Difficult due to length and a few portions with steep stairs

Trail surface: Wide path; mostly dirt with boardwalks and stone stairs

Blaze: Blue

Best season: Spring through fall and in winter after a snowfall

Other trail users: Hikers only

Canine compatibility: Leashed dogs permitted

Water: Available at Old Man's Cave Visitor Center, Cedar Falls parking area, and Ash Cave trailhead

Land status: State park

Nearest town: Logan

Fees and permits: None

Schedule: Open daily year-round

Maps: Buckeye Trail Association section map: Old Man's Cave; USGS quad: South Bloomingville

Trail contact: Hocking Hills State Park, Logan; (740) 385-6842; http://parks.ohiodnr.gov/hockinghills

Special considerations: Hiking off-trail is illegal.

Finding the trailhead: From US 33 in Logan, turn south on SR 664 and travel 10.2 miles. Pass the campground on your left and then turn left into the large parking area, toward the Old Man's Cave Visitor Center. Follow the walkway from the parking area to the visitor center, gift shop, restrooms, and concession and pick up the trailhead to the left (east) of the building. The trail is marked with blue blazes, as this is also part of the Buckeye Trail. *DeLorme: Ohio Atlas & Gazetteer:* Page 79 A5. GPS: N39 26.08' / W82 32.48'.

The Hike

The hike between Old Man's Cave and Ash Cave is rich in both natural and human history, making it a favorite among many hikers. The trail is largely bordered by sandstone walls and features waterfalls, cliffs, hemlock forests, and abundant ferns and wildflowers. If solitude is what you're looking for, try this hike on a weekday or in winter.

The Lower Falls at Old Man's Cave

Beginning at Old Man's Cave, it's 2.7 miles to Cedar Falls, where you can turn around and take the rim trail back or continue on. It's another 2.8 miles to the Ash Cave trailhead. This trail is named after Emma "Grandma" Gatewood, an Ohio native who was the first woman to through-hike the Appalachian Trail (at age sixty-seven) and a charter member of the Buckeye Trail Association.

You can spend half the day exploring the first half-mile of the trail. As soon as you descend into the gorge, walk upstream, passing the Devil's Bathtub whirlpool on your way to the 30-foot upper falls. Turning back and walking downstream, take notice of all the hard work the Works Progress Administration (WPA) put into the park in the 1930s, creating trails, stone stairs, and tunnels leading to Old Man's Cave.

Old Man's Cave is named after a hermit, Richard Roe, who made it his home in the eighteenth century. Actually a recess cave, eroded weaker layers of Blackhand sandstone carved by water through long periods of time have left a large hollow opening in the cliff face. Old Man's is 250 feet long, 85 feet high, and 50 feet deep. From Old Man's Cave, look downstream to view the Sphinx Head rock formation.

Continue walking to the 40-foot lower falls, larger in volume than the upper falls and often flanked by rock-skipping youngsters. As you continue downstream, enjoy

"GRANDMA" GATEWOOD

The trail from Old Man's Cave to Ash Cave is known as the Grandma Gatewood Trail. It's named after Emma "Grandma" Gatewood, an Ohio native who is best known as the first woman to through-hike the Appalachian Trail (AT). But that's where the story just starts to get interesting. Grandma Gatewood completed her through-hike in 1955 at age sixty-seven—and in tennis shoes, to boot! She was clearly unfazed by the demands of keeping up with the latest advancements in gear technology. Her provisions included a blanket, a shower curtain, a tin cup, beef jerky, and cheese. She didn't even carry a backpack; she just slung a sack over one shoulder. Some refer to Grandma Gatewood as "the patron saint of ultralightweight backpackers."

Her advice to other long-distance hikers? "Head is more important than heel." And as if once wasn't enough, this mother of eleven through-hiked the AT again in 1957 and in 1964. Reportedly Old Man's Cave to Ash Cave remained her favorite hike. She began the annual Hocking Hills Winter Hike, now the largest event of the year, and she was a founding member of the Buckeye Trail Association (BTA). She died in 1973 at age eighty-five.

the sandstone walls, ferns, hemlocks, and spring wildflowers, including trillium, wild columbine, jack-in-the-pulpit, Dutchman's-breeches, trout lilies, and violets. In July and August look for the endangered round-leafed catchfly growing out of rocky spots. Its brilliant red color will catch your eye.

As you approach the confluence of Old Man's and Queer Creeks, the valley widens and large water-loving white-barked sycamores fill the valley. Look for the smaller, water-loving musclewood trees as well, identifiable by their smooth, sinewy bark.

The trail turns east and takes you along Queer Creek, where the gorge walls are farther apart and still stunning. Approaching Cedar Falls, the gorge again narrows and the path skirts tall, vertical rock faces. Cedar Falls, 55 feet high, are the largest by volume in the Hocking Hills area. They were misnamed by early white settlers, who mistook the hemlocks for cedars.

From Cedar Falls the trail ascends out of the gorge and becomes a mostly upland path in an oak-hickory forest until it arrives at the lip of Ash Cave. It's especially important to keep an eye on children and pets here and to watch your footing. Peer into the state's largest recess cave, measuring 700 feet long, 100 feet deep, and 90 feet high. It is named for the massive amounts of ashes found by early European settlers, believed to be leftovers from fires made by Native Americans over hundreds of years. Follow the rim and then descend into the cave and enjoy views from within of a trickling waterfall and some of the biggest hemlock trees in the state.

The remainder of the trail is a wheelchair-accessible paved path out to the parking lot, pit toilets, and water. You can return by way of car or bicycle shuttle or by foot the way you came.

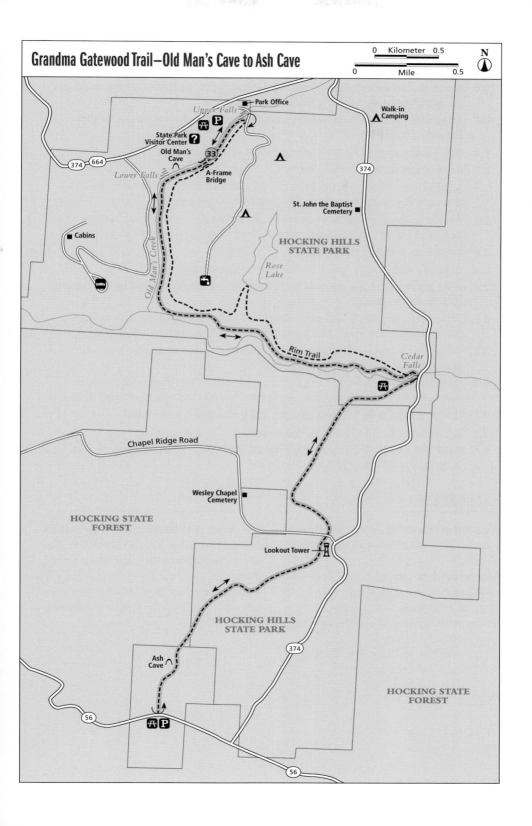

Grandma Gatewood Trail—Old Man's Cave to Ash Cave

0 Kilometer 0.5

0 Mile 0.5

N

Upper Falls

Park Office

Walk-in Camping

State Park Visitor Center

Old Man's Cave

A-Frame Bridge

374 664

Lower Falls

Old Man's Creek

33

374

Cabins

St. John the Baptist Cemetery

HOCKING HILLS STATE PARK

Rose Lake

Rim Trail

Cedar Falls

Chapel Ridge Road

Wesley Chapel Cemetery

HOCKING STATE FOREST

Lookout Tower

HOCKING HILLS STATE PARK

374

Ash Cave

56

HOCKING STATE FOREST

56

Miles and Directions

0.0 Start from the Old Man's Cave Visitor Center. Following the blue blazes, descend steps into the gorge. Take a left and walk upstream to the upper falls.

0.2 Arrive at the upper falls, then turn around and continue downstream, passing the steps you walked down on.

0.5 Walk through a stone tunnel and emerge in front of Old Man's Cave.

0.7 Descend stairs to a view of the lower falls.

1.3 Approach the confluence of Old Man's and Queer Creeks. Take a left, following Queer Creek and the signs to Cedar Falls. Then pass benches and a trail sign.

1.7 The trail moves away from the creek and up and around the hillside. Do not continue straight on the old trail, as conditions are slick and dangerous. Follow the blue blazes.

2.0 Take the stone steps up and to the left.

2.6 Come to a T-intersection. Take a left, following the sign for Cedar Falls.

2.7 Arrive at Cedar Falls. Take the stairs out of the gorge, following signs for Cedar Falls parking (blue and yellow blazes).

2.8 At the top of the stairs, look across the road for a post with a blue blaze. Walk toward the post and then to the orange gate. Walk along the gravel road past the orange gate.

3.2 Come to a junction with another gravel road on the right; continue straight. In about 100 yards the gravel road forks; take the left fork.

3.9 Cross Chapel Ridge Road and walk across a gravel parking lot. Pass an orange gate and walk to the fire tower. The trail continues past the fire tower and then joins a road grade.

4.2 The trail leaves the road grade to the right; look for the double blue blazes.

5.1 Approach the rim of Ash Cave. Take the wooden stairs down into the cave.

5.5 Finish at the Ash Cave trailhead. Return the way you came, or pick up your shuttle here.

10.6 Arrive back at the visitor center.

Hike Information

Local information: Hocking Hills Tourism Association, (800) HOCKING, www.explorehocking hills.com

Accommodations: Hocking Hills State Park campground and cottages; call (866) 644-6727 for reservations.

Restaurants: Hocking Hills State Park dining lodge, (740) 385-2300

Inn and Spa at Cedar Falls, (800) 653-2557, http://innatcedarfalls.com

Hike tours: Naturalist-led hikes are offered in season, including the annual Hocking Hills Winter Hike; contact the park for up-to-date information.

Organizations: Friends of Hocking Hills State Park, (877) 403-4477, www.friendsofhocking hills.org

34 Rim and Gorge Trails

Conkles Hollow State Nature Preserve

One of the state's best trails, Conkles Hollow provides a rarity in Ohio: vistas. From sandstone overlooks, view the hollow, rock outcroppings, and forested ridges unfolding into the distance. Walk around the rim of this beautiful hollow, and be sure to hike the Gorge Trail as well, where wildflowers bloom in springtime profusion. A hemlock forest, diverse wildlife, and a waterfall are other attractions along this 3.1-mile trail system.

Start: Parking lot
Distance: 3.1-mile trail system
Hiking time: About 1 to 2 hours
Difficulty: The Rim Trail is moderate due to a steep ascent out of the gorge and some difficult footing. The Gorge Trail is an easy, short and flat trail.
Trail surface: Dirt
Blaze: None; trails are well traveled and marked at junctions.
Best season: Apr and May for wildflowers, Sept and Oct for fall foliage

Other trail users: Hikers only
Canine compatibility: Dogs not permitted
Water: Available at the parking lot
Land status: State nature preserve
Nearest town: Logan
Fees and permits: None
Schedule: Open daily from dawn to dusk
Maps: USGS quad: South Bloomingville
Trail contact: Conkles Hollow State Nature Preserve, Logan; (614) 265-6453; http://ohiodnr.com/location/conkles_hollow/tabid/884/Default.aspx

Finding the trailhead: From US 33 in Logan, turn south on SR 664 and drive 12 miles (pass the Hocking Hills State Park campground and visitor center) to SR 374. Turn right (north) and travel 1 mile to Big Pine Road. Turn right again and continue 0.2 mile to the parking lot on the left. *DeLorme: Ohio Atlas & Gazetteer:* Page 79 A5. GPS: N39 27.22' / W82 34.42'.

The Hike

One of Ohio's most scenic hikes, Conkles Hollow offers the Rim Loop Trail, which loops 200 feet above the gorge, affording views of nearby and faraway ridges, waterfalls, forests, and sandstone outcroppings. This is not a trail for those with a fear of heights. The out-and-back Gorge Trail, which lies between walls only 100 to 300 feet apart, will take you through some of the most biodiverse areas in the state. You can expect to see as many as fifty wildflower species blooming at once in the springtime while hiking to a beautiful waterfall tumbling into a box canyon.

Conkles Hollow lies several miles beyond the reach of the last glacier to come through Ohio. But like so many other places in the state, the glacier affected this area drastically. Formerly part of the north-flowing Teas River Valley, the waterways in

Rock outcrops at Conkles Hollow

this region were pushed—and sometimes reversed—to their current configuration, flowing south to the Ohio River. This highly biodiverse region offers myriad variations in topography, soils, and microclimes. More than 1,200 plant species grow in the Hocking Hills region.

The hike begins with an ascent to the top of the gorge's rim, where you'll be pleased with a rare treat in Ohio: views from rock outcroppings that allow you to see into the distance. Take in the hardwood forests on the ridgetops, peer into the hollow below, and view the sandstone outcroppings themselves. Just before the turnaround point on the trail, an observation deck allows you to view a 90-foot seasonal waterfall dropping into the gorge.

But don't just hike the Rim Trail and neglect all the life there is to see in the gorge itself. The cool microclime in Conkles Hollow supports towering evergreen hemlock, Canada yew, and yellow birch. Spring wildflowers include Dutchman's-breeches, trillium, Solomon's seal, violets, and a number of native orchid species, to name just a few. An unnamed tributary to Big Pine Creek has carved a narrow gorge through layers of sandstone, providing 200 feet's worth of living geology lesson in how weathering affects different types of rock. The soft layers of Blackhand sandstone have eroded away faster than surrounding rock, leaving recess caves and creating slump blocks, which now lie in the valley. These slump blocks are covered in ferns, wildflowers, and hemlocks.

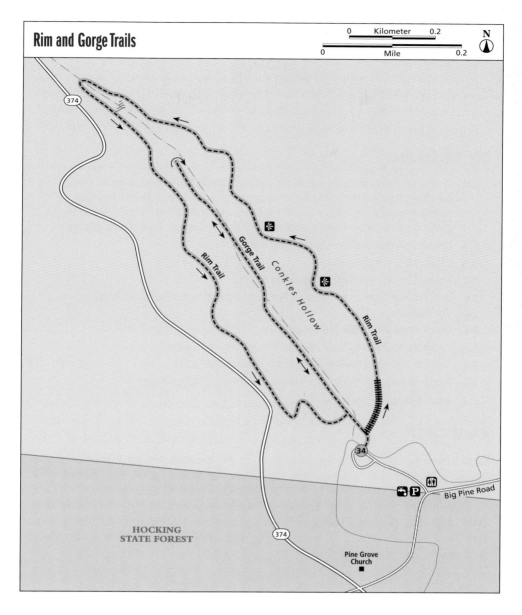

You can hike all the way to the bottom of the waterfall, where it pours into a nar-row, moist greenspace. Stop and listen for a minute to the falling water, breezes, and the many nesting and migrating birds found here, including the flutelike song of the hermit thrush and the intensifying call of the ovenbird.

Humans have inhabited the hollow and its surroundings for generations. Conkles is named after a German immigrant, W. J. Conkle, who carved his initials into the rock in 1797. Reportedly, old-timers remember another carving in the hollow: an arrow marking the spot across the gorge where a treasure of sorts was buried. As the story goes, a small group of Native Americans robbed some European settlers on the Ohio River, then returned to this hollow and stashed the money in a high-up recess cave. They reached the hiding place by felling one of two hemlocks growing near the cave. They used the hemlock as a ladder and then dropped it to the ground, planning to return later and use the second hemlock to access the goods. But when they returned a storm had felled the other hemlock, so the money remains in the cave to this day.

Miles and Directions

0.0 Start at the bridge along the cul-de-sac portion of the far end of the parking lot. Cross the creek and follow the trail to the left as it passes an informational kiosk and then approaches the stairs to begin the Rim Trail. Turn right and ascend the stairs out of the gorge. At the top of the stairs, the trail curves left and makes its way to the gorge's rim.

0.4 Come to the first sandstone outcropping overlook.

0.5 Reach the second overlook.

0.9 Arrive at the wooden overlook above the waterfall.

1.0 Walk over the creek on a footbridge. Return on the west side of the gorge, walking downstream.

1.7 Descend the stairs back into the gorge.

1.9 Reach the trailhead for the Gorge Trail. Turn left and walk upstream.

2.4 Come to the end of the Gorge Trail, at the bottom of the falls.

3.0 Return to the Gorge Trail trailhead the way you came. Continue straight.

3.1 Arrive back at the starting point.

Hike Information

Local information: Hocking Hills Tourism Association, (800) HOCKING, www.explorehocking hills.com

Logan-Hocking Chamber of Commerce, (740) 385-6836, www.logan-hockingchamber .com

Local events and attractions: Hocking Hills State Park (740-385-6842; http://parks.ohio dnr.gov/hockinghills) surrounds Conkles Hollow, a state nature preserve; the park is home to excellent hikes, including Old Man's Cave to Ash Cave, Cantwell Cliffs, and Rockhouse.

Rockbridge State Nature Preserve, Rockbridge; http://ohiodnr.com/location/rockbridge/ tabid/959/Default.aspx

The Washboard Music Festival is held in Logan, usually on Father's Day weekend; www .washboardmusicfestival.com.

Accommodations: Hocking Hills State Park campground and cottages; call (866) 644-6727 for reservations. More than 700 cabin, bed-and-breakfast, and lodge rooms are located in the Hocking Hills region; visit www .explorehockinghills.com for a listing.

Restaurants: Inn & Spa at Cedar Falls, (800) 653-2557, http://innatcedarfalls.com

Hike tours: Naturalist-led hikes are offered throughout the year. Contact the Department of Natural Areas and Preserves for a schedule at (614) 265-6561; www.ohiodnr.com/dnap.

35 Hemlock to Creekside Meadows Loop

Clear Creek Metro Park

As you drive southeast from Columbus on US 33, the flat landscape is abruptly interrupted by short but steep ridges and hollows. This topographic change marks where the last glacier ended—where Midwest gives way to Appalachia. Glacial meltwater created the beautiful Clear Creek, which today is surrounded by a biodiverse forest, sandstone outcroppings, and many bird species that call this place home. Begin and end next to Clear Creek and make a 3-mile loop on the appropriately named Hemlock and Fern Trails—there are about forty fern species in the park.

Start: Pullout/trailhead on Clear Creek Road
Distance: 3-mile loop
Hiking time: About 1 to 1.5 hours
Difficulty: Easy; short and well maintained
Trail surface: Dirt
Blaze: Hemlock Trail, blue hemlock tree; Fern Trail, green fern; Creekside Meadows Trail, yellow flower. Posts with trail maps mark all intersections.
Best season: Apr through Oct
Other trail users: Hikers only

Canine compatibility: Leashed dogs permitted only on the Pet Trail at the Barnebey-Hambleton Day Use Area and in picnic areas
Water: No potable water in the park; bring your own.
Land status: Columbus Metro Park
Nearest towns: Lancaster, Logan
Fees and permits: None
Schedule: Open daily 6:30 a.m. until dark
Maps: USGS quad: Rockbridge
Trail contact: Columbus Metro Parks, Westerville; (614) 508-8000; www.metroparks.net

Finding the trailhead: From US 33 between Lancaster and Logan, turn west onto CR 116 (Clear Creek Road), marked with a small brown sign. Drive 2.4 miles to the fishing access pullout on the left, across from the Hemlock Trailhead. It's marked with a PED XING sign. If you hit the Fern Picnic Area, you've gone too far. *DeLorme: Ohio Atlas & Gazetteer:* Page 69 D5. GPS: N39 35.46' / W82 35.25'.

The Hike

Although it's part of the Columbus Metro Parks system, Clear Creek is located in the Hocking Hills region, 30 miles southeast of the I-270 outerbelt. Metro Parks made a good choice by going a little farther afield to purchase this special land in 1996. Unlike the more urban parks, Clear Creek is arguably underutilized and has a well-maintained system of 12 miles of hiking trails.

Geologists estimate that the Wisconsinan Glacier terminated its advance just north and west of today's Clear Creek Valley some 10,000 to 18,000 years ago. Clear Creek is now the central feature of the valley and the park. Its riffling waters sparkle

Horsetail, aka scouring rush, along the Creekside Meadows Trail

in the sun as anglers fish for brown trout, smallmouth bass, and rock bass. Tributaries to Clear Creek make their way through narrow, verdant drainages, often lined by sandstone cliffs. By hiking the Hemlock Trail and returning by way of the Fern and Creekside Meadows Trails, you can get a nice sampling of all the park has to offer.

Begin near Clear Creek and walk along a ravine. This cool, moist environment is home to its namesake hemlocks and ferns. Naturalists have identified forty fern species in the park. The more common ones you'll see include Christmas, wood, maidenhair, and sensitive fern, as well as ebony spleenwort and polypody fern. As you ascend the 300-foot ridge, conditions get drier and the forest becomes dominated by red and white oak. If you are observant, you may notice some young stump sprouts of American chestnut. These trees will succumb to the chestnut blight before reaching fruit-bearing age. Near the intersection of the Fern and Cemetery Ridge Trails, look for mountain laurel and reindeer moss, species usually associated with Southern Appalachian balds.

After descending again to the creek valley on the Fern Trail, join the Creekside Meadows Trail and follow it back to the trailhead. Notice a thick understory of

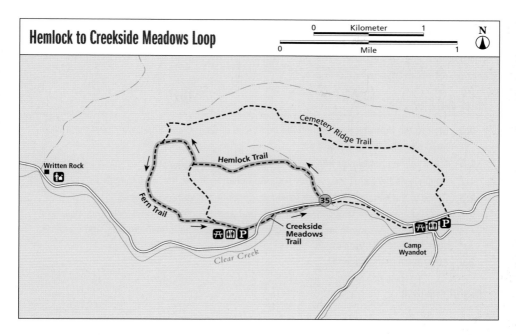

0   Kilometer   1

0   Mile   1

N

Cemetery Ridge Trail

Hemlock Trail

Written Rock

Fern Trail

35

Creekside
Meadows
Trail

Camp
Wyandot

Clear Creek

scouring rush (horsetail) growing alongside the creek, underneath the sycamores that lean over the water in search of sunlight. In the field near the Fern Picnic Area, look for late summer wildflowers such as wingstem, oxeye, sweet William, joe-pye weed, ironweed, and goldenrod.

In addition to the nearly 800 plants that grow in the Clear Creek watershed, more than 100 bird species call this place home (on average, 300 species of birds are found in Ohio each year). The nearby Prairie Warbler Trail allows you a chance to see some of the eighteen species of warbler that nest in the park. Moving up the food chain, deer and beavers are very active in the park. And if you're lucky, you might see a resident bobcat or signs of its presence.

Humans have called the Clear Creek Valley home for thousands of years. In the Written Rock recess cave, located along Clear Creek Road, there are V-shaped grooves cut into a sandstone boulder. Archaeologists believe these were ax polishers, used by the Late Woodland prehistoric peoples. Other evidence of human activity in the cave has been vandalized by more recent humans.

Like so many other preserves today, the fate of the land in the Clear Creek Valley could have easily been very different. Oscar Barnebey and the families of Allen F. Beck and Emily Benua owned much of the land in the Clear Creek Valley before it became a park. In the 1960s there was a proposal to dam the valley and create a reservoir. The project was defeated, however, and these individuals and families began donating land to Ohio State University and the Franklin County Metro Parks.

The Metro Parks system plans to keep Clear Creek in a "semiprimitive" condition, which means it will be protected from most development, even recreation-related development such as campgrounds and miniature golf. Several trails allow visitors to explore much of the park, but some areas are off-limits in order to protect rare and endangered species. Contact the park to learn about naturalist-led backcountry hikes that go off-trail and into these areas.

Miles and Directions

0.0 Start at the Hemlock trailhead on the north side of Clear Creek Road. Walk past the trailhead sign and follow the stream.

1.5 Come to the intersection with the Fern Trail. Turn right.

1.7 Continue straight past the junction with the Cemetery Ridge Trail on the right.

2.3 Come to the junction of the Fern Trail loop. Continue straight (downslope).

2.5 Arrive at Clear Creek Road. Cross the road and walk through the Fern Picnic Area. Pick up the Creekside Meadows Trail in the picnic area, marked with a trailhead sign, and continue straight, heading downstream.

3.0 Arrive back at the trailhead.

Hike Information

Local information: Hocking Hills Tourism Association, (800) HOCKING, www.explorehocking hills.com

Logan-Hocking Chamber of Commerce, (740) 385-6836, www.logan-hockingchamber .com

Local events and attractions: Nearby parks with excellent hikes include Rockbridge and Conkles Hollow Nature Preserves; (614) 265-6561 or www.ohiodnr.com/dnap.

Hocking Hills State Park is home to a number of excellent hikes, including short forays into Rock House and Cantwell Cliffs; (740) 385-4402 or http://parks.ohiodnr.gov/hockinghills.

The Washboard Music Festival is held in Logan, usually on Father's Day weekend; www .washboardmusicfestival.com.

Accommodations: Hocking Hills State Park campground and cottages; call (866) 644-6727 for reservations. More than 700 cabin, bed-and-breakfast, and lodge rooms are located in the Hocking Hills region; visit www .explorehockinghills.com for a listing.

Restaurants: Inn & Spa at Cedar Falls, (800) 653-2557, http://innatcedarfalls.com

Hike tours: Park naturalist programs are held evenings and on weekends. Contact the park for information; (614) 508-8000.

36 Peninsula to Olds Hollow Trail

Lake Hope State Park and Zaleski State Forest

Lake Hope is a dammed, salamander-shaped body of water that's the central feature of this state park, which is adjacent to Zaleski State Forest. Begin a 4.2-mile day hike from the Hope Furnace, a leftover from the region's bygone iron-smelting days. Walk along the lakeshore in a nice second-growth oak-hickory forest. Then head into the forest and walk by a recess cave and a pioneer cemetery and into a mini gorge before returning in a wetland area.

Start: Lake Hope Furnace parking lot
Distance: 4.2-mile figure eight
Hiking time: About 1.5 to 2.5 hours
Difficulty: Moderate due to length and hills, including a descent into a narrow and sometimes slick gorge
Trail surface: Dirt
Blaze: None, but part of Olds Hollow Trail follows Zaleski Backpack Trail, blazed orange.
Best season: Mid-Apr through mid-Oct
Other trail users: Hikers only

Canine compatibility: Leashed dogs permitted
Water: Available at the parking lot
Land status: State park
Nearest towns: Zaleski, McArthur
Fees and permits: None
Schedule: Open daily from dawn to dusk
Maps: USGS quad: Mineral
Trail contact: Lake Hope State Park, McArthur; (740) 596-4938; http://parks.ohiodnr.gov/lakehope

Finding the trailhead: From SR 56 south of Nelsonville, turn south onto SR 278 and travel 4.6 miles to the Hope Furnace parking lot on the right. *DeLorme: Ohio Atlas & Gazetteer:* Page 79 B7. GPS: N39 19.87' / W82 20.46'.

The Hike

Begin and end your hike at Lake Hope State Park at the namesake Hope Furnace, built in the nineteenth century as an iron ore smelter. Ohio was once one of the nation's leading iron producers, and some of the items made from the ore in this area included munitions for the Union Army during the Civil War. The forests here were cleared in order to fuel these furnaces, most of which had shut down by 1900. Since then a second-growth oak-hickory forest has come back nicely.

After exploring the furnace you will begin the Peninsula Trail by walking along the edge of Lake Hope, a salamander-shaped body of water created by an earthen dam stopping up Big Sandy Creek (also called Sandy Run), just upstream from its confluence with Raccoon Creek. All lakes in southeast Ohio are human-made, since the topography does not support natural lakes. They all take on the familiar look of dammed hollows. Although you are hiking along the water's edge, you will find

Lake Hope

yourself in an upland oak-hickory forest because this is actually an upland trail. Look along the lakeshore for signs of a very active beaver population. You should see their dens as well as dams and stumps. This path forms a circle around the dining lodge and cabins, making it very accessible to guests.

You can pick up the Olds Hollow Trail at the end of the Peninsula Trail. Cross the road and begin hiking both the Olds Hollow and Zaleski Backpack Trails. The Olds Hollow Trail diverges from the backpack trail and takes you to some interesting sights, including recess caves and an old pioneer cemetery, where the sandstone grave inscriptions are slowly eroding. This secluded hike also takes you through a small yet striking gorge. In springtime look on the forest floor for wildflowers, including such common species as wild geranium, bloodroot, and blue-eyed Mary. The rare yellow lady's slipper also blooms here. As you complete this loop you will walk parallel to a wetland area. Look here for water-loving birds, including ducks, kingfishers, and great blue herons. And as always, keep an eye out for wild turkeys and white-tailed deer.

▶ **Raccoon Creek, 99 miles long, is said to be the world's longest creek. One hundred miles would make it a river.**

Many other hiking options are available in Lake Hope State Park and Zaleski State Forest, including a 23.5-mile backpack loop with a nice 10-mile day-hike option along the backpack trail.

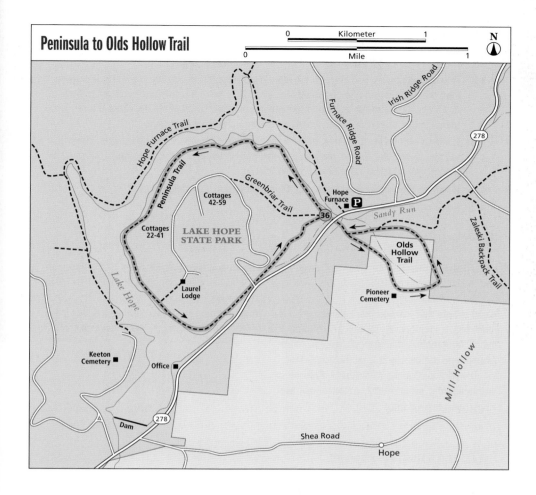

Peninsula to Olds Hollow Trail

Miles and Directions

0.0   Start at the Hope Furnace. After exploring the furnace walk to the road and turn right (south). Walk over the bridge, then look for wooden stairs to your right. Ascend the stairs and follow the path to a wooden footbridge. The trailhead is here, marked with a wooden sign. Walk into the woods. In less than 0.1 mile, cross a footbridge and then come to a fork. The Peninsula Trail goes both ways. Take the right fork.

1.6   Pass a connector trail to the lodge on the left. Continue straight, paralleling the lake.

1.9   Cross a footbridge and continue straight; the trail here moves away from the lake.

2.1   Cross the lodge road and follow the grass about 150 feet past the Welcome to Lake Hope State Park sign. You will see a wooden trailhead where you reenter the woods.

2.6   Hit a T-intersection and a wooden signpost directing you right to stay on the Peninsula Trail (left on the Greenbriar to the cabins and lodge).

2.9   Return to the first trail junction. Turn right across the footbridge and come out at the road.

3.0 Cross the road and pick up the trailhead for both the Olds Hollow Trail and the Zaleski Backpack Trail. Cross the footbridge and turn left.

3.1 Come to a fork. Follow the sign right onto the Olds Hollow Trail.

3.5 Pass an old pioneer cemetery on the right. The trail continues slightly to the left and down from the cemetery. In a few hundred feet, you will come to a sandstone-lined gorge. Walk down the steps into the gorge and turn left, passing two small waterfalls. Cross a footbridge to the other side of the stream and continue walking along it.

3.6 Come to with a fork. The Kings Hollow Trail (the Zaleski Backpack Trail) goes right. Take the left fork. In about 100 feet, pass an informal trail on the right. Continue straight, crossing a footbridge and following blue and orange blazes.

4.1 Return to the junction that began the Olds Hollow loop. Continue straight.

4.2 Arrive back at the trailhead.

Hike Information

Local information: Vinton County Convention and Visitors Bureau, (740) 596-5033, www.vintoncountytravel.com

Local events and attractions: Lake Hope State Park has a number of facilities, including a beach, boat rentals, dining lodge, cabins, campground, and the nearby Zaleski Backpack Trail.

The Vinton County Wild Turkey Festival is an annual May event; http://vintoncountytravel.com/turkeyfestival.htm.

Accommodations: Lake Hope State Park cabins and campground; call (866) 644-6727 for reservations.

Restaurants: Lake Hope State Park dining lodge, (740) 596-0601, http://lakehopelodge.com

THE MOONVILLE GHOST

Stories about the ghost of Moonville Tunnel, located in Zaleski State Forest, are a mixture of fact and fiction. (But, as they say, never let the facts get in the way of a good story.) Moonville was once a stop on the Marietta and Cincinnati Railroad and was home to up to one hundred people, mostly employed by the furnaces and the coal mines. In 1859 a man was, in fact, killed when he was run over by a train. Who he was and exactly what happened, however, are less clear. Perhaps the most popular story claims that Moonville was in the throes of a plague-like epidemic. Fearing exposure, the train's crew refused to stop in town. But supplies in Moonville were dwindling, so the town appointed one man to stop the train in order to save them all—but the train ran him down.

Over the years there have been a number of reported sightings of the Moonville Ghost. If you're brave, you might follow the bed of the tracks to the sandstone-and-brick tunnel at night. If not, well, there's a reason they're called day hikes.

37 Rockhouse to Athens Trail Loop

Sells Park, Riddle State Nature Preserve, and Strouds Run State Park

With help from the state's Clean Ohio Fund and the Athens Conservancy, the city of Athens was able to purchase the "missing link" property between the city-owned Sells Park and Strouds Run State Park. The result? Nearly 30 miles of hiking and biking trails, all accessible from a trailhead at the end of a neighborhood street, just minutes from this hip college town's main shopping district. On this hike, walk around a small pond, past rock outcroppings, and to a recess cave before returning on the ridgetop that overlooks an old-growth forest to the north.

Start: Rockhouse Trail trailhead in Sells Park

Distance: 4.1-mile loop

Hiking time: About 2 hours

Difficulty: Moderate due to length and a ridge climb

Trail surface: Dirt

Blaze: Rockhouse Trail, white arch on orange background; Athens Trail, white arrow on red background

Best season: Pawpaw trees fruit in the fall.

Other trail users: Mountain bikers, runners, and rock climbers

Canine compatibility: Leashed dogs permitted

Water: Available in summer at Sells Park trailhead

Land status: City park, state nature preserve, and state park

Nearest town: Athens

Fees and permits: None

Schedule: Open daily from dawn to dusk, unless you are camping in the backcountry site

Maps: Download a trail map at www.athens trails.org. USGS quad: Athens.

Trail contacts: Athens Arts, Parks, and Recreation Department, (740) 592-3325, www.ci.athens.oh.us; Strouds Run State Park, (740) 767-3570, http://parks.ohiodnr.gov/stroudsrun

Finding the trailhead: From US 33 in Athens, take the East State Street exit and travel east on East State Street 0.3 mile to Avon Place on the left. Turn north onto Avon Place and go 0.4 mile to the end of the street and the Sells Park parking. *DeLorme: Ohio Atlas & Gazetteer:* Page 80 B2. GPS: N39 30.61' / W84 42.91'.

The Hike

For years, locals enjoyed the trails in Athens's Sells Park while both locals and out-of-towners took advantage of the many trails in Strouds Run State Park. Though less than half a mile of land separated these two parks, the fact that it was held in private ownership made a Sells-to-Strouds trek out of the question. The private land, known as Hawk Woods, was also familiar to botanists because of its status as an old-growth forest.

Turtlehead Cave, aka Blue Ash Cave

When the owner of Hawk Woods passed away, Riddle Forest Products purchased the property. Riddle and the city of Athens worked together and, with money from the statewide Clean Ohio Fund, the city purchased the property and worked with the state to establish the Dale and Jackie Riddle State Nature Preserve, managed by the city of Athens.

Today you can hop on the Rockhouse Trail and walk around a small pond that is the central feature of Sells Park. Then, as you enter Riddle Preserve and Strouds Run, walk along the base of the ridge, often passing sandstone rock outcroppings. These rocks are popular locally with those who boulder—that is, climb on the short rocks (boulders) without going high or using ropes. The trail is also popular with mountain bikers and dog walkers. Most trails in this area are named for natural features. The Pawpaw Trail is especially appropriate, as this area is loaded with pawpaw trees in the understory. Look for this edible native fruit from late August to early October.

Past the junction with the White Ash Trail, look to the right of the trail for a large chestnut oak. A few steps down the trail, a massive black oak makes the first one seem small. Both of these are county champion trees—that is, the largest tree of this species in Athens County. At mile 2.6 come to a connector trail for a recess cave that is reminiscent of the nearby Hocking Hills region. After checking out the cave, return to the trail where it climbs to the top of the ridge (this is technically a connector trail, but seamlessly joins the Rockhouse and Athens Trails). At the top of the ridge, join the Athens Trail and take a left to return to Sells Park.

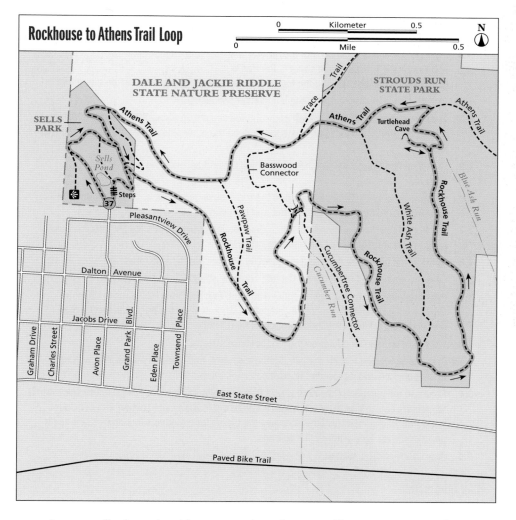

Rockhouse to Athens Trail Loop

As you walk along the ridge among the oaks, you will again see signs indicating when you leave the state park for the Riddle State Nature Preserve. At this point, look right (north) and you will see Hawk Woods, which is home to an old-growth forest that includes some trees 150 to 200 years old. Finish by descending the ridge back down to Sells Park.

Miles and Directions

0.0 Start at the Rockhouse Trail trailhead in Sells Park. A sign by the parking lot on the west side of the park marks the Rockhouse Trail, blazed with a white arch on an orange background. The trail ascends to the pond in about 100 feet and forks by the earthen dam. Take a left; do not cross the dam.

0.2 Come to a fork by a footbridge. Take a right and cross the footbridge.

0.25 Arrive at a three-way junction with the Athens Trail. Go straight and trend right.

> **The pawpaw was named Ohio's state native fruit in 2009.**

0.3 Come to a four-way junction with the Athens Trail and Sourwood Trail. Continue straight. The trail is very level; ignore side trails to the rock outcroppings—all formal trail junction are marked.

0.75 Pass the Pawpaw Connector on the left; continue straight.

1.25 Pass the Basswood Trail on the left and continue straight. In about 200 feet, cross a footbridge over a drainage and come to a fork on the other side of the bridge. Take the left fork.

1.9 The White Ash Connector switches back to the left and ascends the ridge. Continue straight.

2.6 Come to a connector trail on the left to the rock house/recess cave. Check out this geologic formation, then return to this spot and continue.

2.7 The Rockhouse Trail ends and the White Oak Connector begins at a left switchback. This section of trail takes you to the top of the ridge.

2.8 Arrive at the top of the ridge and the junction with the Athens Trail. Take a left.

3.0 Pass the White Ash Connector on the left; continue straight.

3.2 Pass the Trace Trail on the right; continue straight. **FYI:** The Trace Trail leads to Chestnut Grove (walk-in) camp. To reach the campsite, take a right on the Trace Trail for 0.7 mile and then take a left on the Tunnel Rock Trail for 0.1 mile.

3.4 Pass the Pawpaw Connector on the left; continue straight.

3.75 Pass the Sourwood Trail on the left. Continue straight, but soon the Athens Trail switches back to the left and descends the ridge.

3.9 Return to the junction of the Athens and Rockhouse Trails. This time take a left to finish on the Athens Trail. In less than 100 yards return to the four-way intersection with the Sourwood Trail. Take a right this time, following the blazes for the Athens Trail down to the pond and parking lot. Ignore informal side trails.

4.1 Arrive back at the trailhead.

Hike Information

Local information: Athens County Convention and Visitors Bureau, (740) 592-1819 or (800) 878-9767, www.athensohio.com

Local events and attractions: The Athens Farmers Market is one of the best in the nation; (740) 593-6763 or www.athensfarmersmarket.org.

The Hockhocking Adena Bikeway is a 20-mile paved path between Athens and Nelsonville and beyond; www.seorf.ohiou.edu/~xx088.

Accommodations: Strouds Run State Park campground; call (740) 594-2628. There is a backcountry campsite open to hikers and cyclists (it's reserved for hunters during the one-week deer gun season in the fall); www.athensconservancy.org/campsite.html.

Restaurants: Casa Nueva in Athens is a worker-owned Mexican-American restaurant with plenty of vegetarian and vegan options; (740) 592-2016 or www.casanueva.com

Village Bakery and Cafe; (740) 594-7311 or www.dellazona.com

Organizations: Athens Conservancy, www.athensconservancy.org

Athens Trails, (740) 593-6572, www.gasp.athens.oh.us/trails.shtml

38 Lakeview Trail

Burr Oak State Park

There are plenty of options for hiking around Burr Oak Lake, since some 50 miles of trail exist here where state park meets national forest. Hikes vary from short to long day hikes as well as an 18-mile backpack trail. Adjacent to the state park is Wayne National Forest and the 15-mile Wildcat Hollow Backpack Trail. Try the highlight: a 5.8-mile out-and-back hike between Tom Jenkins Dam and Dock 4. Views are consistently good on this truly lakeside trail.

Start: Tom Jenkins Dam
Distance: 5.8-mile out-and-back or 2.9-mile point-to-point
Hiking time: About 2 to 3 hours
Difficulty: Easy; short and flat
Trail surface: Mostly flat dirt trail
Blaze: Yellow
Best season: Apr through Oct
Other trail users: Hunters (in season)
Canine compatibility: Leashed dogs permitted

Water: Available at Tom Jenkins Dam
Land status: State park
Nearest town: Glouster
Fees and permits: None
Schedule: Open daily from dawn to dusk
Maps: State park map; USGS quad: Corning
Trail contact: Burr Oak State Park, Glouster; (740) 767-3570; http://parks.ohiodnr.gov/burroak

Finding the trailhead: From the junction of SR 13 and SR 78 north of Glouster, continue north on SR 13 for 2.7 miles to the railroad tracks. Past the tracks, look for a right turn to the Tom Jenkins Dam at mile 2.9. Go 0.2 mile and park in the lot atop the dam. *DeLorme: Ohio Atlas & Gazetteer:* Page 70 D2. GPS: N39 32.60' / W82 03.48'.
   Option: If you choose to shuttle, continue north on SR 13 a half mile from the dam and turn right (east) onto CR 107. Drive 1 mile and turn right onto Beach Road, marked by a huge state park sign. Drive 1.2 miles to the bottom of the hill and turn right into the parking lot at Dock 4. The trailhead is at the far end of the lot, marked with a sign.

The Hike

Burr Oak State Park is named for this particular winged-branch, large-acorn oak tree. The forests here are dominated by a variety of oaks as well as hickories. The center-piece of the park is Burr Oak Lake, a dammed salamander-shaped body of water that is surrounded by 29 miles of trails just within park boundaries—and more beyond. A campground, cabins, and a lodge make this a popular multiday destination for hikers and other fun-seekers.

   The Lakeview Trail begins at the Tom Jenkins Dam picnic area. In 1950 the Army Corps of Engineers dammed the East Branch of Sunday Creek to create Burr Oak

The Lakeview Trail near Tom Jenkins Dam

Lake. A rock outcropping over the water here was a favorite spot for jumping in—now signs indicate it is illegal to swim here. To take a dip, go to the beach area by the lodge. The trail parallels the lakeshore among oak, hickory, and beech trees. Watch for the yellow blazes to help you stay on track when you see informal side trails. Spring wildflowers and fall foliage make this an especially nice walk. In the spring look for spring beauty, Dutchman's-breeches, trillium, hepatica, and bloodroot.

As you hike you're likely to see anglers and boaters enjoying Burr Oak Lake. Looking inland, you might see the abundant white-tailed deer and wild turkey. The trail often follows the very edge of the lake, so views are consistently good. You will watch the dam disappear slowly behind as you take in some new vistas. Toward the end of this section near Dock 4, Burr Oak Lodge comes into spectacular view across the lake to the east. This is best seen in the evening light.

Miles and Directions

0.0   Start at the Tom Jenkins Dam. From the parking lot, look to the sign for the backpacking trail. Do not follow the sign. Instead, walk past it and straight through the picnic area. Just past the picnic shelter, you will see the wooden trailhead sign for the Lakeview Trail.

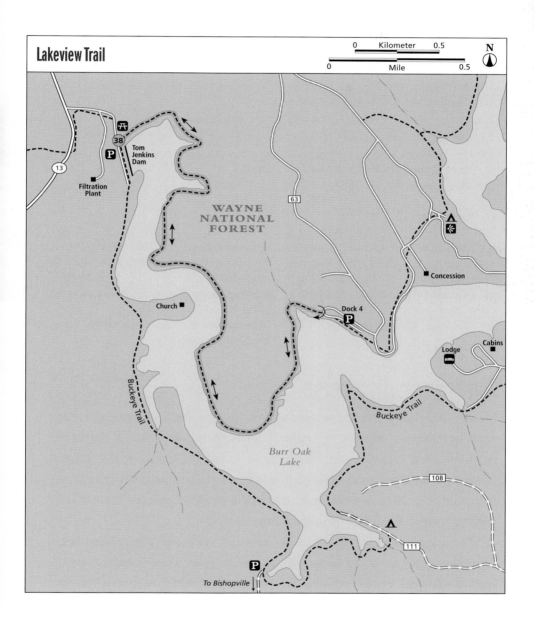

Lakeview Trail

Kilometer 0 — 0.5
Mile 0 — 0.5

N

13

Filtration
Plant

38

Tom
Jenkins
Dam

Church ■

Buckeye Trail

WAYNE
NATIONAL
FOREST

63

Dock 4

Concession ■

Lodge

Cabins ■

Buckeye Trail

108

Burr Oak
Lake

111

To Bishopville

0.2 The trail veers away from the lake, edging the stream. At this point you will pick up white diamond blazes in addition to the yellow blazes. When you see the double white blaze, cross the stream and head back to the main body of the lake.

0.7 You will cross a large stream. (**Note:** The stream crossing occurs before the blazes.) In a few hundred feet you will cross another stream. Cross and walk slightly to the left, ascending the ridge. Continue ascending about halfway up the ridge. The trail stays there for a while, crossing some more drainages.

1.2 The trail cuts to the left, crossing a ridge, and then immediately descends. The blazes are not apparent here.

1.5 The trail finishes its descent to the lakeside.

2.0 Cross a couple of footbridges, then walk through some brambles.

2.6 The lodge will come into view across the lake, and Dock 4 will be visible straight ahead.

2.9 The trail curves eastward and finishes at Dock 4. Turn around and return the way you came. **Option:** Finish the hike here if you shuttled.

5.8 Arrive back at the dam trailhead.

Hike Information

Local information: Athens County Convention and Visitors Bureau, (800) 878-9767, www .athensohio.com

Local events and attractions: Muskingum River Parkway State Park, (740) 453-4377, http:// parks.ohiodnr.gov/muskingumriver

Accommodations: Burr Oak Getaway Rentals and campground; call (866) 644-6727 for reservations.

Restaurants: Bonnie's Home Cooking, Glouster; (740) 767-4777

Organizations: Sunday Creek Watershed Group, www.sundaycreek.org

WHY LEAVES CHANGE COLOR

The Burr Oak Lakeview Trail is especially popular in fall, when the bright colors of turning leaves accent the landscape. But what makes leaves change color in the fall? As most of us remember from grade school, photosynthesis is the process by which plants turn sunlight into sugar for food. The chemical chlorophyll, an integral part of photosynthesis, gives leaves their green color. Other chemicals are associated with the other colors you see in leaves: carotenoids with yellow and orange; anthocyanins with red.

These chemicals are present in leaves all along, but the chlorophyll green masks them during the growing season. As the days shorten and the nights approach freezing, plants begin to shut down the photosynthesis process. As the chlorophyll disappears from the leaves, the reds and yellows can come through. Maple trees are best known for their fall color, with red maple turning red; sugar maple turning yellow, orange, and red; and black maple turning yellow.

39 River Loop to Scenic River Trail

Wayne National Forest–Athens District–Marietta Unit

Think Appalachia—hollows, coal mines, bluegrass music, rural life. Now think Appalachian Ohio. Yep, there is such a thing, and Wayne National Forest lies in the heart of Ohio's hill country. Hike the River Loop to Scenic River Trail and walk through a microcosm of the natural, human, and resource history that defines this region. Start from the banks of the Ohio River and ascend to the ridgetop through a mixed mesophytic forest. Walk past gas pumps and through rock gardens before returning to the river. Hike it in a day or make it into an overnighter, since backcountry camping is allowed in the national forest.

Start: Leith Run Recreation Area
Distance: 11.4-mile lollipop
Hiking time: About 4 to 6 hours
Difficulty: Difficult due to length and hills
Trail surface: A dirt path with a paved access trail
Blaze: Yellow diamond; access trail, white diamond
Best season: Mid-Apr through mid-Oct
Other trail users: Mountain bikers and hunters (in season)
Canine compatibility: Leashed dogs permitted
Water: Available at Leith Run Recreation Area
Land status: National forest

Nearest town: Newport
Fees and permits: None
Schedule: Wayne National Forest trails are open 24 hours a day, 365 days a year. Day hikes are best done from dawn to dusk.
Maps: A brochure with topo maps of hiking and backpacking trails in the Wayne is available for purchase at Wayne National Forest offices. USGS quad: Raven Rock
Trail contact: Wayne National Forest, Athens District–Marietta Unit, Marietta; (740) 373-9055; www.fs.usda.gov/wayne

Finding the trailhead: From I-77 exit 1 in Marietta, take SR 7 north 20 miles to Leith Run Recreation Area on the right (river) side of the road. Park by the restroom and pick up the paved path between the restroom and the playground. *DeLorme: Ohio Atlas & Gazetteer:* Page 73 D7. GPS: N39 26.70' / W81 9.02'.

The Hike

The USDA Forest Service started purchasing land here in the 1930s, when much of it had already been largely depleted of its timber and other natural resources. Today the Wayne National Forest comprises more than 240,000 acres within a purchase boundary of 834,000 acres. The Wayne's purchase boundaries are the lines Congress has drawn within which the Forest Service can buy land.

Along the River Loop Trail

It seems vast, but in reality the Wayne's actual holdings look more like the shotgun blasts you see on target-practice road signs here. Private inholdings make up most of the area within purchase boundaries. The Wayne's management plan is an attempt to satisfy all industry and public desires. Timbering, oil and gas development, and coal-mining proposals exist side by side with legal and illegal ATV, equestrian, mountain bike, and hiking trails. Some locals resent the Wayne because of the lack of a tax base. But other locals, as well as the Wayne's many visitors, take advantage of the many recreational opportunities it provides.

Among these trail users are members of the River Valley Mountain Bike Association. RVMBA volunteers worked with Wayne staff to rehab and rebuild neglected and nearly abandoned trails, specifically the River Loop Trail, which is also known as the Greenwood Trail. More than 600 hours of volunteer labor resulted in this well-built (to International Mountain Bike Association standards) trail loop. RVMBA has been hosting races on this course since 2008. Bicycle traffic helps to keep such a long trail in a remote area well established.

The hike starts and ends at Leith Run Recreation Area, which is a day-use area and a campground. The first portion of the hike is a connector trail from the recreation

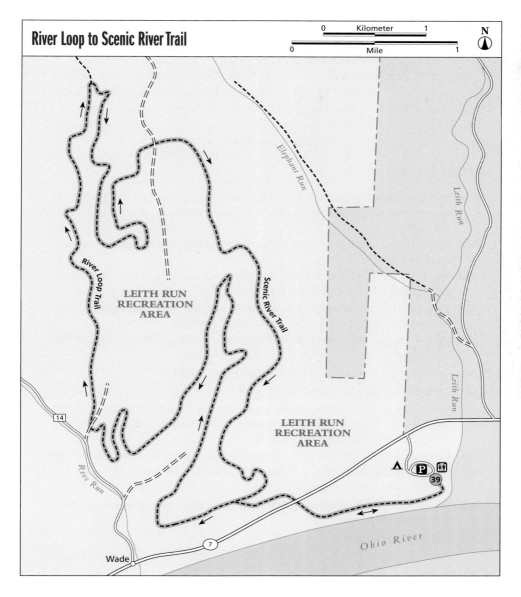

0   Kilometer   1

0   Mile   1

N

LEITH RUN
RECREATION
AREA

River Loop Trail

Scenic River Trail

Elephant Run

Leith Run

Leith Run

LEITH RUN
RECREATION
AREA

14

Rees Run

7

Wade

Ohio River

39

area. It parallels the Ohio River before turning away from the river and crossing the road, then ascending the ridge. Rock outcroppings throughout the trail make it an interesting hike, and late fall through early spring you can get views of the Ohio River from the ridge. The mixed mesophytic forest has no dominant tree species, but some attractive sections are thick with pawpaws and buckeyes.

If you make the 11.4-mile hike into an overnighter, listen for the incessant call of the whip-poor-will until you hear the hooves of white-tailed deer just outside the tent. But this is a very doable, if difficult, day hike. Walk quietly and keep an eye out for fox. Look on the trail for signs of raccoons and wild turkey scratch—they often kick up large areas of leaf litter while looking for grub. In the spring, look for the many wildflowers that bloom here, including Virginia bluebell and trillium.

By way of connector trails, the Scenic River Trail leads all the way to the 9.5-mile Archers Fork Trail (hike Y) and the Covered Bridge Trail (hike W). Included in the local web of trails is a portion of the 4,600-mile North Country Trail. Day and overnight hiking options in this section of the Wayne are almost limitless, though you should plan ahead to find a filterable water supply.

Miles and Directions

0.0 Start on the paved footpath in Leith Run Recreation Area; you can pick it up by either of the restrooms. Walk toward the Ohio River. Continue on the paved path until it gives way to a dirt path.

0.3 Pass two paved access trails on the right and come to a fork. Take the left fork and walk along the boardwalk.

0.75 Pass by an old gas pump on the left and a doubletrack coming in on the right. Continue straight, looking for the white diamond blaze.

0.9 Cross SR 7. In a couple hundred feet, pass an access trail (from the Brown House trail-head) on the left. Continue straight; you are now on the Scenic River Trail.

1.25 Come to the junction with the River Loop Trail, marked with a sign. Continue straight. This begins the loop.

2.1 Cross the most prominent of several dirt doubletracks (roads).

4.5 Cross a private gravel road; trend left and down.

8.0 Come to the northern junction with the Scenic River Trail, marked with a sign. Take a right switchback, continuing up the ridge. At the top of the ridge, cross a dirt road. Continue straight, following the yellow diamond blaze.

8.5 Cross over a couple more dirt roads. Continue straight, following the yellow diamond blaze.

9.7 Pass an old doubletrack dirt road on the left, marked with a white blaze. Go straight, following the yellow diamond blaze.

10.2 Return to the original junction with the River Loop Trail. Take a left and retrace your steps from the start of the hike.

11.4 Arrive back at the trailhead.

Hike Information

Local information: Marietta/Washington County Convention and Visitors Bureau, (800) 288-2577, www.mariettaohio.org

Local events and attractions: The Lamping Homestead, Covered Bridge, and Ohio View Trails are also located in the Marietta Unit of Wayne National Forest.

Accommodations: Leith Run Recreation Area has a seasonal campground with showers; (740) 373-9055 or www.fs.usda.gov/recarea/wayne/recarea/?recid=6215 for information; (877) 444-6777 or www.recreation.gov for reservations. Backcountry camping is permitted in Wayne National Forest.

Organizations: River Valley Mountain Bike Association, www.rvmba.com

North Country National Scenic Trail, www.northcountrytrail.org

40 Lamping Homestead Trail

Wayne National Forest–Athens District–Marietta Unit

This 3.5-mile loop trail is one of the most secluded in the state. Begin the hike at the nineteenth-century Lamping family homestead. Walk around a small fishable pond and into a deciduous forest dotted here and there with white pine plantations. Ascend ridges 300 to 400 feet above the river valleys, and walk in biodiverse hollows. Overlook Clear Fork and return to where you started, passing by the old Lamping family cemetery.

Start: Picnic area next to the parking lot
Distance: 3.5-mile loop
Hiking time: About 1.5 hours
Difficulty: Moderate due to some steep sections and some difficult footing
Trail surface: Dirt
Blaze: White diamond
Best season: Apr through Oct
Other trail users: Hunters (in season)
Canine compatibility: Leashed dogs permitted
Water: None available; bring your own.
Land status: National forest
Nearest town: Graysville

Fees and permits: None
Schedule: Wayne National Forest trails are open 24 hours a day, 365 days a year. Day hikes are best done from dawn to dusk.
Maps: A brochure with topo maps of hiking and backpacking trails in the Wayne is available for purchase at Wayne National Forest offices. USGS quad: Rinard Mills.
Trail contact: Wayne National Forest, Athens Ranger District–Marietta Unit, Marietta; (740) 373-9055; www.fs.usda.gov/wayne

Finding the trailhead: From Marietta, take SR 26 north 35.3 miles to SR 537. Turn left (west) and drive 1.6 miles to Township Road 307. Take a left and drive 0.2 mile to the sign for the Lamping Homestead picnic area. Turn left into the parking lot. *DeLorme: Ohio Atlas & Gazetteer:* Page 72 C2. GPS: N39 37.85' / W81 11.37'.

The Hike

The Lamping Homestead Trail is one of the most secluded hiking trails in Wayne National Forest, if not the state. Not only is it far from just about anywhere, but the trail never crosses a road or suffers from a lot of human intrusion. Wayne National Forest literature suggests that this old homestead still looks much as it did in the early 1800s, when the Lamping family lived here. Astronomers bring their telescopes here seeking dark sky conditions.

Situated well into the Western Allegheny–Appalachian Plateau, the Lamping Homestead and much of Morgan County are home to some of the steepest ridges in Ohio, with 300- to 400-foot elevation gain from creek to ridgetop. This is the land where the last glacier pushed the flow of the former Teas and Steubenville Rivers backward into the newly created (geologically speaking) Ohio River, which cuts a

Lamping cemetery

valley through the Appalachian Plateau. Monroe County has historically been known as Little Switzerland—but not because of the steep slopes. Rather it's because this area was heavily settled by Swiss immigrants.

The hike begins at a picnic area situated where the homestead once was. Walk through a small white pine plantation and begin circling around a fishable pond created by a small earthen dam. The trail soon turns away from the pond and follows an attractive stream that feeds the pond. Look for beech and maple trees lower down and oak trees on the ridgetops. Understory species include pawpaw and spicebush. Springtime brings common wildflowers such as spring beauty, trillium, and wild geranium.

Ascend to a small opening and walk by the only gas well you'll see on the hike and then through another white pine plantation. Soon you will have the option to take a shorter loop back to the picnic area. Continuing on, the trail works its way along other small tributaries to the Clear Fork, an attractive creek that flows into the Little Muskingum River. There are some views of the Clear Fork Valley. The forest is lush and ferns grow in the cool, damp drainages. Walk quietly and keep an eye out for white-tailed deer, wild turkey, ruffed grouse, and fox.

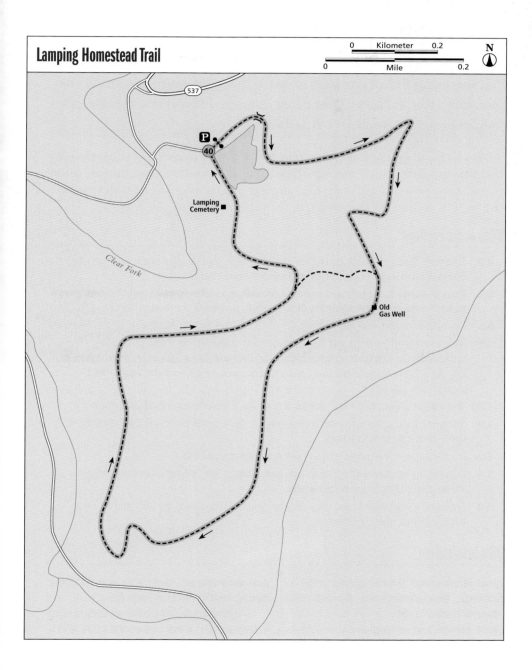

Lamping Homestead Trail

537

P
40

Lamping
Cemetery ■

Clear Fork

Old
Gas Well ■

0   Kilometer   0.2

0   Mile   0.2

N

MIXED MESOPHYTIC FORESTS

A mixed mesophytic forest is one in which about twenty to twenty-five tree species are common, but none dominate the canopy. Trees found in a mixed mesophytic forest include beech, tulip tree, basswood, sugar maple, red oak, white oak, and hemlock. Depending on where you are, some species drop out while others come in, including birch, cherry, ash, magnolia, sour gum, black walnut, and hickory. Mixed mesophytic forests are known to be very biologically rich, often containing more than 1,000 plant species.

As you approach the end of this loop, you will see evidence of the people who lived here long before the Lampings. The trail skirts the base of a large, natural conical mound. Look for a side trail to the old Lamping cemetery atop the mound. Finish the hike by walking over the dam and back to the picnic area.

Miles and Directions

0.0 Start from the picnic area next to the parking lot. Walk past the gate and toward the lake. Take a left and walk through the pines, following white blazes.

0.2 The trail curves to the right and crosses a footbridge. In a few hundred feet, the trail turns away from the pond and slowly ascends the ridge, paralleling the stream.

0.5 Turn right and cross over the stream.

0.9 Reach the top of the ridge and then approach a wooden sign for the short loop. To continue on the long loop, walk straight ahead. (**Option:** Take a right to return on the short loop for a 1.8-mile round-trip hike.) You will soon cross an old road and walk through another pine plantation.

1.25 The trail turns sharply left and crosses a drainage. It then begins a gradual descent.

1.8 The trail curves to the right and ascends slightly. You can see Clear Fork Creek from here. Soon cross a steep doubletrack.

2.5 The trail takes a sharp right turn just before a large downed tree.

3.1 Come to the junction with the short loop trail, entering from the right. Continue straight ahead, descending to the bottomlands.

3.5 Approach a large mound and circle halfway around it. Then cross the dam and return to the picnic area where you started.

Hike Information

Local information: Monroe County Office of Economic Development and Tourism, www.monroecountyohio.net

Local events and attractions: The Archers Fork, Covered Bridge, and Ohio View Trails are also located in the Marietta Unit of Wayne National Forest.

Accommodations: There is a nice primitive campground at Lamping Homestead.

Neighboring Clearwater Creek Campground in Graysville has electric sites; (740) 934-2331.

41 Red and Blue Trails

Dysart Woods

For all the times your eyes scanned a landscape and you thought, *I wonder what it was like to discover this place,* go to Dysart Woods and indulge this daydream. Home to Ohio's largest remaining tract of virgin forest, Dysart Woods allows you to get a glimpse of what the eastern hardwood forests looked like to Native Americans and, later, European settlers. Trees 300 to 400 years old continue to live in this 50-acre National Natural Landmark.

Start: Parking area
Distance: 1.5-mile figure eight
Hiking time: About 1 hour
Difficulty: Moderate due to a lot of ups and downs and several large fallen tree trunks over the trail
Trail surface: Hilly dirt trail occasionally blocked by fallen logs
Blaze: Red Trail, red; Blue Trail, blue
Best season: Apr through Oct
Other trail users: Hikers only
Canine compatibility: Dogs not permitted
Water: None available; bring your own.

Land status: Owned by Ohio University; open to the public
Nearest town: St. Clairsville
Fees and permits: None
Schedule: Open daily from dawn to dusk
Maps: Download a trail map at http://www.ohio.edu/plantbio/Assets/documents/pdf/Brochure.pdf. USGS quads: Armstrong Mills, Hunter.
Trail contact: Ohio University, Athens; www.plantbio.ohiou.edu/index.php/facilities/dysart
Special considerations: No smoking is allowed in Dysart Woods.

Finding the trailhead: From I-77 in St. Clairsville, turn south onto SR 9 (exit 216) and travel 7.8 miles to SR 147. Turn right (west) and drive 1 mile to Ault Dysart Road, marked by a large wooden sign. Turn left (south) and travel 0.2 mile to a fork. Take the right fork, following the large sign for Dysart Woods. Drive 0.8 mile to a small gravel parking lot on the left. Look downhill for two blue markers indicating the trailhead. *DeLorme: Ohio Atlas & Gazetteer:* Page 72 A4. GPS: N39 58.93' / W80 59.93'.

The Hike

Beginning on the Blue Trail, walk down into a ravine. You will see a rich mixed mesophytic forest, common in this part of the state. Pay close attention and you will begin to notice the characteristics that make this forest special. Most obvious are the smattering of trees as large as 5 feet in diameter. A number of these giants are concentrated on the small loop of the Blue Trail, so be sure to take it.

Some of the most noticeable here are tulip trees, so called in reference to their yellow-and-orange tulip-like flowers. Look on the trail for petals in springtime,

A tree hugger at Dysart Woods

because you probably won't see the flowers growing in the trees. Tulips are tall, straight, self-pruning trees whose first branches in dense woods are 40 to 50 feet from the ground. Scientists refer to tulip poplars as tulip trees because they are not actually in the poplar family. Giant snags make good homes for a number of animal species. Look for the squared-off holes of the pileated woodpecker.

The Blue Trail ends at Ault Dysart Road. Both the road and the woods are named after the Dysart family, who for several generations preserved the woods they owned before handing ownership over to the Nature Conservancy and then Ohio University. When you cross the road and begin the Red Trail, you will descend into the valley. On the other (upland) side of the stream, approach some of the biggest trees at Dysart. The largest tree in Dysart used to be a tulip tree located here. It was struck by lightning, but the base still remains on the ground as coarse woody debris. Because the core was rotten when it fell, no one knows the tree's exact age, but it was estimated to be about 400 years old.

Standing snags and fallen trees left to rot are notably common here. The forest is left untouched in an effort to preserve its natural state. What makes this a "virgin" forest is that it has encountered little or no human disturbance. The forest has never been logged or thinned; it hasn't been occupied by a homestead, fenced, used for grazing animals, farmed, or otherwise disturbed by humans (except, of course, for this hiking trail).

Due to the shade cast by a dense canopy, the understory of this forest is clearer than in a younger forest. Common understory plants include witch hazel, pawpaw, and spicebush. In spring look for such flowers as trout lily, trillium, and spring beauty. In summer look for sweet cicely. Mosses, ferns, and fungi tend to be more widespread here than in a disturbed forest.

Researchers use Dysart Woods as a laboratory for studying forest ecosystems. These remnant old-growth forests are the best measure we have today for how a healthy, functioning forest ecosystem works and how natural disturbances affect them. These forests tend to be reserves of biological diversity and also serve as living museums that provide a climatic history of the area. Tree rings indicate periods of drought, fire, and human impact.

Finally, as you stroll through these magnificent woods, ponder the philosophical questions that surround the place. How do we measure the worth of a forest? In

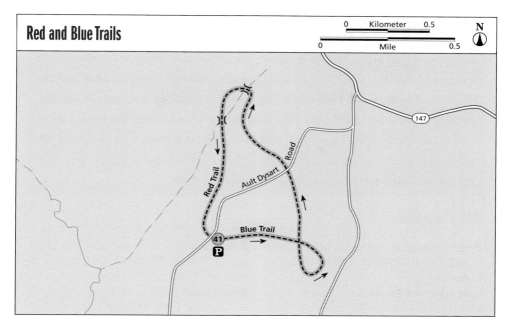

board feet? In biological diversity? Intrinsic value? What are the roles humans have played in the demise of the eastern hardwood forests, and what is our role in preserving what's left and being stewards of the forests that are still growing?

Miles and Directions

0.0 Start at the parking area. Look downhill to two blue markers that indicate the Blue Trail trailhead.

0.2 Come to a junction. Turn right to walk a small loop on the Blue Trail. This loop contains some of the preserve's larger trees.

0.5 Return to the junction of the Blue Trail loop. Take a right, following signs for the Red Trail.

0.7 The Blue Trail ends at Ault Dysart Road. Cross the road; angle off to the left a bit and pick up the Red Trail, marked with a sign.

0.9 Cross the stream over two footbridges and then begin to ascend the ridge.

1.0 Come to what was once the forest's largest tulip tree. Its woody remains lie on the ground. In about 75 feet approach a giant white oak. The trail continues to the left (downslope) of the oak, not to the right.

1.1 Cross the stream again over a footbridge. The rest of the trail is uphill. Look for the red blazes. You will have to climb over some large fallen logs.

1.5 Arrive back at Ault Dysart Road and the parking area.

"UNDERMINING" DYSART WOODS

After years of legal battles between the Ohio Valley Coal Company and environmental groups, the company gained a permit to mine under Dysart Woods. Coal mining took place directly beneath the woods in 2005 utilizing a form of mining known as room-and-pillar mining, designed to cause less immediate surface damage. Within the following few years, a higher than normal number of the big old trees died. Though mining is suspected as the cause, scientists have not determined mining to be the definitive cause. Either way, in an aging stand like this, it's always best to plan a trip sooner rather than later.

Hike Information

Local information: Belmont County Tourism Council, (740) 695-4359, www.belmontcounty tourism.org

Local events and attractions: Barnesville Pumpkin Festival; www.barnesvillepumpkinfestival.com

Accommodations: Barkcamp State Park campground, Belmont; (800) 644-6727 for reservations; http://parks.ohiodnr.gov/barkcamp

Restaurants: Gasber's Fine Day Restaurant, St. Clairsville; (740) 695-0125; www.facebook.com/gasbers

Honorable Mentions

Southeast Ohio

T Buckeye Trail through Hocking Hills State Forest

Love the Hocking Hills but hate the crowds? The statewide Buckeye Trail (BT) traces a path through Hocking Hills State Forest, and while some sections are mobbed (think Old Man's Cave to Cedar Falls), others are hardly even known. A case in point is the 2.5-mile section between Rocky Fork and Kreashbaum Roads. Starting from a small pullout along Rocky Fork Road, walk into a dense hemlock forest. Downslope is Rocky Fork, and upslope to your left are some nice sandstone outcroppings. The understory is relatively bare, so don't think about flowering plants; rather, look for the easy-to-see mushrooms that grow on the many rotting logs and stumps here. The trail dips down and crosses Rocky Fork at an attractive spot of sandstone outcroppings, small caves, and a fern-covered floor. You can continue to Kreashbaum Road, but the trail quality goes downhill between the creek and Kreashbaum as it travels through younger successional forests and then skirts a former clear-cut. But definitely take the BT as far as the creek bed and a little beyond, then return for a nearly 5-mile round-trip. You probably won't see another soul.

Trail contact: Hocking State Forest, Rockbridge; (740) 385-4402; http://ohiodnr.com/DNN/forests/hocking/tabid/5156/Default.aspx

Finding the trailhead: From US 33 west of Logan, turn onto SR 180 West and drive 3.9 miles to the junction with SR 678 South. Turn left and drive 1.3 miles to Kreashbaum Road, on the left. Turn onto Kreashbaum and drive 0.7 mile to Rocky Fork Road (Township Road 232) on the left. Make a sharp left turn onto this gravel road and drive 1 mile to a pullout on the right, marked with a double blue blaze that indicates a turn onto the Buckeye Trail. *DeLorme: Ohio Atlas & Gazetteer:* Page 69 D6 and Page 79 A5. GPS: N39 30.07' / W82 31.92'.

U Rockbridge State Nature Preserve

The main attraction at this preserve is Ohio's longest natural bridge, measuring nearly 100 feet long and featuring a 50-foot waterfall. Both of the preserve's trails can be combined to make a 2.6-mile hike. Begin by walking a long, narrow right-of-way between two farm fields and then enter the woods, where you will see spring wildflowers such as crested dwarf iris, trillium, bloodroot, and trailing arbutus. Other attractions include migrating warblers, views of the Hocking River, and more rock features, including a small rock shelter. There is also canoe access to the Hocking River. This spot was popular with Wyandot Indians and, later, Hocking Canal travelers. Be sure to stay on designated trails; you will be near private property at all times. Hunters may be on adjacent private property, so be aware of hunting season dates.

Trail contact: Rockbridge State Nature Preserve, Rockbridge; http://ohiodnr .com/location/rockbridge/tabid/959/Default.aspx

Finding the trailhead: From US 33 in Hocking County (near the state rest area), turn north onto Township Road 124/503 (Dalton Road). Take an immediate right and follow the signs 0.7 mile to a parking area on the left. The trail is located just past the information kiosk. *DeLorme: Ohio Atlas & Gazetteer:* Page 69 D6. GPS: N39 33.98' / W82 29.96'.

V Lakeview Trail, Strouds Run State Park

A lot of trail development has been happening at Strouds in recent years, including a trail to a backcountry campsite and mountain bike trails. But the old standard is still the Lakeview Trail. Walk around Dow Lake in an attractive, healthy second-growth oak-hickory forest on the ridgetops and beech-maple in the valleys. Walk through white pine plantations, near a Native American mound, and by a pioneer cemetery. Look for the active beaver population. Spring wildflowers and fall foliage are highlights of this 6.8-mile horseshoe trail in a state park just 5 miles from Ohio's funkiest small town.

Trail contact: Strouds Run State Park, Athens; (740) 767-3570; http://parks .ohiodnr.gov/stroudsrun

Finding the trailhead: From US 33 in Athens, exit south onto Columbus Road (exit 13) and drive 2.1 miles to Columbia Avenue (at the top of the hill with a traffic light). Turn left (east) and drive 1.1 miles to a fork at the third stop sign. Take the right fork and continue 0.3 mile to a T-intersection with CR 20 (Strouds Run Road). Turn right (east) and drive 3.2 miles to the beach entrance on the right. From the beach parking lot, continue to the small gravel lot beyond it. The trailhead is on the far side of the gravel lot, marked with a sign. **Option:** Just past the park entrance sign on the right is a small parking lot at the terminal trailhead. You can drop off a bicycle or car here if you want to set up a shuttle. *DeLorme: Ohio Atlas & Gazetteer:* Page 80 B2. GPS: N39 20.79' / W82 02.00'.

W Covered Bridge Trail, Wayne National Forest–Athens District–Marietta Unit

The highlight of this 5-mile point-to-point trail is what lies at each end: a century-old covered bridge. Once numbering in the thousands, only about 140 covered bridges exist in Ohio today. Each bridge/trailhead crosses the scenic Little Muskingum River where steep wooded slopes meet farmland in the river valley. The trail itself moves away from the river to upland oak-hickory forests and crosses some attractive tributaries. From the Covered Bridge Trail, you can take a connector trail to Archers Fork and the North Country Trail. Stay on the designated trail, since private land abuts the Wayne throughout this portion of the national forest. Primitive campgrounds are located at either trailhead, but vandalism is a threat in this remote area.

Trail contact: Wayne National Forest, Athens District–Marietta Unit; (740) 373-9055; www.fs.usda.gov/wayne

Hune Bridge

Finding the trailhead: From the junction of SR 7 and SR 60 in Marietta, take SR 26 north 17.7 miles to a brown Forest Service trailhead sign on the right that reads CANOE ACCESS HUNE BRIDGE. Take a right onto Duff Road and leave your car in the camping area. *DeLorme: Ohio Atlas & Gazetteer:* Page 72 D2. GPS: N39 30.58' / W81 15.03'.

To shuttle, return to SR 26 and continue north another 3 miles to the Rinard Bridge, visible right next to the road. Turn right onto Tice Run Road (CR 406) and cross the river. Take a right onto Haught Run Road (Township Road 407) and drive 0.4 mile to the campground. The trailhead is marked with a COVERED BRIDGE TRAIL sign. GPS: N39 31.90' / W81 13.52'.

✕ Ohio View Trail, Wayne National Forest–Athens District–Marietta Unit

The 7-mile point-to-point Ohio View Trail could be better described as the Ohio Glimpse Trail. And the glimpse you do get is overlooking an industrial complex! But don't be discouraged, this well-designed trail weaves through mature oak-hickory forests on the slopes and beech-maple forests in the bottomlands. Wind your way around a number of attractive streams and drainages. Go in springtime to see a riot of wildflowers and in autumn for the striking colors of fall foliage. Get a permit to collect some non-timber forest products like morel and chicken-of-the-woods mushrooms, pawpaw fruits, and medicinal plants like yellowroot, bloodroot, blue cohosh, and black cohosh. Watch closely for blazes toward the northern end of this trail; the route sometimes deviates from the Forest Service map due to changes in oil and gas access roads.

Trail contact: Wayne National Forest, Athens District–Marietta Unit; (740) 373-9055; www.fs.usda.gov/wayne

Finding the trailhead: The trailhead is marked with a sign on SR 7 in Beavertown. To shuttle, continue north to New Matamoras, where you turn onto SR 260 and travel west 2 miles to the trailhead on the left. The trailhead sign is easy to miss; if you hit CR 9, you've gone too far. *DeLorme: Ohio Atlas & Gazetteer:* Page 73 C7. GPS: (SR 260) N39 31.44' / W81 6.15'; (SR 7) N39 28.32' / W81 6.34'.

⅄ Archers Fork Trail, Wayne National Forest–Athens District-Marietta Unit

This 9.3-mile loop trail offers a sampling of the natural, resource, and human history that defines Ohio's Appalachian region. The highlight is the Irish Run natural bridge, which measures 51 feet long. Start from an old cemetery and walk along ridgetops and in hollows. Pass two attractive runs, the natural bridge, recess caves, and rock outcroppings surrounded by mountain laurel. Spring wildflowers in this mixed mesophytic forest are outstanding. Hike it in a day or break it into two, since backcountry camping is allowed in the national forest.

Trail contact: Wayne National Forest, Athens District–Marietta Unit; (740) 373-9055; www.fs.usda.gov/wayne

Finding the trailhead: From SR 260 between Bloomfield and New Matamoras, turn south onto Shay Ridge Road (Township Road 34). Drive 1.4 miles to the brown North Country Scenic Trail sign. Turn left and park by the cemetery on the left. Do not try to continue along the road past the cemetery; it's deeply rutted and there's no parking farther down. *DeLorme: Ohio Atlas & Gazetteer:* Page 72 D2. GPS: N39 31.41' / W81 10.86'.

▶ There are approximately forty known rock bridges in Ohio. It's possible that more have yet to be documented.

In Addition: Selected Ohio Backpack Trails

If you're looking for a few more miles, a backcountry experience, or a secluded camping spot, try one of Ohio's backpack trails. Most backpack trailheads do not have maps stocked, so contact the appropriate agency before heading out. Also bring a water purifier, since reliable water sources can be few and far between. Most of these trails require a free backcountry permit or self-registration at the trailhead.

Buckeye Trail, AEP ReCreation Lands

Ohio's newest backpacking trail is courtesy of the Buckeye Trail Association, whose volunteers built 26 miles through American Electric Power (AEP) ReCreation Lands. Yes, ReCreation is a double entendre. These 60,000 acres owned by AEP were (and continue to be) surface mined for coal. Much environmental reclamation, in the form of planting grasses and trees, has been AEP's attempt at re-creating a landscape, which they have in turn opened up for public recreation; you simply need to download and fill out a free permit beforehand (www.aep.com/environmental/recreation/recland/permit.aspx).

Completed in 2012, this linear section of trail begins north of campsite K and ends south of campsite H (or the other way around, of course). This means you can walk for three days, sleeping two nights at free campsites with potable water. Not bad. The scenery is nothing stellar, but the trail is thoughtfully routed in the woods and through the campsites with some pond views along the way. You can purchase the Stockport trail section map from the Buckeye Trail Association for detailed directions.

Trail contact: Buckeye Trail Association, Worthington; (740) 832-1BTA; www.buckeyetrail.org

Finding the trailhead (north): From Cumberland, take SR 83 south 2.7 miles to CR 20. Take a left (east) and go 4.5 miles to a spot where the Buckeye Trail enters the woods. Look for the blue blaze. Parking here is difficult; get dropped off or find a spot where you can leave your car by the side of the road. *DeLorme: Ohio Atlas & Gazetteer:* Page 71 C5. GPS: N39 43.15' / W81 40.09'.

Finding the trailhead (south): From the junction of SR 83 and SR 78, take SR 78 west 0.7 mile to a pullout on the right (north) side of the road. There is parking and a trailhead bulletin board here. If you cross the bridge over Dyes Fork, you've gone too far. GPS: N39 43.28' / W81 40.20'.

Burr Oak Backpack Trail

Walk around the perimeter of Burr Oak Lake on a 23-mile trail that provides some excellent views of the lake from the comfortable shade of a maturing forest. There are some nice rock features and even a supposed Native American signal tree—an old tree that Native Americans bent down as a sapling to mark a direction on a long-distance route. Begin from the ranger station and take the Buckeye Trail along the east side of the lake or the Burr Oak Backpack Trail along the west side of the lake to one of several primitive campsites or the main campground. Alternately, begin along the north side of the lake, at the campground or at the Wildcat Hollow trailhead, and spend the night at one of the cottages near the lodge.

Trail contact: Burr Oak State Park, Glouster; (740) 767-3570; http://parks .ohiodnr.gov/burroak

Finding the trailhead: From SR 13 north of Glouster, turn east onto SR 78 and drive 4.1 miles to the park entrance on the left, marked with a sign. Take a left onto the park drive and drive 0.2 mile straight to the ranger office. The backpack trail trailhead is marked and visible from the ranger station parking. *DeLorme: Ohio Atlas & Gazetteer:* Page 70 D2. GPS: N39 31.74' / W82 1.59'.

East Fork State Park Trails

There are three lengthy trails on the south side of East Fork Lake. Combine them any way you want to make an overnighter or a several-day trip. Try the Buckeye Trail (blue blaze) to backcountry site 2 and return on the Backpack Trail (red blaze) for an overnight loop. Closest to the lakeshore is the 14-mile Backpack Trail. Paralleling that and circling the entire lake is the 32-mile Steve Newman Worldwalker Perimeter Trail, named after a native son who became the first person to circle the globe entirely on foot. He spent the last night of his travels in East Fork State Park before returning home. Largely sharing the same route with the Perimeter Trail

▶ If you arrive at park or forest headquarters during office hours and they're not too busy, you may be able to get somebody to drop you off at a trailhead in order to set up a shuttle. This is especially true in more-remote areas, where vandalism is more of a threat to unattended vehicles.

is the Buckeye–North Country–American Discovery Trail. This multi-named trail continues beyond park boundaries to the east and west. There are four backcountry campsites available; get a permit from the park office. Horses are permitted on the Perimeter Trail, and illegal equestrian use has extended to the Backpack Trail as well.

Trail contact: East Fork State Park, Bethel; (513) 734-4323; http://parks.ohiodnr .gov/eastfork

Finding the trailhead: From I-275 in Cincinnati, travel east on SR 32 for 10 miles to Half Acre Road. Turn right (south) and drive 0.8 mile to Old SR 32. Take a left and drive 0.1 mile to the park entrance on the right. Drive straight ahead to the park office. Trailhead parking is near the office. *DeLorme: Ohio Atlas & Gazetteer:* Page 75 D7. GPS: N39 00.26' / W84 08.43'.

Mohican-Memorial State Forest Bridle Trails

The day hikes in Mohican State Park feature the area's main attractions: the Clear Fork of the Mohican River, Big and Little Lyons Falls, and a covered bridge. Two developed

Backpacking the Twin Valley Trail

campgrounds are in the park. But if you want to get a backcountry experience, head out on the combined state park and adjacent Mohican-Memorial State Forest's 45 miles of hiking, mountain biking, and bridle trails. Start at the group camping area near the forest office and hike to a backcountry campsite along the Hickory Ridge Trail. Return along the Hemlock Gorge Trail. You'll pass both car campgrounds along the way. Check in with the state forest office to self-register and get information about backcountry campsites. Dogs are not allowed in backcountry campsites.

Trail contact: Mohican-Memorial State Forest, New Philadelphia; (330) 339-2205; www.dnr.state.oh.us/forests/mohican/tabid/5160/Default.aspx

Finding the trailhead: From I-71 south of Mansfield, exit on SR 96 and drive about 16 miles to Park Road on the left. Take Park Road 0.5 mile to the state forest office on the left. *DeLorme: Ohio Atlas & Gazetteer:* Page 49 D7. GPS: N40 36.21' / W82 18.64'.

Twin Valley Backpacking Trail

Five Rivers MetroParks is working steadily to make Dayton the adventure capital of the Midwest. Exhibit A: the Twin Valley Backpacking Trail, opened in 2008 with the creation of backcountry campsites and a connector trail between the existing trails in Germantown and Twin Creek MetroParks. Get a permit ahead of time and head out on some or all of the 22 miles of trail—you can make loops of varying lengths. Expect to hike mostly in second-growth woods, along the relatively clean Twin Creek, through some meadows, and minimally on the road—all just twenty minutes from downtown Dayton. Try this for a weekend: Start Friday from the Germantown overnight parking (Boomershine Road) trailhead and hike down the west side of Twin Creek to the Oak Ridge backcountry campsite (2 miles). Saturday, continue to the Cedar Ridge backcountry site (4.6 miles). Sunday, return up the east side of Twin Creek and back to the Boomershine Road trailhead (8.6 miles).

Trail contact: Five Rivers MetroParks, Dayton; (937) 275-PARK; www.metro parks.org

Finding the trailhead: From the junction of SR 4 and SR 725 in Germantown, take SR 725 west 4.1 miles to Boomershine Road. Turn north onto Boomershine Road and go 1.8 miles to the parking lot on the right. *DeLorme: Ohio Atlas & Gazetteer:* Page 65 C4. GPS: N39 39.29' / W84 25.87'.

Vesuvius Backpack Trail

If you enjoyed the Lakeshore Trail at Lake Vesuvius in the Ironton Ranger District of Wayne National Forest, take it up a notch and head out on the Vesuvius Backpack Trail, a 16-mile loop that shares the Lakeshore Trail but then extends out into the forest along ridges and creek valleys. The redbuds and dogwoods blooming in springtime make a great show. Wildflowers and rock outcroppings in the Hanging Rock region are impressive as well.

Trail contact: Wayne National Forest, Ironton Ranger District, Pedro; (740) 532-3223; www.fs.usda.gov/wayne

Finding the trailhead: From Ironton, travel north on SR 93 for 6.5 miles and turn right (east) onto CR 29. (If you get to the forest headquarters, you've gone too far.) Follow the signs 0.9 mile to the furnace parking lot. *DeLorme: Ohio Atlas & Gazetteer:* Page 85 D7. GPS: N38 35.04' / W82 38.22'.

Wildcat Hollow Backpack Trail

This popular trail in the Athens District of Wayne National Forest largely follows ridgetops and features excellent spring wildflowers and fall foliage. Attractions include an old one-room schoolhouse and an old farmhouse. Expect also to see oil wells and access roads. In dry weather it may be difficult to find a good water source. The trail is a 15-mile loop with an optional 5-mile day hike.

Trail contact: Wayne National Forest, Athens Ranger District; (740) 753-0101; www.fs.usda.gov/wayne

Finding the trailhead: From SR 13 between Corning and Glouster, turn east onto Irish Ridge Road (CR 16). Drive 0.1 mile to a junction, where Irish Ridge turns left. Take the left here and drive 1.9 miles to a second junction. Turn right onto Dew Road (it changes name to Sunday Creek Road after a mile) and drive 1.6 miles

BICYCLE SHUTTLING

For some point-to-point hikes, a bike shuttle makes a lot more sense than bringing two cars. A bike shuttle is a fairly straightforward proposition. Bring your bike, helmet, lock, extra water, and a road map. Stash your bike at the end of the trail and then drive to the trailhead. When you finish the hike, turn a three-hour return hike into a thirty-minute return ride. Don't forget the car keys!

to the trailhead parking lot on the left. All turns starting from SR 13 are marked with a brown trail sign. *DeLorme: Ohio Atlas & Gazetteer:* Page 75 D7. GPS: N39 34.38' / W82 1.97'.

Zaleski Backpack Trail

Only about ninety minutes from Columbus, the 23.5-mile Zaleski State Forest Backpack Trail is perhaps the most popular backpack trail in the state. From the official trailhead at the Hope Furnace, you can start on a Friday night and make it to the first campsite just 1.5 miles into the trail. There are three backcountry sites in total, and you are required to camp at a designated site. All sites have tanks filled with potable water. Several access points allow you to trim the mileage when necessary, including a 10-mile day hike that also starts from the Hope Furnace. Hike in mature second-growth forest, near a decade-old clear-cut, and through a former strip mine site. Walk through a young successional forest and a pine plantation. A side loop takes you past a pioneer cemetery and through a mini gorge. There's even an overlook where you might glimpse the Moonville Ghost's swinging lantern at night.

Trail contact: Zaleski State Forest, Zaleski; (740) 596-5781; http://ohiodnr .com/forests/zaleski/tabid/5171/Default.aspx

Finding the trailhead: From SR 56 south of Nelsonville, turn south onto SR 278 and travel 4.6 miles to the Zaleski backpacking parking lot on the left. Walk south on the road to cross the creek. Take a left off the road to a footbridge and the trailhead. *DeLorme: Ohio Atlas & Gazetteer:* Page 79 B7. GPS: N39 19.86' / W82 20.46'.

In Addition: Ohio's Long Trails

Buckeye Trail

When Emma "Grandma" Gatewood finished becoming the first woman to through-hike the Appalachian Trail, she returned to her home state of Ohio and hatched a new plan. With a few other dedicated folks, the Buckeye Trail Association (BTA) formed in 1959 with a mission to connect the Ohio River to Lake Erie with a footpath.

At 1,450 miles in length, the Buckeye Trail (BT)—Ohio's official state trail—is the longest hiking trail within one state in the country. The BT's southern terminus is along the Ohio River at Cincinnati's Eden Park. From there the trail circles around the state to the northern terminus at Headlands Beach in Mentor, on Lake Erie. The trail then completes the circle back down to the Ohio. In the meantime it crosses forty counties in just about every fashion possible: through state parks and forests, along abandoned railroad rights-of-way, through private lands, on bike paths, and along the road. The scenery is equally diverse: deep forests to farmland, rocky outcrops to lakeshore, boardwalks to waterfalls.

The entire trail is completed and marked, and about half of the trail is off-road. You can simply "follow the blue blazes" for the BT's entire length, or you can purchase section maps that detail the route in increments of about 50 miles each. Many organized hikes allow you to join other hikers along the trail for outings.

The Buckeye Trail is made possible with the many hours of work provided by its tireless volunteers. To help with trail building or maintenance, to make a donation, or to get information on group hikes, contact the BTA at (740) 832-1BTA or visit www.buckeyetrail.org.

North Country Trail

Following the successful completion of the Appalachian Trail and the Pacific Crest Trail, Congress designated these two mountainous footpaths as National Scenic Trails in 1968. At about the same time, the USDA Forest Service came up with a plan to build the North Country National Scenic Trail (NCT). In March 1980 Congress passed legislation authorizing the trail. The NCT is 4,600 miles that weave through seven northern states: North Dakota, Minnesota, Wisconsin, Michigan, Ohio, Pennsylvania, and New York.

A full 1,050 of these miles are in Ohio, and much of the NCT follows the same path as the Buckeye Trail (BT). The NCT's characteristics are varied, combining natural, recreational, historic, and cultural features.

The NCT enters northwest Ohio from Michigan, west of Toledo. It joins the BT and follows the Miami and Erie Canal towpath down toward Cincinnati, where it turns east through southern Ohio. The NCT continues through the Marietta Unit of

Wayne National Forest. It then veers northward to Beaver Creek State Park, where it takes an eastward turn and continues to Pennsylvania.

Chapters in several states further the aims of the NCT. Log on to their website for more information: www.northcountrytrail.org.

American Discovery Trail

The American Discovery Trail (ADT) is the nation's only coast-to-coast nonmotorized trail. Spanning from Cape Henlopen State Park in Delaware to Point Reyes National Seashore near San Francisco, the trail has a total length of 6,800 miles. The ADT connects five National Scenic Trails and ten National Historic Trails along the way. Like the Buckeye and the North Country Trails, it combines wilderness with urban experiences and links everything in between.

Coming from the west, optional north and south routes of the ADT converge in Elizabethtown, Ohio, west of Cincinnati. The ADT then follows the path of the Buckeye Trail for most of southern Ohio before diverging in the southeast part of the state, where it continues to Belpre before crossing the Ohio River into West Virginia. For route, volunteer, and other information, visit www.discoverytrail.org.

The Art of Hiking

When standing nose to snout with a bear, you're probably not too concerned with the issue of ethical behavior in the wild. But let's be honest. How often are you nose to snout with a bear? For most of us, a hike into the "wild" means loading up the SUV with everything North Face and driving to a toileted trailhead. Sure, you can mourn how civilized we've become—how GPS units have replaced natural instinct and Gore-Tex, true-grit—but the silly gadgets of civilization aside, we have plenty of reason to take pride in how we've matured. With survival now on the back burner, we've begun to reason—and it's about time—that we have a responsibility to protect, no longer just conquer, our wild places; that they, not we, are at risk. So please, do what you can.

Now, in keeping with our chronic tendency to reduce everything to a list, here are some rules to remember.

Zero impact. Always leave an area just like you found it—if not better than you found it. Avoid camping in fragile meadows and along the banks of streams and lakes. Use a lightweight camp stove versus building a wood fire. Pack up all of your trash and extra food, and carry it out with you. Pack out or bury human waste at least 200 feet from water sources and under 6 to 8 inches of topsoil. Don't bathe with soap (even biodegradable soap) in a lake or stream. Even your body oils (especially if you're wearing sunscreen) can contaminate water sources, so try to take water in a container at least 200 feet from water sources and wash and rinse there. Remember to dump the wastewater away from water sources. Another option is to use prepackaged moistened towels to wipe off sweat and dirt.

Leave no weeds. Noxious weeds tend to outcompete (overtake) our native flora, which in turn affects animals and birds that depend on them for food. Noxious weeds can be harmful to wildlife. Yes, just like birds and furry critters, we humans can carry weed seeds from one place to another. Here are a couple of things hikers can do to minimize the spread of noxious weeds: First, learn to identify noxious weeds and exotic species. You can obtain information pamphlets from the USDA Forest Service or Ohio State University Cooperative Extension (http://extension.osu.edu). Second, regularly clean your boots, tents, packs, and hiking poles of mud and seeds. Brush your dog to remove any weed seed. Avoid camping and traveling in weed-infested areas.

Stay on the trail. It's true, a path anywhere leads nowhere new, but purists will just have to get over it. Paths serve an important purpose: They limit our impact on natural areas. Straying from a designated trail may seem innocent, but it can cause damage to sensitive areas—damage that may take years to recover, if it can recover at all. Even simple shortcuts can be destructive. So please, stay on the trail.

Keep your dog under control. You can buy a flexi-lead that allows your dog to go exploring along the trail, while allowing you the ability to reel him in should another hiker approach or should he decide to chase a deer. Always obey leash laws, and be sure to bury your dog's waste or pack it out in plastic bags. Don't let your dog harass wildlife; a dog on leash may also alert you to nearby wildlife you might otherwise miss.

Respect other trail users. Often you're not the only one on the trail. With the rise in popularity of multiuse trails, you'll have to learn a new kind of respect, beyond the nod and "hello" approach you're used to. You should first investigate whether you're on a multiuse trail, and assume the appropriate precautions. When you encounter motorized vehicles (ATVs, motorcycles, and four-wheel drives), be acutely aware. Though they should always yield to the hiker, often they're going too fast or are lost in the buzz of their engine to react to your presence. If you hear activity ahead, step off the trail just to be safe. Now, you're not likely to hear a mountain biker coming, so the best bet is to know whether you share the trail with them. Cyclists should always yield to hikers, but that's of little comfort to the hiker. Be aware. When you approach horses or pack animals on the trail, always step quietly off the trail, preferably on the downhill side, and let them pass. If you're wearing a large backpack, it's often a good idea to sit down.

Preparedness

It's been said that failing to plan means planning to fail, so do take the necessary time to plan your trip. Whether going on a short day hike or an extended backpack trip, always prepare for the worst. Simply remembering to pack a copy of the *US Army Survival Manual* is not preparedness. Although it's not a bad idea if you plan on entering truly wild places, it's merely the tourniquet answer to a problem. You need to do your best to prevent the problem from arising in the first place. These days the word *survival* is often replaced with the pathetically feeble term *comfort*. In order to remain comfortable (and to survive if you really want to push it), you need to concern yourself with the basics: water, food, and shelter. Don't go on a hike without having these bases covered. And don't go on a hike expecting to find these items in the woods.

Water. Even in frigid conditions, you need at least 2 quarts of water a day to function efficiently. Add heat and/or taxing terrain, and you can bump that figure up to 1 gallon. That's simply a base to work from—your metabolism and your level of conditioning can raise or lower that amount. Unless you know your level, assume that you need 1 gallon of water a day. Now, where do you plan on getting the water?

Natural water sources can be loaded with intestinal disturbers, such as bacteria and viruses. *Giardia lamblia*, the most common of these disturbers, is a protozoan parasite that lives part of its life cycle as a cyst in water sources. The parasite spreads when mammals (humans included) defecate in water sources. Giardia can induce cramping, diarrhea, vomiting, and fatigue within two days to two weeks after ingestion. Giardiasis is treatable with the prescription drug Flagyl. Fluid loss due to diarrhea can be helped by drinking an electrolyte solution, such as Gatorade. If you believe you've contracted giardiasis, see a doctor immediately.

Treating water. The best and easiest solution to avoid polluted water is to carry your water with you. Yet, depending on the nature of your hike and the duration, this may not be an option—seeing as 1 gallon of water weighs 8.5 pounds. In that case, you'll need to look into treating water. Regardless of which method you choose, you should always carry some water with you, in case of an emergency. Save this reserve until you absolutely need it.

There are three methods of treating water: boiling, chemical treatment, and filtering. Boiling is the safest, if not simplest, method because it's not dependent on variables (i.e., brand name or proper dosage). If you boil water, it's recommended that you do so for ten to fifteen minutes, though some will say just bringing the water to a boil is enough. Many may find this method impractical, however, since you're forced to exhaust a good deal of your fuel supply.

You can opt for chemical treatment (e.g., Potable Aqua), which will kill giardia but will not take care of other chemical pollutants. Other drawbacks to chemical treatments are the unpleasant taste of the water after it's treated and the length of time it takes for them to be effective. You can remedy the former by adding powdered drink mix to the water.

Filters are the preferred method for treating water. Filters remove giardia and other organic and inorganic contaminants (check the instructions to make sure) and don't leave an aftertaste. Some filters also remove viruses. Water filters are far from perfect, however, as they can easily become clogged or leak if a gasket wears out. It's always a good idea to carry a backup supply of chemical treatment tablets in case your filter decides to quit on you.

Food. If we're talking about "survival," you can go days without food, as long as you have water. But we're talking about "comfort" here. Try to avoid foods that are high in sugar and fat, like candy bars and potato chips. These food types are harder to digest and are low in nutritional value. Instead, bring along foods that are easy to pack, nutritious, and high in energy (e.g., bagels, nutrition bars, dehydrated fruit, gorp, and jerky). Complex carbohydrates and protein are your best food friends. If you are on an overnight trip, easy-to-fix dinners include rice or pasta dinners and soup mixes. A few lightweight spices can really perk up a meal. Freeze-dried meals are nice for long trips, but are expensive and bulky. If you do a lot of long backpacks, invest in a dehydrator. For a tasty breakfast, you can fix hot oatmeal with brown sugar and reconstituted milk powder topped off with banana chips. If you like a hot drink in the morning, bring along herbal tea bags or hot chocolate. If you are a coffee junkie, you can purchase coffee that is packaged like tea bags.

Prepackage all of your meals in heavy-duty resealable plastic bags to keep food from spilling in your pack. These bags can be reused to pack out trash. Prepackaging also minimizes extra trash in the form of boxes and cans. Avoid bringing glass containers into the backcountry, as broken glass can pose some serious problems. A good book on backcountry cooking is *Wilderness Ranger Cookbook* by Brunell and Swain, Globe Pequot Press.

Shelter. The type of shelter you choose depends less on the conditions than on your tolerance for discomfort. Shelter comes in many forms—tent, tarp, lean-to, bivy sack, cabin, cave, etc. If you're camping in the desert, a bivy sack may suffice, but if you're near tree line and a storm is approaching, a better choice is a three- or four-season tent. Tents are the logical and most popular choice for most backpackers as they're lightweight and packable—and you can rest assured that you always have shelter from the elements. Before you leave on your trip, anticipate what the weather and terrain will be like and bring the type of shelter that will work best for your comfort level.

Finding a campsite. If there are established campsites, stick to those. If not, start looking for a campsite early—like around 3:30 or 4 p.m. Stop at the first appropriate site you see, remembering that good campsites are found and not made. Depending on the area, it could be a long time before you find another suitable location. Pitch your camp in an area that's reasonably level and clear of underbrush, which can harbor insects and conceal approaching animals. Make sure the area is at least 200 feet from fragile areas like lakeshores, meadows, and stream banks. Tree saplings and flowering plants are easily damaged, so avoid plopping your tent on top of them. In addition, watch out for poison ivy and thorny plants like greenbrier and multiflora rose.

If you are camping in stormy, rainy weather, look for a rock outcrop or a shelter in the trees to keep the wind from blowing your tent all night. Be sure that you don't camp under trees with dead limbs that might break off on top of you. Also, try to find an area that has an absorbent surface, such as sandy soil or forest duff. This, in addition to camping on a surface with a slight angle, will provide better drainage. By all means, don't dig trenches to provide drainage around your tent—remember you're practicing minimum-impact camping.

If you're in bear country, steer clear of creek beds or animal paths. If you see any signs of a bear's presence (e.g., scat, footprints), relocate. You'll need to find a campsite near a tall tree where you can hang your food and other items that may attract bears such as deodorant, toothpaste, or soap. Carry a lightweight nylon rope with which to hang your food. As a rule, you should hang your food at least 15 feet from the ground and 4 feet away from the tree trunk. You can put food and other items in a waterproof stuff sack and tie one end of the rope to the sack. To get the other end of the rope over the tree branch, tie a good-size rock to it and gently toss the rock over the tree branch. Pull the stuff sack up until it reaches the top of the branch, and tie it off securely. Don't hang your food near your tent! If possible, hang your food at least 100 feet away from your campsite. Alternatives to hanging your food are bear-proof plastic tubes and metal bear boxes. Chipmunks, ground squirrels, and raccoons will also steal your food if you don't hang it.

Lastly, think of comfort. Lie down on the ground where you intend to sleep and see if it's a good fit. Bring along an insulating pad for warmth and extra comfort. The days of using pine boughs or digging a hip depression in the ground are long gone. And for the final touch, have your tent face east. You'll appreciate the warmth of the morning sun and have a nice view to wake up to.

First Aid

If you plan to spend a lot of time outdoors hiking, spend a few hours and bucks to take a good wilderness first-aid class. You'll not only learn first-aid basics, but how to be creative miles from nowhere. The Red Cross offers basic first-aid and CPR classes. Some outdoor organizations and universities offer Wilderness First Response courses. Find the nearest Red Cross office by going to http://chapters.redcross.org/oh/ohiostate.

Now, we know you're tough, but get 10 miles into the woods and develop a blister, and you'll wish you had carried a first-aid kit. Face it: It's just plain good sense. Many companies produce lightweight, compact first-aid kits; just make sure yours contains at least the following:

- Band-Aids
- Moleskin, duct tape or athletic tape, and/or Band-Aid's Blister Relief
- Compeed
- Various sterile gauzes and dressings
- White surgical tape
- An ACE bandage
- An antihistamine
- Aspirin, ibuprofen, or acetaminophen
- Betadine solution
- First-aid book
- Antacid tablets
- Tweezers
- Scissors
- Antibacterial wipes
- Triple-antibiotic ointment
- Plastic gloves
- Sterile cotton-tip applicators
- A thermometer

Here are a few tips for dealing with and hopefully preventing certain ailments.

Sunburn. To avoid sunburn, wear sunscreen (SPF 15 or higher), protective clothing, and a wide-brimmed hat when you are hiking in sunny weather. If you do get sunburned, treat the area with aloe vera gel and protect the area from further sun exposure. Protect your eyes by wearing sunglasses with UV protection, too!

Blisters. First, try to prevent blisters. Break in your boots, wear appropriate socks, and then, if you're prone to blisters, apply moleskin, Compeed, Bodyglide (www.bodyglide.com), duct tape, or athletic tape before you start hiking to help decrease friction to that area. In the event a blister develops despite your careful precautions, an effective way to treat it is to cut out a circle of moleskin and remove the center—like a donut—and place it over the blistered area. Cutting the center out will reduce the pressure applied to the sensitive skin. Then put Second Skin in the hole and tape over the whole mess. Second Skin (made by Spenco) is applied to the blister after it has popped and acts as a "second skin" to help prevent further irritation.

Insect bites and stings. The most troublesome of Ohio's insects are mosquitoes and yellow jackets. A simple treatment for most insect bites and stings is to apply hydrocortisone 1 percent cream topically and to take a pain medication such as ibuprofen or acetaminophen to reduce swelling. If you forgot to pack these items, a cold compress or a paste of mud and ashes can sometimes assuage the itching and discomfort. Remove any stingers by using tweezers or scraping the area with your fingernail or a knife blade. Don't pinch the area, as you'll only spread the venom.

Some hikers are highly sensitive to bites and stings and may have a serious allergic reaction that can be life-threatening. Symptoms of a serious allergic reaction can include wheezing, an asthmatic attack, and shock. The treatment for this severe type of reaction is epinephrine (adrenaline). If you know that you are sensitive to bites and stings, carry a prepackaged kit of epinephrine (e.g., Anakit), which can be obtained only by prescription from your doctor. Also carry an antihistamine such as Benadryl.

Ticks. As you well know, ticks can carry disease, such as Lyme disease. The best defense is, of course, prevention. If you know you're going to be hiking through an area littered with ticks, wear long pants and a long-sleeved shirt. At the end of your hike, do a spot check for ticks (and insects in general). If you do find a tick, coat the insect with Vaseline or tree sap to cut off its air supply. The tick should release its hold, but if it doesn't, grab the head of the tick firmly—with a pair of tweezers if you have them—and gently pull it away from the skin with a twisting motion. Sometimes the mouthparts linger, embedded in your skin. If this happens, try to remove them with a disinfected needle. Clean the affected area with an antibacterial cleanser and then apply triple antibiotic ointment. Monitor the area for a few days. Lyme disease is a serious tick-borne illness. If, after hiking, you find a bull's-eye rash on your skin combined with flulike symptoms, seek medical attention right away. Lyme disease is very treatable if you catch it early.

Poison ivy. This skin irritant can be found most anywhere in North America and comes in the form of a vine or bush, having leaflets in groups of three. Learn how to identify the plant. The oil it secretes can cause an allergic reaction in the form of blisters, usually about twelve hours after exposure. The itchy rash can last from ten days to several weeks. The best defense against poison ivy is to wear protective clothing and to apply a nonprescription product called IvyBlock to exposed skin. This lotion is meant to guard against the effects of poison ivy and can be washed off with soap and water.

If you know you've been exposed, look for some jewelweed (spotted touch-me-not). Crush the juicy stem and leaves, and apply to your skin. Only do this if you're in an area where it's legal to pick plants and where there is an abundant supply. Thin the stand carefully by taking a small plant that will likely be outcompeted anyway. Jewelweed is an effective antidote to poison ivy for many people.

After you return home, wash the area as soon as possible with soap and cool water. Taking a cool shower after you return home from your hike will also help remove any lingering oil from your skin (hot water opens your pores). Should you contract a rash from poison ivy, use Benadryl or a similar product to reduce the itching. If the rash is localized, hydrocortisone cream or calamine lotion can help reduce itching and dry up the area. If the rash has spread, either tough it out or see your doctor about getting a dose of cortisone (available both orally and by injection).

Snakebites. First off, snakebites are rare in North America. Unless startled or provoked, the majority of snakes will not bite. If you are wise to their habitats and keep a careful eye on the trail, you should be just fine. Though your chances of being struck are slim, it's wise to know what to do in the event you are.

If a nonvenomous snake bites you, allow the wound to bleed a small amount and then cleanse the wounded area with a Betadine solution (10 percent povidone iodine). Rinse the wound with clean water (preferably) or fresh urine (it might sound ugly, but it's sterile). Once the area is clean, cover it with triple antibiotic ointment and a clean bandage. Remember, most residual damage from snakebites, venomous or otherwise, comes from infection, not the snake's venom. Keep the area as clean as possible and get medical attention immediately.

If you are bitten by a venomous snake, remove the toxin with a suctioning device, found in a snakebite kit (like the Sawyer Extractor). If you do not have such a device, squeeze the wound—don't cut it and do not use your mouth for suction, as the venom will enter your bloodstream through the vessels under the tongue and head straight for your heart. Then, clean the wound just as you would a nonpoisonous bite. Tie a clean band of cloth snuggly around the afflicted appendage, about an inch or so above the bite (or the rim of the swelling). This is not a tourniquet—you want to simply slow the blood flow, not cut it off. Loosen the band if numbness ensues. Remove the band for a minute and reapply a little higher every ten minutes. (Do not try to apply ice to the bite wound to achieve slower blood flow.)

If it is your friend who's been bitten, treat him for shock—make him comfortable, have him lie down, elevate the legs, and keep him warm. Immobilize the affected area and remove any constricting items such as rings, watches, or restrictive clothing—swelling may occur. Splint the extremity that was bitten and keep it lower than the heart. Monitor for shock. Keep your friend hydrated but avoid painkillers and alcohol. Once your friend is stable and relatively calm, hike out to get help. The victim should get treatment within twelve hours, ideally, which usually consists of a tetanus shot, antivenin, and antibiotics.

Now, if you are alone and struck by a venomous snake, stay calm. Hysteria will only quicken the venom's spread. Follow the procedure above and do your best to reach help. When hiking out, don't run—you'll only increase the flow of blood throughout your system. Instead, walk calmly.

Ohio is home to only three venomous snakes: the copperhead, the eastern massasauga, and the timber rattlesnake. The timber rattlesnake is an endangered species, and you are far more likely to get struck by lightning than bitten by one of these. The massasauga and the timber are both rattlers, and all three of these species have two defining characteristics: triangular heads and elliptical pupils. Copperheads tend to bite more than any other species, but their bites are rarely fatal.

Dehydration. Have you ever hiked in hot weather and had a roaring headache and felt fatigued after only a few miles? More than likely you were dehydrated. Symptoms of dehydration include fatigue, headache, and decreased coordination and judgment. Dehydration can also make you more susceptible to hypothermia and frostbite. When you are hiking, your body's rate of fluid loss depends on the outside temperature, humidity, altitude, and your activity level. On average, a hiker walking in warm weather will lose 4 liters of fluid a day. That fluid loss is easily replaced by normal consumption of liquids and food. However, if a hiker is walking briskly in hot, dry weather and hauling a heavy pack, he can lose 1 to 3 liters of water an hour. It's important to always carry plenty of water and to stop often and drink fluids regularly, even if you aren't thirsty.

One way to tell if you're adequately hydrated is to check the color of your urine. It should be clear. The darker yellow it is, the more dehydrated you are. With a little creativity, you can check the color in the backcountry. You can also pinch the skin on the back of your hand. If it quickly lowers itself, you're okay. If it remains in a peak, you're dehydrated.

Heat exhaustion. Heat exhaustion is the result of a loss of large amounts of electrolytes and often occurs if a hiker is dehydrated and has been under heavy exertion. Common symptoms of heat exhaustion include cramping, exhaustion, fatigue, lightheadedness, and nausea. You can treat heat exhaustion by getting out of the sun, eating high-energy foods, and drinking an electrolyte solution made up of 1 teaspoon of salt and 1 tablespoon of sugar dissolved in 1 liter of water. Drink this solution slowly over a period of an hour.

Drinking plenty of fluids (preferably an electrolyte solution like Gatorade) can also prevent heat exhaustion. When drinking a lot of water, remember to snack while you drink. If you don't, you'll disrupt the electrolyte balance as you lose body salt through sweating, and possibly develop hyponatremia (water intoxication). Symptoms include nausea, vomiting, frequent urination, and an altered mental state. Avoid hiking during the hottest parts of the day and wear breathable clothing, a wide brimmed hat, and sunglasses.

Hypothermia. Hypothermia is one of the biggest dangers in the backcountry—especially for day hikers in mild weather. That may sound strange, but imagine starting out on a hike in spring when it's sunny and 60 degrees Fahrenheit out. You're clad in nylon pants and a cotton T-shirt. About halfway through your hike, the sky begins to cloud up and in the next hour a light drizzle begins to fall and the wind starts to pick up. Before you know it, you are soaking wet and shivering—the perfect recipe for hypothermia. More advanced signs include decreased coordination, slurred speech, and blurred vision. When a victim's temperature falls below 91 degrees, the blood pressure, breathing, and pulse plummet, possibly leading to coma and death.

To avoid hypothermia, always bring a windproof/rainproof shell, a fleece jacket, Capilene tights or rain pants, gloves, and hat when you are hiking in the mountains. Avoid wearing 100 percent cotton clothing, as it does not dry easily and provides no warmth when wet. Learn to adjust your clothing layers based on the temperature. If you are climbing uphill at a moderate pace, you will stay warm, but when you stop for a break, you'll become cold quickly unless you add more layers of clothing. Keeping hydrated and well nourished are also important in avoiding hypothermia.

If a hiker is showing advanced signs of hypothermia, dress her in dry clothes and make sure she is wearing a hat and gloves. Place her in a sleeping bag in a tent or shelter that will protect her from the wind and other elements. Give her warm fluids to drink and keep her awake. Put water bottles filled with warm water in the crotch and armpits to help warm her.

Frostbite. When the mercury dips below 32 degrees Fahrenheit, your extremities begin to chill. If a persistent chill attacks a localized area, say your hands or your toes, the circulatory system reacts by cutting off blood flow to the affected area—the idea being to protect and preserve the body's overall temperature. And so it's death by attrition for the affected area. Ice crystals start to form from the water in the cells of the neglected tissue. Deprived of heat, nourishment, and now water, the tissue literally starves. This is frostbite.

Prevention is your best defense against this situation. Most prone to frostbite are your face, hands, and feet—so protect these areas well. Wool is the material of choice because it provides ample air space for insulation and draws moisture away from the skin. However, synthetic fabrics have recently made great strides in the cold-weather clothing market. Do your research. A pair of light silk or polypro liners under your regular gloves or mittens is a good trick for keeping warm. They afford some additional warmth, but more importantly they'll allow you to remove your mitts for intricate work without exposing the skin.

Now, if your feet or hands start to feel cold or numb due to the elements, warm them as quickly as possible. Place cold hands under your armpits or bury them in your crotch. Carry hand and foot warmers if you can. If your feet are cold, change your socks. If there's room in your boots, add another pair of socks. Do remember, though, that constricting your feet in tight boots can restrict blood flow and actually make your feet colder more quickly. Your socks need to have breathing room if they're going to be effective. Dead air provides insulation. If your face is cold, place your warm hands over your face or simply wear a head stocking (called a balaclava).

Should your skin go numb and start to appear white and waxy but is still cold and soft, chances are you've got superficial frostbite. Rewarm as quickly as possible with skin-to-skin contact. No damage should occur. Do not let the area get frostbitten again!

If your skin is white and waxy but dents when you press on it, you have partial thickness frostbite. Rewarm as you would for superficial frostbite, but expect swelling and blisters to form. Don't massage the affected area, but do take ibuprofen for pain and reduction of tissue damage. If blisters form, you need to leave the backcountry.

If your skin is frozen hard like an ice cube, you have full thickness frostbite. Don't try to thaw the area unless you can maintain the warmth. In other words, don't stop to warm up your frostbitten feet only to head back on the trail. You'll do more damage than good. Tests have shown that hikers who walked on thawed feet did more harm, and endured more pain, than hikers who left the affected areas alone. Do your best to get out of the cold entirely and seek medical attention—which usually consists of performing a rapid rewarming in warm water (104 to 108 degrees) for twenty to thirty minutes. Get to a doctor as soon as possible.

The overall objective in preventing both hypothermia and frostbite is to keep the body's core warm. Protect key areas where heat escapes, like the top of the head, and maintain the proper nutrition and hydration levels. Foods that are high in calories aid the body in producing heat. Never smoke or drink alcohol when you're in situations where the cold is threatening. By affecting blood flow, these activities ultimately cool the body's core temperature.

Natural Hazards

Besides tripping over a rock or tree root on the trail, there are some real hazards to be aware of while hiking.

Lightning. Thunderstorms are common to Ohio in the spring and summer and also occur in the fall. Lightning is generated by thunderheads and can strike without warning, even several miles away from the nearest overhead cloud. Keep an eye on cloud formation and don't underestimate how fast a storm can build. The bigger they get, the more likely a thunderstorm will happen.

Lightning takes the path of least resistance, so if you're the high point, it might chose you. Ducking under a rock overhang is likewise dangerous, as you form the shortest path between the rock and ground. Avoid standing under the only or the tallest tree. If you have an insulating pad, squat on it. Avoid having both your hands and feet touching the ground at once, and never lay flat. Minimize yourself as a target. If you hear a buzzing sound or feel your hair standing on end, move quickly, as an electrical charge is building up. For additional information, check out the National Lightning Safety Institute's website at www.lightningsafety.com.

Flash floods. The spooky thing about flash floods is that they can appear out of nowhere from a storm many miles away. Always climb to safety if danger threatens. Flash floods usually subside quickly, so be patient and don't cross a swollen stream.

Bears. The black bear is making a comeback in the eastern part of Ohio. Here are some tips in case you and a bear scare each other: Most of all, avoid scaring a bear. Watch for bear tracks (five toes) and droppings (sizable, with leaves, partly digested berries, seeds, and/or animal fur). Talk or sing where visibility or hearing are limited.

Keep a clean camp, hang food, and don't sleep in the clothes you wore while cooking. Be especially careful in spring to avoid getting between a mother and her cubs. In late summer and fall, bears are busy eating berries and acorns to fatten up for winter, so be extra careful around berry bushes and oak brush.

If you do encounter a bear, move away slowly while facing the bear, talk softly, and avoid direct eye contact. Give the bear room to escape. Since bears are very curious, it might stand upright to get a better whiff of you, and it may even charge you to try to intimidate you. Try to stay calm. If a bear does attack you, fight back with anything you have handy. Unleashed dogs have been known to come running back to their owners with a bear close behind. Keep your dog on a leash or leave him at home.

Hunting. Hunting is a popular sport in Ohio, and it seems as if it's always one sort of hunting season or another. Contact the Ohio Department of Natural Resources Division of Wildlife for information on hunting seasons at (800) WILDLIFE or go to www.ohiodnr.com/wildlife. When it comes to the one-week gun season for deer (usually in November or December), just avoid the public lands where hunting is allowed (you will be considerably outnumbered by people with guns in their hands) and opt for parks and preserves where hunting is not allowed. It's always a good idea to wear at least one article of clothing that's hunter orange.

Trip Planning

Planning your hiking adventure begins with letting a friend or relative know your trip itinerary so they can call for help if you don't return at your scheduled time. Your next task is to make sure you are outfitted to experience the risks and rewards of the trail. This section highlights gear and clothing you may want to take with you to get the most out of your hike.

Day Hikes

- Daypack
- Water and water bottles/water hydration system
- Food and high-energy snacks
- First-aid kit
- Headlamp/flashlight with extra batteries and bulbs
- Maps and compass/GPS unit
- Knife/multipurpose tool
- Sunscreen and sunglasses
- Matches in waterproof container and fire starter
- Insulating top and bottom layers (fleece, wool, etc.)
- Raingear
- Winter hat and gloves
- Wide-brimmed sun hat

- Insect repellent
- Backpacker's trowel, toilet paper, and resealable plastic bags
- Whistle and/or mirror
- Space blanket/bag
- Camera
- Guidebook
- Watch
- Water treatment tablets
- Wet Ones or other wet wipes
- Hand and foot warmers for cold weather hiking
- Duct tape for repairs
- Extra socks
- Gaiters, depending on season

Overnight Trip (in addition to what's listed for day hikes)
- Backpack and waterproof rain cover
- Bandanna
- Biodegradable soap
- Collapsible water container (2- to 3-gallon capacity)
- Clothing (extra wool socks, shirt and shorts, long pants)
- Cook set/utensils and pot scrubber
- Stuff sacks to store gear
- Extra plastic resealable bags
- Garbage bags
- Journal and pen
- Nylon rope to hang food
- Long underwear
- Permit (if required)
- Repair kit (tent, stove, pack, etc.)
- Sandals or running shoes to wear around camp and to ford streams
- Sleeping bag
- Waterproof stuff sacks (one for hanging food)
- Insulating ground pad
- Hand towel
- Stove and fuel
- Tent and ground cloth
- Toiletry items
- Water filter

Appendix A: Hike Index

Best Hikes for Birding

Best Hikes to See Native American Earthworks

Best Kid-Friendly Hikes

G. Rocky River Reservation (NE)

17. Terrace to Ancient Trail Loop, Battelle Darby Creek Metro Park (C)

Best Hikes along Rivers and Streams

16. Blackhand to Quarry Rim Trail Loop, Blackhand Gorge State Nature (C)

28. Fort to Gorge Trail Loop, Fort Hill State Memorial (SW)

20. Glen Helen Loop Trail, Glen Helen Nature Preserve (SW)

H. Glens Trail, Gorge Metro Park (NE)

S. Gorge Trail, Sharon Woods (SW)

23. Harkers Run to Bachelor Preserve East Loop, Miami University Natural Areas (SW)

35. Hemlock to Creekside Meadows Loop, Clear Creek Metro Park (SE)

13. Hemlock Gorge to Lyons Falls Trail, Mohican State Park (NE)

19. Little Miami River Loop, Clifton Gorge State Nature Preserve and John Bryan State Park (SW)

B. Miami and Erie Canal: Farnsworth Metro Park to Providence Metropark (NW)

8. Stanford House to Brandywine Falls Loop, Cuyahoga Valley National Park (NE)

P. Valley of the Ancients to Etawah Woods Trail, Highlands Nature Sanctuary (SW)

12. Vondergreen Trail, Beaver Creek State Park (NE)

Best Hikes to View Rock Features

Y. Archers Fork Trail, Wayne National Forest (SE)

16. Blackhand to Quarry Rim Trail Loop, Blackhand Gorge State Nature (C)

11. Cascade Falls to Devil's Icebox, Nelson–Kennedy Ledges State Park (NE)

24. Flat Fork Ridge Trail to Pioneer Village, Caesar Creek State Park (SW)

28. Fort to Gorge Trail Loop, Fort Hill State Memorial (SW)

20. Glen Helen Loop Trail, Glen Helen Nature Preserve (SW)

H. Glens Trail, Gorge Metro Park (NE)

33. Grandma Gatewood Trail, Hocking Hills State Park (SE)

35. Hemlock to Creekside Meadows Loop, Clear Creek Metro Park (SE)

6. Hinckley Lake to Whipps Ledges Trail Loop, Hinckley Reservation (NE)

30. Lake Vesuvius Lakeshore Trail, Wayne National Forest (SE)

9. Ledges Trail, Cuyahoga Valley National Park (NE)

L. Ledges Trail, Liberty Park, Summit County Parks (NE)

19. Little Miami River Loop, Clifton Gorge State Nature Preserve and John Bryan State Park (SW)

5. North Shore Loop, North Pond, and East Quarry Trails, Kelleys Island State Park (NW)

14. Overlook and Dripping Rock Trails, Highbanks Metro Park (C)
39. River Loop to Scenic River Trail, Wayne National Forest—Athens District–Marietta Unit (SE)
U. Rockbridge State Nature Preserve (SE)
37. Rockhouse to Athens Trail Loop, Sells Park, Riddle State Nature Preserve (SE)
R. Trail to Buzzardroost Rock, Edge of Appalachia Preserve (SW)
P. Valley of the Ancients to Etawah Woods Trail, Highlands Nature Sanctuary (SW)

Best Hikes for Solitude

Y. Archers Fork Trail, Wayne National Forest (SE)
W. Covered Bridge Trail, Wayne National Forest (SE)
29. Day Hike Trail, Shawnee State Forest (SW)
40. Lamping Homestead Trail, Wayne National Forest (SE)
32. Logan Hollow Trail—North Loop, Tar Hollow State Forest and State Park (SE)
2. Oak Openings Hiking Trail, Oak Openings Preserve Metropark (NW)
X. Ohio View Trail, Wayne National Forest (SE)
39. River Loop to Scenic River Trail, Wayne National Forest (SE)

Best Hikes to See Old-Growth Forests or Trees

22. Big Woods and Sugar Bush Trails, Hueston Woods State Nature Preserve (SW)
1. Cottonwood to Toadshade Loop, Goll Woods State Nature Preserve (NW)
28. Fort to Gorge Trail Loop, Fort Hill State Memorial (SW)
13. Hemlock Gorge to Lyons Falls Trail, Mohican State Park (NE)
41. Red and Blue Trails, Dysart Woods (SE)
17. Terrace to Ancient Trail Loop, Battelle Darby Creek Metro Park (C)

Best Trails with Vistas

3. Boardwalk Trail, Maumee Bay State Park (NW)
18. Five Oaks to Kokomo Wetland Trail, Slate Run Metro Park (C)
15. Lake Trail with Japanese Garden spur, The Dawes Arboretum (C)
30. Lake Vesuvius Lakeshore Trail, Wayne National Forest (SE)
38. Lakeview Trail, Burr Oak State Park (SE)
9. Ledges Trail, Cuyahoga Valley National Park (NE)
5. North Shore Loop, North Pond, and East Quarry Trails, Kelleys Island State Park (NW)
N. Ridge to Meadows Trail Loop, Chestnut Ridge Metro Park (C)
34. Rim and Gorge Trails, Conkles Hollow State Nature Preserve (SE)
C. Sheldon Marsh State Nature Preserve (NW)
R. Trail to Buzzardroost Rock, Edge of Appalachia Preserve (SW)

Best Trails to See Waterfalls

7. Buckeye Trail: Red Lock to Blue Hen Falls to Boston Store, Cuyahoga Valley National Park (NE)
31. Calico Bush and Salt Creek Trails, Lake Katharine Nature Preserve (SE)
11. Cascade Falls to Devil's Icebox, Nelson-Kennedy Ledges State Park (NE)
28. Fort to Gorge Trail Loop, Fort Hill State Memorial (SW)
20. Glen Helen Loop Trail, Glen Helen Nature Preserve (SW)
S. Gorge Trail, Sharon Woods (SW)
33. Grandma Gatewood Trail—Old Man's Cave to Ash Cave, Hocking Hills State Park (SE)
13. Hemlock Gorge to Lyons Falls Trail, Mohican State Park (NE)
19. Little Miami River Loop, Clifton Gorge State Nature Preserve and John Bryan State Park (SW)
U. Rockbridge State Nature Preserve (SE)
8. Stanford House to Brandywine Falls Loop, Cuyahoga Valley National Park (NE)

Best Wheelchair-Accessible Hikes

33. Ash Cave Trail, Hocking Hills State Park (SE)
3. Boardwalk Trail, Maumee Bay State Park (NW)
19. Little Miami River Loop, Clifton Gorge State Nature Preserve (SW)
5. North Pond Trail, Kelleys Island State Park (NW)
C. Sheldon Marsh State Nature Preserve (NW)

Best Long Hikes

33. Grandma Gatewood Trail—Old Man's Cave to Ash Cave, Hocking Hills State Park (SE)
13. Hemlock Gorge to Lyons Falls Trail, Mohican State Park (NE)
32. Logan Trail—North Loop, Tar Hollow State Forest and State Park (SE)
2. Oak Openings Hiking Trail, Oak Openings Preserve Metropark (NW)
39. River Loop to Scenic River Trail, Wayne National Forest—Athens District–Marietta Unit (SE)
12. Vondergreen Trail, Beaver Creek State Park (NE)

Appendix B: Resources (Government, State, and Local Groups)

Public Land Management Agencies

Ohio Department of Natural Resources
Division of Forestry
Columbus, OH
(614) 265-6694 or (877) 247-8733
http://ohiodnr.com/forestry

Ohio Department of Natural Resources
Ohio State Parks
Columbus, OH
http://parks.ohiodnr.gov

Ohio Division of Soil and Water Conservation
Columbus, OH
(614) 265-6610
www.ohiodnr.com/soilandwater

Wayne National Forest
Nelsonville, OH
(740) 753-0101
www.fs.usda.gov/wayne

Hiking and Trail Groups

American Discovery Trail
(540) 720-5489 or (800) 663-2387
www.discoverytrail.org

Athens Trails
Athens, OH
(740) 593-6572
www. athenstrails.org

Boy Scouts
There are several local Boy Scout chapters; find a local chapter at www.scouting.org.

Buckeye Trail Association
Worthington, OH
(740) 832-1BTA
www.buckeyetrail.org

Cleveland Hiking Club
www.clevelandhikingclub.com

Columbus Outdoor Pursuits
Columbus, OH
(614) 447-1006
www.outdoor-pursuits.org

Cuyahoga Valley Trails Council
www.cvtrailscouncil.org

Dayton Hikers
www.daytonhikers.org

Maumee Valley Volkssporters
http://www.ava.org/gen3/data/clubevents_results.asp?club=AVA-0532

Miami Valley Outdoor Club
www.miamivalleyoutdoorclub.org

Mohican Trails Club
http://groups.yahoo.com/group/mohican_trails

North Country Scenic Trail
www.northcountrytrail.org
(866) 445-3628

Ohio Parks and Recreation Association
Westerville, OH
(614) 895-2222
www.opraonline.org

Statewide Environmental and Conservation Groups

Audubon Ohio
Columbus, OH
(614) 545-5475
oh.audubon.org

Buckeye Forest Council
Columbus, OH
(614) 487-9290
www.buckeyeforestcouncil.org

Environmental Education Council of Ohio
Lancaster, OH
(740) 653-2649
www.eeco-online.org

The Nature Conservancy
Ohio Chapter Main Office
Dublin, OH
(614) 717-2770
www.nature.org/ourinitiatives/regions/northamerica/unitedstates/ohio/index.htm

Ohio Ecological Food and Farm Association
Columbus, OH
(614) 421-2022
www.oeffa.org

Ohio Environmental Council
Columbus, OH
(614) 487-7506
www.theoec.org

Rivers Unlimited
Cincinnati, OH
(513) 761-4003
www.riversunlimited.org

Sierra Club—Ohio Chapter
Columbus, OH
ohio.sierraclub.org

Appendix C: Further Reading

Braun, Emma Lucy. *The Woody Plants of Ohio: Trees, Shrubs, and Wood Climbers Native, Naturalized, and Escaped* (Ohio State University Press).

Collective authors. *Ohio Birds* (Globe Pequot Press).

Dean, Tanya West, and W. David Speas. George W. Knepper, ed. *Along the Ohio Trail* (Ohio Auditor of State).

Eckert, Allan W. *That Dark and Bloody River: Chronicles of the Ohio River* (Bantam Doubleday Dell).

Genheimer, Robert A., ed. *Cultures Before Contact: The Late Prehistory of Ohio and Surrounding Regions* (Ohio Archaeological Council Inc.).

Gross, W. H. "Chip." *Ohio Wildlife Viewing Guide* (Globe Pequot Press).

Lafferty, Michael B., ed. *Ohio's Natural Heritage* (Ohio Academy of Science).

Minardi, Kay Wert. *Short Bike Rides in Ohio* (Globe Pequot Press).

Newcomb, Lawrence, and Gordon Morrison. *Newcomb's Wildflower Guide* (Little, Brown & Company).

Ostrander, Stephen, ed. *The Ohio Nature Almanac: An Encyclopedia of Indispensable Information About the Natural Buckeye Universe* (Orange Frazer Press).

Pacheco, Paul J., ed. *A View from the Core: A Synthesis of Ohio Hopewell Archaeology* (Ohio Archaeological Council Inc.).

Quinley, Mary. *52 Ohio Weekends* (McGraw-Hill/Contemporary Books).

Ramey, Ralph. *50 Hikes in Ohio* (Countryman Press).

Romain, William F. *Mysteries of the Hopewell: Astronomers, Geometers, and Magicians of the Eastern Woodlands* (University of Akron Press).

Sibley, David Allen. *The Sibley Guide to Birds* (National Audubon Society).

Vincent, Adam. *Mountain Bike America Ohio* (Globe Pequot Press).

Vonada, Damaine, ed. *The Ohio Almanac* (Orange Frazer Press).

Wharton, Mary E., and Roger W. Barbour. *A Guide to the Wildflowers and Ferns of Kentucky* (University Press of Kentucky).

———. *Trees and Shrubs of Kentucky* (University Press of Kentucky).

Woodward, Susan, and Jerry N. McDonald. *Indian Mounds of the Middle Ohio Valley* (McDonald and Woodward Publishing Co.).

Woodyard, Chris. *Haunted Ohio,* vols. I–IV (Kestrel Publishing).

Zimmermann, George and Carol. *Ohio Off the Beaten Path* (Globe Pequot Press).

About the Author

Mary Reed is a freelance journalist and photographer based in Athens, Ohio. Her work has appeared in *Backpacker, Ohio Magazine, Orion Afield, New River Gorge Guide,* and many other publications. She is also the author of *Hiking West Virginia, 2nd* (FalconGuides).